RENEWALS 458-4574

THE MACEDONIAN CONFLICT

THE MACEDONIAN CONFLICT

ETHNIC NATIONALISM IN A
TRANSNATIONAL WORLD

Loring M. Danforth

PRINCETON UNIVERSITY PRESS   PRINCETON, NEW JERSEY

Library of Congress Cataloging-in-Publication Data

Danforth, Loring M., 1949–
The Macedonian conflict : ethnic nationalism in a
transnational world / Loring M. Danforth.
Includes bibliographical references and index.
ISBN 0-691-04357-4 (cl : alk. paper)
1. Macedonia—Ethnic relations. 2. Greece—Ethnic relations.
3. Australia—Ethnic relations. 4. Nationalism—Macedonia.
5. Nationalism—Greece. 6. Macedonia—Name. 7. Macedonians—
Australia. 8. Greeks—Australia. 9. Immigrants—Australia.
I. Title.
DR2173.D36   1995
949.5′6—dc20   95-13319   CIP

This book has been composed in Palatino

Princeton University Press books are printed
on acid-free paper and meet the guidelines
for permanence and durability of the Committee
on Production Guidelines for Book Longevity
of the Council on Library Resources

Printed in the United States of America by Princeton Academic Press

3 5 7 9 10 8 6 4

For Nicholas and Ann

Contents

Illustrations

Maps

MY FIRST introduction to the controversial subject of ethnic identity in northern Greece occurred in 1975–76 while I was doing fieldwork as a graduate student in a village near Serres—a village inhabited by Thracian refugees and "local Macedonians." When I spoke to a Greek folklorist in Athens about the "local Macedonians" who lived in this village, he replied firmly that there were no "Macedonians" in Greece, only "Slavophone Greeks." I did not fully understand the significance of his comment then. I understand it much better now.

An invitation to participate in the First International Congress on Macedonian Studies in Melbourne, Australia, in 1988 changed the course of my scholarly career and led me to focus my research for the next six years on the Macedonian conflict. A primary goal of this conference, which was simultaneously one of the most ethnographically interesting and ethically troubling experiences in my career, was to assert the essential Greekness of Macedonia and refute "the propaganda" of "the Slavs" who were attempting to "distort history" by claiming that they were the "real" Macedonians. The Macedonian community of Melbourne mounted a protest against this conference in order to "defend the rights of Macedonians in multicultural Australia." After witnessing firsthand both the intensity and the complexity of the conflict between Greeks and Macedonians over which group had the right to identify itself as Macedonian, I decided to return to Australia and investigate the subject further. This book is the result of my investigations.

Given the transnational nature of the Macedonian conflict, my research on it has of necessity been transnational as well. The fieldwork on which this book is based has been carried out in four different countries on three different continents. Throughout my research I have made an effort to work closely with people on both sides of the issue so that I could understand both the Greek *and* the Macedonian perspectives on the Macedonian conflict.

In June 1989, I conducted fieldwork at a conference entitled "Macedonia: History, Culture, Art," which was held in New York City at Columbia University. I spoke with Greek scholars who participated in the conference as well as with Macedonians who attended it. A year later, in June 1990, I spent two weeks doing research in the region of Florina in northern Greece. I worked primarily with members of the Macedonian human rights movement there, but I also spoke with people who had other, very different points of view. Then in March 1991, I spent a week in Toronto, Canada, where I attended the celebration of Greek Independence Day on March 25, as well as a Macedonian protest march, which was held the same day.

The most important period of fieldwork on which this book is based, however, was carried out in Melbourne, Australia, from September 1991 through July 1992. During this time I spoke with a variety of people in both the Greek and the Macedonian communities there—university professors and construction workers, lawyers and milk bar owners, consular officials and human rights activists, elementary school teachers and high school students. I attended an equally wide range of political, cultural, and community events—demonstrations and protest marches, folklore festivals and parades, academic conferences and lectures, and dances, picnics, and barbecues sponsored by village associations of immigrants from northern Greece. In addition, I followed media coverage of the Macedonian conflict—in newspapers, on radio, and on television—and not only in the mainstream Australian media, but also in both the Greek and the Macedonian "ethnic" media as well. Finally, throughout my fieldwork in Melbourne I listened to, and inevitably participated in, innumerable discussions about ethnic identity in general and Macedonian identity in particular. Given my fluency in Greek and my fairly limited knowledge of Macedonian, my interviews with immigrants from the region of Florina were conducted either in Greek or in English. Given the politically charged nature of the topic, I did not use a tape recorder during most of these interviews. I did, however, keep detailed notes during all of them. It is on these notes that the majority of the material presented here is based.

In the six years I have been working on the Macedonian conflict I have benefited from the financial, intellectual, and emotional support of many organizations and many people. I am deeply indebted to them all. The short periods of fieldwork I conducted in New York, Florina, and Toronto were supported by Bates College through two Roger C. Schmutz Faculty Research Grants. My year of fieldwork in Melbourne was made possible by a Fulbright Scholar Award, and I am extremely grateful to the Council for International Exchange of Scholars in Washington and the Australian-American Educational Foundation in Canberra for giving me and my family the opportunity to live for a year in Australia. Upon completion of my fieldwork in Melbourne I was able to spend the 1992–93 academic year writing the first draft of this book thanks to a grant from the National Endowment for the Humanities. Don Harward, Carl Straub, and Martha Crunkleton of Bates College have supported this project by granting me the leaves of absence that have enabled me to complete it. I thank them as well.

During my stay in Melbourne the Department of Anthropology and the Australian Centre at the University of Melbourne graciously served as my hosts, providing me with an office and the other privileges of a Visiting Research Fellow. I would particularly like to thank Roger Just, Douglas Lewis, Homer Le Grand, and Chris Wallace-Crabbe, as well as Howard Nicholas of La Trobe University, for their hospitality and support.

Over the years many friends and colleagues in anthropology, modern Greek studies, Slavic studies, and classics have helped me tremendously in my work on the Macedonian conflict by answering my questions, reading drafts of this book, and helping me avoid at least some of the pitfalls that lay in my path. Many thanks to Gene Borza, Keith Brown, Victor Friedman, Michael Herzfeld, John Iatrides, Gregory Jusdanis, Christina Kramer, and Lillian Petroff. I have also benefited greatly from the advice and support of two other anthropologists who have studied the construction of Macedonian identity in northern Greece and done fieldwork in the Florina area: Riki van Boeschoten, who participated with me in the 1988 conference in Melbourne and worked with me in Florina in 1990, and Anastasia Karakasidou, who as a result of her research on the Macedonian conflict has been the target of death threats both in Greece and the United States. More than anyone else they can appreciate the frustrations and the rewards of working with a group of people, the Macedonian minority of northern Greece, whose existence the Greek government adamantly denies. Needless to say, I am completely responsible for all the views expressed here on this most controversial of topics.

Unquestionably I owe my greatest debt of gratitude to the people from Florina and other parts of Macedonia who shared their experiences with me. Whether they identified themselves as Greeks or Macedonians, and whether they lived in Florina, Toronto, or Melbourne, they spoke with me—sometimes eagerly, sometimes reluctantly—about the Macedonian conflict and the impact it has had on their lives. Because of the sensitive nature of this subject I have only used the real names of people who themselves have chosen to take a public stand on the issue and whose real names have already appeared in various media accounts and human rights publications. Some of the people I spoke with saw me as an advocate; others as a threat. With this book I may have disappointed some of the former and surprised some of the latter. In any event, I am sure that what I have written will please no one entirely. That is the fate of anthropologists, who must ultimately stand at least partially outside the communities whose worlds they try to understand.

Several other people have contributed in important ways to the completion of this book: Joyce Caron of Bates College, who always seemed to finish revisions of the manuscript more quickly than she said she would; Brian MacDonald, who edited the manuscript; and Mary Murrell of Princeton University Press, who carefully supervised the entire publication process.

On a more personal note I would like to thank my wife, Peggy Rotundo, who shared with me both the pleasures of living in Australia and the frustrations of writing in Lewiston. Finally, I would like to dedicate this book to my two children: Nicholas, who is beginning to understand what it means to write a book, and Ann, who knew that whenever I left the house to interview someone in Melbourne and whenever I went to my office at Bates to write, I was really going to Macedonia.

Note on Transliteration

IN TRANSLITERATING Greek words and phrases in the text I have been guided by a desire to approximate modern pronunciation. Bibliographical references and some proper names, however, appear in more conventional transcription.

In transliterating Macedonian words and phrases I have adopted standard scholarly practice in which the symbols used are pronounced as follows:

ǵ = gy as in "argue"
ž = zh as in "pleasure"
j = y as in "you"
ǩ = ky as in "cute"
c = ts as in "bits"
č = ch as in "chart"
š = sh as in "show"

THE MACEDONIAN CONFLICT

Introduction

THE PRESPA LAKES lie in a quiet valley surrounded by rugged mountains high in western Macedonia. All that separates the two lakes is a narrow isthmus of sand flanked on one side by a tall bed of reeds. On a bright sunny day in May 1981, I stood in the middle of a grassy field looking north across the calm blue waters of Great Prespa Lake. In the distance I could see a row of small white buoys running out from the eastern shore of the lake until it faded from sight to the west somewhere in the center of the lake. I knew that this line of buoys marked the border between Yugoslavia and Greece. I also knew that somewhere in the center of the lake this line of buoys intersected another line of buoys running north and south which marked the border separating Yugoslavia and Greece, on one side, from Albania, on the other. The territories of three sovereign and independent states met at this point—at a buoy in the middle of a lake in western Macedonia.

From where I stood I could see the village of Ayios Yermanos on the Greek side of the border. A few kilometers further north along the shore of the lake I could also make out the village of Ljubojno on the Yugoslav side of the border. Years ago the inhabitants of these two villages had been able to ride their bicycles across the border to work in their fields or to visit relatives who lived on the other side. Now this was impossible; the border was closed. Watch towers, barbed wire, and sentries separated the two communities.

Other reminders of the hostile relations that have often existed between Yugoslavia and Greece lay in the uneven terrain around me. Depressions in the ground and large mounds of sand were all that remained of the foxholes, trenches, and earthworks constructed during the Greek Civil War, when the Greek government had fought against the Communists, who, for a time at least, had enjoyed the support of Tito and the Communist Party of Yugoslavia.

I looked up from the ground in time to see a kettle of huge white Dalmatian pelicans rising slowly from their nests in the nearby marsh. When they had climbed high enough, they soared gracefully out over Great Prespa Lake on their way to feed. In just a few minutes they had flown out over the row of white buoys in the middle of the lake and disappeared from sight against the mountains of Yugoslavia rising in the distance to the north.

This was one of the most powerful experiences I have had in Macedonia. It is part of what Macedonia means to me. But Macedonia means many different things to many different people. Sometimes it seems as if Macedonia means too many things. Whenever I tell someone that I have done research in Macedonia, the same questions always seem to arise: What is Macedonia? Where exactly is it? Whom does it belong to? What country is it part of? Who are the Macedonians? And finally—what is the conflict all about?

In the introduction to his 1951 book, *Maps and Politics: A Review of the Ethnographic Cartography of Macedonia*, Henry R. Wilkinson wrote that "Macedonia defies definition." Ignoring this somewhat bald assertion—at my peril perhaps—in the present book I will attempt to answer some of these basic, but very difficult questions.

Anyone who consults a dictionary or encyclopedia to find out what Macedonia means will encounter a fairly consistent set of definitions. Macedonia is usually defined first somewhat vaguely as a geographical region located somewhere in the Balkans. The *Oxford English Dictionary*, for example, defines Macedonia as a "geographical area in the central Balkans lying astride the frontiers of southern Yugoslavia, northern Greece, and southwestern Bulgaria." The second entry in many dictionaries and encyclopedias defines Macedonia as "ancient Macedonia," "an ancient country north of Greece," or "an ancient kingdom in northern Greece." Still other definitions state that Macedonia is a part of Greece. One of the entries on Macedonia in the *Encyclopedia Britannica*, for example, defines Macedonia as "a traditional region of Greece, comprising the northern and northeastern portions of that country."

It is often only in the final entry that Macedonia is defined as "the Socialist Republic of Macedonia," the most southern of the six constituent republics of the federal state of Yugoslavia. In order to find Macedonia identified as "the Republic of Macedonia," a newly independent Balkan state, it is necessary to consult one of the most recent editions of the various almanacs that are published every year.

To the question, Who are the Macedonians? a similar range of answers can be found. They are the people who live in Macedonia; they are the ancient people ruled over by Philip of Macedon and Alexander the Great; they are Greeks; they are Slavs; they are the citizens of the Republic of Macedonia.

While I resist conceding that Macedonia defies definition, it is clear that the meaning of the terms "Macedonia" and "Macedonian" is sharply contested. They have many contradictory and mutually exclusive definitions, and none of them alone is satisfactory.

Defining Macedonia as a geographical region "lying astride the frontiers" of Bulgaria, Yugoslavia, and Greece eliminates Macedonia from contemporary maps of the Balkans. It makes Macedonia "an area without boundaries that lies between countries, without being either inside or outside them." It makes Macedonia "vanish to the point where the frontiers of Bulgaria, Greece, and Yugoslavia intersect" (Brown 1992: 6–7). Yet this definition is completely accurate; the center of the geographical region of Macedonia *does* lie along the borders of other Balkan states. Macedonia *is* located in the margins, in the interstices between other Balkan states. I have heard Macedonian nationalists jokingly refer to the old border between Yugoslavia and Greece as the border between Macedonia and Macedonia. I have also been told that there are signs on each side of what is now the border between the Republic of Macedonia and Greek Macedonia that read "Welcome to Macedonia!"

As long as Macedonia was not an independent state, but only a geographical region, it suffered the same fate as places like Palestine and Kurdistan. It did not really exist; it had no place in a world composed of states. This situation came about as a result of the successful nationalist campaigns of the older Balkan states, which were able to exclude Macedonia from the map of the Balkans. The Balkans were just too crowded; their history too full. It was difficult to find room for another state or another nation. All the glorious ancestors, all the famous heroes, and all the powerful symbols had already been claimed.

Problems arise with the other definitions of Macedonia as well. Defining Macedonia as ancient Macedonia deprives it of any existence in the present by locating it exclusively in the past. Defining Macedonia as a region in northern Greece fails to take into consideration either the Republic of Macedonia, which declared its independence in 1991, or its predecessor, the Socialist Republic of Macedonia, which became one of the constituent republics of the former Yugoslavia in 1944 (and which was known from then until 1963 as the People's Republic of Macedonia). Defining Macedonia as a region in northern Greece also ignores the existence of the Macedonian language, a Slavic language whose distinctiveness from Bulgarian and Serbo-Croatian has been asserted for over a century and which became standardized and internationally recognized as a distinct language fifty years ago. Finally, defining Macedonia as the Republic of Macedonia ignores the existence of the part of Greece known as Macedonia. It fails to take into consideration the fact that the Greek language and Greek culture more generally have enjoyed a long history, from antiquity to the present, in Macedonia.

This book is about the conflicting claims to Macedonian identity asserted by both Greeks and Macedonians. The conflict between Greeks and Macedonians over which group has the right to identify itself as Macedonian is a dispute over names, flags, history, and territory. Ultimately, however, it is a dispute over meaning. Who will control the meaning of the word "Macedonian?" Who will define it? Who will determine which of its many contradictory and mutually exclusive definitions will prevail in diplomatic circles, at scholarly conferences, and in public opinion around the world?

In both Greek and Macedonian nationalist discourse "Macedonia" can mean one and only one thing. Greek nationalists claim that "Macedonia is, was, and always will be Greek," that all Macedonians are Greeks, and that only Greeks can be Macedonians. Macedonians, on the other hand, assert equally forcefully that Macedonians are not Greeks, but are a unique people with their own language, culture, history, and national identity. Neither side acknowledges the legitimacy of the other's claims to Macedonian identity. From an anthropological perspective, however, "Macedonia" can have many different meanings, many different definitions. It is also possible, from an anthropological perspective, for more than one group of people to identify itself as Macedonian. Given the controversy that surrounds the use of the term "Macedonian," it is important that I explain here as clearly as possible how I use the term in the present book.

The term "Macedonian" has three basic meanings. It is used most frequently in this book and in general political, scholarly, and journalistic discourse in a *national* sense to refer to people with a Macedonian national identity. When it is used in this way, "Macedonian" contrasts with other categories of national identity, such as "Serbian," "Bulgarian," and "Greek." According to this usage, "Macedonian" and "Greek" are mutually exclusive categories referring to people with two different national identities. While Greek nationalists object to this use of "Macedonian," each group finds these names acceptable as terms of self-designation. Their use, therefore, is completely consistent with the standard anthropological practice of employing indigenous categories and labels when referring to cultural groups of any kind.

The word "Macedonian" is also used in what I would call a *regional* sense to refer to people with a Greek national identity who come from Macedonia. These people often refer to themselves as "Greek-Macedonians." Although some Macedonian nationalists object to this use of "Macedonian," it also enjoys wide acceptance in a variety of contexts. Finally, in northern Greece the word "Macedonian" is used in a much more restricted sense with what I would call an *ethnic* meaning to refer to the indigenous people of Macedonia (who may speak Greek or Macedonian or both), in contrast to the many other ethnic groups that live in the area. For the sake of clarity, and because they also call themselves "locals," I use the term "local Macedonian" to designate this group. Most local Macedonians have developed a Greek national identity; some, however, have developed a Macedonian national identity. These are some of the different kinds of Macedonians whose identities and lives will be explored in this book.

Ethnic nationalism lies at the heart of the Macedonian conflict. Chapter 1, therefore, begins with a theoretical discussion of ethnic nationalism and the construction of national identities and cultures. It focuses particularly on the process of nation formation and on the role states play in the construction of nations. It concludes with an examination of the challenges facing anthropologists in their study of national cultures.

Chapter 2 outlines both the Greek and the Macedonian positions on the Macedonian Question. These two diametrically opposed nationalist ideologies and the histories that legitimate them are presented from the perspectives of Greek and Macedonian nationalists themselves, with very little commentary on my part. Chapter 3 offers a third history of Macedonia, a history of the construction of Macedonian national identity from an anthropological perspective. It represents an attempt to deconstruct both nationalist positions, to show how they both reify national identities and cultures in their efforts to lay claim to Macedonian identity. This account focuses on the construction of Macedonian national identity among the Slavic-speaking people of northern Greece because their identity has been an extremely sensitive issue in the larger Macedonian conflict.

In the global world of the late twentieth century, the subject of ethnic nationalism must be approached from a transnational perspective. The Macedonian conflict is not simply a dispute between two Balkan states, Greece and Macedonia. It is a "global cultural war" (Featherstone 1990a:10) that involves (in addition to these two states) ethnic minorities, diaspora communities, and international organizations like the United Nations and the European Union. This book, therefore, does not have a single geographic focus; it is not a study of one community or one culture. Instead it attempts to track the global cultural war between Greeks and Macedonians as it plays itself out in Athens and Skopje, in New York and Brussels, in Toronto and Melbourne, as well as in villages in northern Greece. Whenever I am asked why I went to Australia to study the Macedonian conflict, I repeat a statement made by the Greek consul in Melbourne in 1991: "Australia is the first line of defense in the battle for Macedonia." Chapter 4, therefore, explores the phenomena of transnationalism and globalization. It documents the construction of transnational national communities of Greeks and Macedonians, describes the relationships that exist between the two diaspora communities and their respective national homelands, and demonstrates how the battle for Macedonia is being waged on a world-wide scale.

In the following chapters I examine the two major issues involved in the Macedonian conflict: the human rights of the Macedonian minority in Greece and the recognition of the newly independent Republic of Macedonia. Chapter 5 deals with the Macedonian minority of northern Greece and its treatment at the hands of the Greek government. There follows an account of the Macedonian minority's struggle for human rights both in the Greek court system and at a meeting of the Conference on Security and Cooperation in Europe. Chapter 6 describes the problems that arose after the Republic of Macedonia declared its independence from Yugoslavia in 1991. The stability of the new republic was challenged almost immediately by its large Albanian minority and by Greek attempts to prevent Macedonia from being recognized by the European Union and the United Nations. Major points of contention in the conflict at this level were the name of the new republic, its flag, and the issue of whether it had irredentist designs on Greek territory.

Chapters 7 and 8 focus on the construction of national identity at the individual level among local Macedonians from northern Greece who have emigrated to Australia. These are people whose villages and families—whose very identities—have literally been torn apart by the Macedonian conflict. These are people whose lives have been decentered or displaced in two important ways. When they lived near the border between Greece and Yugoslavia, their national identity was ambiguous, their political loyalties suspect. They were never fully accepted as Greeks *or* as Macedonians. As immigrants to Australia, as members of diaspora communities, they have been doubly displaced; they have been marginalized even further from the national communities to which many of them would like to belong.

Chapter 7 presents a narrative account of the process by which Ted Yannas, an immigrant from northern Greece to Australia who earlier in his life had a Greek national identity, gradually developed a Macedonian national identity. As a result of this "conversion experience" Ted became estranged from his brother Jim and the rest of his family, who all retained their Greek national identity.

Chapter 8 explores from a more theoretical perspective how national identities are constructed at the individual level by considering how it is possible for two brothers to develop different national identities and to disagree about what nationality they both really are. Important issues dealt with here are the role of choice and the complex factors constraining choice in the construction of national identities among transnational migrants in multicultural societies. This chapter also examines the categories and the theories that immigrants from northern Greece to Australia use to construct the different identities that so powerfully shape their lives.

On a hot summer evening in January 1992, members of the Kelli Family Association were holding a dance at the parish hall of the Greek Orthodox Church of Saints Cyril and Methodius in Preston, a working-class suburb north of Melbourne. The village of Kelli lies in the district of Florina in northern Greece at the foot of Mount Kaimaktsalan, whose jagged peaks form the border between Greece and the former Yugoslavia. Three or four hundred families still live in Kelli; the rest have left. After the Greek Civil War a hundred families settled in Skopje. Now there are over a hundred families from Kelli living in Toronto, and even more in Melbourne.

The men collecting tickets for the dance were upset. It was already nine o'clock, and only forty people had arrived. Several years ago three hundred people would come to the Kelli dances. But then "the worm entered the village." Some villagers started saying they were not Greek; they "became Macedonians." People started arguing about whether to play Greek or Macedonian music at village dances and whether to send out invitations to the dances in Greek or Macedonian. But the issue that really split the village was whether to use Kelli (the Greek name) or Gorničevo (the Macedonian name) in the official title of the village association. That was what finally destroyed the village.

Inside the church hall, whose walls were decorated with posters of heroes of the Greek War of Independence, forty people—couples and families—sat at long tables talking and eating olives and cheese. A disk jockey sat on stage playing Greek music over a loudspeaker system, but no one was dancing. It was early in the evening; the men at the door hoped that more people would come soon.

That very same evening the Gorničevo-Kelli Community was holding its first dinner dance at Eden Receptions right next to the big Goodyear Tyre and Rubber factory in the nearby suburb of Thomastown. There were about 250 people present, some of them from other villages near Florina. They were eating dinner at tables arranged around a large dance floor.

After dinner the band—a singer, backed up by an electric guitar, a clarinet, a keyboard, and a bouzouki—began to play. The band played some old Macedonian folk songs about driving the Turks out of Macedonia and some new "patriotic" songs about "the children of Macedonia" who were separated from their families and live scattered around the world, as well as a few popular American songs like "Long Tall Sally," and "You've Lost That Lovin' Feeling."

Late in the evening during one of the "patriotic" songs a group of men knelt in a circle around a man named Panko. They clapped for him as he danced intensely, whirling a red handkerchief over his head. Panko had been born in Gorničevo during the Greek Civil War, just before his parents, who were accused of supporting the Communists, fled the village. His parents died several years later, and Panko grew up alone in Skopje. He had lived all over eastern Europe; he had even spent seven years in the Philippines. A few months after he came to Melbourne, he attended the big picnic that the Macedonian community holds every year. There he met someone from Gorničevo and learned that he had cousins living in Melbourne he had never met before.

"I'm flying," he said. "I have two hearts now, because I've found my cousins."

CHAPTER I

Ethnic Nationalism: The Construction of National Identities and Cultures

WHILE many people hoped that the early 1990s would be celebrated as the time when long-cherished dreams of European integration and unification were finally realized, it seems more likely now that these years will be remembered as a period of dramatic, and often violent, disintegration and fragmentation. The collapse of the Soviet Union and the break up of Yugoslavia, in addition to the separatist movements of western Europe and the ethnic politics of the United States, Canada, and Australia, testify to the fact that ethnic nationalism continues to be a major political force in the Western world in the final decade of the twentieth century. What Anthony Smith (1981) has called "the ethnic revival"—the surge of support for ethnic minorities demanding cultural freedoms, human rights, political autonomy, and even national independence—shows every sign of increasing in both intensity and scope.

Various reasons are cited to explain this resurgence of ethnic nationalism. Although the power of nationalist ideologies themselves has tended to seduce us with the myth that European states are ethnically homogeneous, closer examination clearly reveals the existence of many politically mobilized ethnic groups that pose a range of threats to the stability of the states in which they live. The contradiction between the widespread theoretical acceptance of the right to national self-determination and the equally widespread practical refusal of states to tolerate their own dismemberment has been a major cause of this resurgence. Other contributing factors include the recent wave of democratization that has spread through eastern Europe; alienation from increasingly impersonal, bureaucratic, and centralized states; and the declining importance of class-based political parties and movements. Uneven economic development has often frustrated the desires of regionally based ethnic groups for educational and occupational mobility and an improved standard of living. Finally, improvements in mass communication have enabled states to impose dominant national cultures and symbols more effectively on the private lives of members of minority groups. Ethnic nationalism can therefore be seen as an attempt to maintain or to recreate a sense of identity and community in the face of the threat of cultural assimilation or annihilation.[1]

Although in many ways the recent wave of ethnic nationalism is a continuation of a process that began in the late eighteenth century, Eric Hobsbawm has pointed out one important difference. Nineteenth-century national movements, which were often directed against huge multinational empires, were engaged in the building of nations; their goal was seen to be national unification and expansion. Furthermore, they were governed by what Hobsbawm (1990:31) has called a "threshold principle"—the principle that the right to national self-determination applied only to nations that were of sufficient size to form viable political and economic units. More recent national movements, however, which are often directed against the very states that came into being as a result of earlier national movements, are frequently accused of destroying nations; their goal is seen to be separatist and divisive. The threshold principle has been abandoned; there seems to be no limit to how small new nations can be.

Macedonia provides a tragically apt example of what Clifford Geertz (1973d:276) has described as the "self-reinforcing whirlpools of primordial discontent" that swirl around newly emerging states. After the violent breakup of Yugoslavia, the Republic of Macedonia declared its independence on September 8, 1991. Almost immediately, however, the survival of Macedonia as a sovereign and independent state was seriously threatened both on the domestic and the international fronts by a variety of nationalist ideologies and movements. In January 1992, the Albanian minority in Macedonia, which makes up over one-fifth of the republic's population, held a referendum and voted overwhelmingly in favor of "the political and territorial autonomy of the Albanians in Macedonia" and the formation of their own state, the Republic of Ilirida.

Even more ominous, however, has been the response of Macedonia's Balkan neighbors. Bulgaria, while it recognizes the existence of a Macedonian state, refuses to recognize the existence of a Macedonian nation on the grounds that Macedonians are really Bulgarians. Serbia, where some nationalists refer to Macedonia as "South Serbia," has refused to recognize the Republic of Macedonia. Finally, Greece refuses to recognize either a Macedonian state or a Macedonian nation on the grounds that everything Macedonian—the name, the people, the history, and the territory—is exclusively Greek. From a Greek perspective international recognition of the Republic of Macedonia constitutes a

---

[1] For further discussion of these general issues, see Connor (1973, 1977); Esman (1977); Guideri, Pellizzi, and Tambiah (1988); Smith (1981, 1983, 1986); Stack (1981); and Tambiah (1989).

threat to the cultural heritage of the Greek nation as well as the territorial integrity of the Greek state.

In this book I am concerned with precisely this aspect of the Macedonian conflict—the dispute between Greeks and Macedonians over which group has the right to identify itself as Macedonian.

ETHNIC NATIONALISM

A great deal of ambiguity and confusion surrounds the use of terms like "ethnic group," "nation," "state," and "nationalism." Because they are employed with a variety of related but different meanings in scholarly articles, nationalist rhetoric, and everyday language, it seems appropriate to introduce this discussion of ethnic nationalism with some general definitions and brief explanatory comments.

Before the pioneering work of Fredrik Barth ethnic groups were generally understood to be social groups that shared a common origin, history, language, and culture. Barth's contribution to the study of ethnicity was to reject this reifying and essentializing approach, which suggests an equivalence between a race, a culture, a society, and an ethnic group, and offer an alternative approach in which ethnic groups are defined as "categories of ascription and identification" that people use to classify both themselves and others (1969:10). Barth's aproach allows us to understand how ethnic boundaries are defined and maintained even in situations where there are no "objective" cultural criteria distinguishing between groups, as well as in situations where individuals are able to change their identity by crossing ethnic boundaries and passing from one group to another.[2]

Nations, like ethnic groups, have traditionally been defined in terms of what they share. Hugh Seton-Watson, for example, defines a nation as "a community of people, whose members are bound together by a sense of solidarity, a commmon culture, a national consciousness" (1977:1). Images of common origin, descent, and history also serve to unite people who define themselves as members of the same nation. Ernest Gellner (1983:7) offers two definitions of a nation. The first— "two men are of the same nation if and only if they share the same culture"—suffers from the same reifying tendencies as traditional definitions of ethnicity. The second—"two men are of the same nation if and only if they *recognize* each other as belonging to the same nation"— is sensitive to the issues of self-ascription and ascription by others emphasized by Barth. Anderson's well-known definition of a nation as

[2] Other important anthropological works on ethnicity include De Vos and Romanucci-Ross (1975), Nash (1989), and Royce (1982).

"an imagined political community" (1983:15) also stresses the fact that nations are socially and culturally constructed through complex historical and political processes.

In spite of the similarities that exist between the concept of the ethnic group and that of the nation, several important differences between the two should be noted as well. These differences generally involve size, degree of politicization, and relationship to a specific territory. Nations are large, politicized ethnic groups associated with specific territories over which they seek some degree of autonomy. Nations, as opposed to ethnic groups, in other words, are people who exercise, or hope one day to exercise, sovereignty over a given territory.

The distinction between a "nation" and a "state" is extremely important. This is particularly true given the misleading way the word "nation" is used in such common expressions as "the United *Nations*" and "inter*national* affairs." Strictly speaking, in both these phrases the word "state," rather than "nation," would be more appropriate. While a nation is, or perhaps more accurately, claims to be a culturally homogeneous social group, a state is "a legal and political organization with the power to require obedience and loyalty from its citizens" (Seton-Watson 1977:1); it is "the major political subdivision of the globe" (Connor 1978:379). While states (like the former Soviet Union or the former Yugoslavia) may contain more than one nation, nations (like the Kurds or the Palestinians) may live in several states, none of which are their own.

Nationalism is the political principle according to which "the political and the national unit should be congruent" (Gellner 1983:1). Nations, in other words, should have the right of self-determination, the right to exist as sovereign and independent states. Nationalist ideologies, as Handler (1988:154) points out, are based on assumptions concerning "the existence of a geographically, historically, and culturally unique nation," which "is believed to be 'born of' and indissolubly linked to a bounded territory and a particular history." The goal of nationalist movements is to "turn the ethnic group into that more abstract and politicised category, the 'nation,' and then to establish the latter as the sole criterion of statehood" (Smith 1981:xii). Their goal, in other words, is to create a territorially bounded political unit, a state, out of a homogeneous cultural community, a nation. A state that emerges from a successful nationalist movement is known as a nation-state—a state, that is, whose political boundaries are the same as those of the nation, a state whose population is homogeneous, whose inhabitants are all members of the same nation.

It is important to remember, as Smith (1981) and Connor (1978) point out, that this ideal-typical nation-state is nowhere nearly as common as successful nationalist ideologies have led us to believe. Many countries that are usually considered to be nation-states, such as France or Spain, in actuality contain one or more ethnic or national minorities. It is a testament to the power of nationalist ideologies that such countries can continue to see themselves, and be seen by others, as ethnically homogeneous nation-states, in spite of the internal nationalist movements that occasionally challenge their legitimacy and at times even threaten their stability.[3]

The power of nationalist ideologies also poses one of the greatest challenges to the anthropological analysis of nationalism. From a nationalist perspective nations are regarded as natural phenomena of great antiquity, whereas from an anthropological perspective nations are human constructions, cultural products of relatively recent historical processes. In Gellner's words, "Nations as a natural, God-given way of classifying men, as an inherent though long-delayed political destiny, are a myth; nationalism, which sometimes takes pre-existing cultures and turns them into nations, sometimes invents them, and often obliterates pre-existing cultures: *that* is a reality" (1983:48).

The anthropology of nationalism must avoid being taken in or co-opted by the persuasiveness of nationalist myths. The anthropologist's task is to dereify the nation, to deconstruct and expose nationalist myths of the nation waiting, Sleeping Beauty–like, to be awakened from its slumber.[4] This can be done by analyzing the process of nation formation, the process by which nations, as well as national ideologies, cultures, and identities, are constructed from preexisting cultural forms. These preexisting cultural forms include conceptions of shared blood, race, language, place of origin, and religion. They are what Geertz (1973d:259) has called "primordial attachments . . . the 'givens'—or more precisely, as culture is inevitably involved in such matters, the assumed 'givens'—of social existence." As Geertz's qualification duly notes, and as the anthropology of nationalism must constantly stress, the idea that the preexisting cultural forms from which nations are built are in fact "primordial" or "naturally given" is itself one of nationalism's most powerful and most insidious constructions.

---

[3] Connor (1978:382) estimates that only 12 of the 132 states in the world "can justifiably be described as nation-states." However, because of the importance of self-perception and self-ascription in discussions of ethnic and national identity, I find it useful to continue to use the term "nation-state" for countries that *define themselves* as such, in contrast to multicultural or multinational states, such as Australia or the former Yugoslavia, that do not define themselves in this way.

[4] The image of the nation "awakening from sleep" is a common one in nationalist ideologies (Anderson 1991:195). In scholarly discourse, however, this image should be avoided. Because national identity is a matter of self-ascription, it either "exists or it does not; it cannot be asleep and then be awakened" (Greenfeld 1992:13).

When exposing these widespread and popularly accepted nationalist myths anthropologists must be careful not to go to the opposite extreme and imply that nations are created anew from absolutely nothing. To say that "nationalism invents nations where they do not exist," as Gellner does (1964:169), fails to take into account the many regional, ethnic, religious, and class identities that existed well before the age of nationalism.[5] If nations were totally new phenomena, if national traditions were completely discontinuous with the past, then they would not exert such power over people's lives. Any successful analysis of nationalism must, therefore, balance an emphasis on the obvious modernity of nationalism as a political principle with the equally obvious preexistence of the identities, traditions, and cultures from which it draws. Nationalism's strength lies in its ability to draw on these preexisting cultural forms, to reshape them, and to fashion from them new identities, new communities, which are nonetheless perceived to be continuous with the past. As Steven Kemper (1991:7) suggests, "nationalism needs to be seen as a conversation the present holds with the past," a conversation that "includes several voices in the present arguing about exactly what kind of past actually existed."

How then are nation-states produced? What is the relationship between nation formation and state formation? And how precisely is a national community imagined?

In its early stages a national movement must construct "an imagined community" (Anderson 1983) from a diversity of ethnic groups, social classes, and regional cultures in what is often a self-conscious and deliberate political process. It must also construct a viable state that will be able to play a part on the stage of world affairs. These two processes exist in a dialectical relationship to one another. While it is important to point out that contrary to many nationalist ideologies it is not nations that make states, it is equally important not to reverse the argument and simply claim the opposite—that states make nations. Hobsbawm, for example, falls into this trap when he states that "nations do not make states and nationalisms but the other way round," and again when he cites with approval the slogan "It is the state which makes the nation and not the nation the state" (1990:10, 44–45). In fact, both are at least partially true. The state clearly participates in the process of building the nation, but the nation, as a reality and an ideal, plays an equally important part in the process of creating the state.[6]

[5] On the existence of "nations" before nationalism, see Armstrong (1982).

[6] The relative importance of the roles of the state and the nation in the development of the nation-state will obviously vary a great deal from case to case.

The successful end result of this dialectical process is the emergence of a new nation-state in which the bonds of race, ethnicity, language, and religion, which together define the nation, are raised to the level of political principles that define the state. These bonds are domesticated, reconciled with the new civil order, and placed at the service of the new state. The result is the integration of the personally meaningful and emotionally powerful nation with the impersonal, distant, but politically powerful state. If, however, the tensions between these "primordial sentiments" and civil politics are not satisfactorily resolved in what Clifford Geertz calls the "integrative revolution," if the leaders of newly formed nation-states are not able to "construct a civil politics of primordial compromise" (1973d:308), then these new states will quickly be destroyed by the very forces that brought them into being.

Once an ethnic group has been politicized and comes to define itself as a nation, it may embark on a quest for self-determination by seeking some degree of autonomy or even outright sovereignty over a national homeland. When this goal is achieved and the nation has aquired political status as an independent state, then the entire range of organizations, institutions, and bureaucratic techniques at the disposal of the state becomes available for the further consolidation and homogenization of the nation. The creation of a state, which is the ultimate goal of a nationalist movement, contributes, therefore, in a dialectical manner to the creation of the nation, which is seen from within the nationalist movement as having created the state.

The state is created by means of an appeal to the right of national self-determination. State power is then used to complete the process of constructing the nation. The goal of such a process, which is often based on a racist or xenophobic nationalist ideology, is the assimilation and homogenization of the population of the new state so that all its citizens are also by definition members of the nation that the state embodies. Since the state is equated with the nation, being a citizen of the state is equated with being a member of the nation.

There are a variety of tools available to a newly formed state with which to create, or at least consolidate, the desired nation. Anderson (1983) points out the decisive role played by print-capitalism and the development of standardized national languages, both of which create national communities of people who read the same print language. Improved systems of transportation, modern forms of mass communication, and the implementation of large-scale programs of public works are other means by which states engage in the process of nation building. In addition state bureaucracies, particulary in the form of educational systems and the military, play an important part in politicizing unmobilized groups such as the rural peasantry or the urban working class. This process is facilitated by the rise of commercial or industrial bourgeoisies, who often constitute the elite of nationalist movements and articulate most forcefully their political demands.

War may also contribute significantly to the process of nation formation. As Anthony Smith (1981:74–78) suggests, while it is often argued that wars are fought between nations or as a result of nationalist sentiments, it is equally true that wars themselves create nations by transforming a vague sense of ethnic difference into sharply opposed and crystallized national identities. Wars accomplish this most dubious of tasks by focusing attention on the precise territorial boundaries of the nation-states involved and by creating homogeneous, bounded national communities in opposition to "enemies of the nation," who are the epitome of otherness. Again it is important to emphasize that nation building is not entirely an official process emanating from above in the form of ideological engineering and state propaganda. It is a dialectical phenomenon involving as well an unofficial process emanating from below in the form of popular enthusiasm and national sentiment. The fact that a state plays a part in the construction of a nation does not mean that all nationalists can be dismissed as agents of the state.

The ideologies that inspire and guide nationalist movements can be understood, following Geertz (1973b:207), as systems of symbols through which these movements are able to accomplish the task of collective self-redefinition and create new national cultures from preexisting regional and ethnic ones. The symbols, images, and metaphors that constituted these preexisting cultures are politicized, generalized, and reduced to the lowest common denominator, in order to create a homogeneous or generic national culture designed to encompass all the specific regional or ethnic cultures that preceded it. Old symbols are given new meanings, and new symbols are introduced. Widely diverse oral and local traditions are replaced by a more standardized literate and national tradition. Paradoxically, then, although nationalist ideologies claim to defend and preserve traditional folk cultures, in fact they actually integrate and consolidate them into a new national culture (Gellner 1983:124).

Intellectuals and scholars from disciplines such as history, archaeology, linguistics, literature, and folklore create "the symbolic capital" (Bourdieu 1977) from which a national culture is formed. This national culture is then disseminated to the citizens of a new state through the educational system. In this way a national canon is created in a variety of disciplines. A national history is written, the material culture of national ancestors is excavated, a national language is created, a canon of national literature is defined, and a body of national folklore is collected. This symbolic capital constitutes a national culture, which serves to legitimate a nation's existence as well as its claims to a specific identity, history, and territory.[7]

In *The Invention of Tradition*, a book frequently cited by anthropologists interested in the construction of national cultures, Hobsbawm and Ranger demonstrate that many "traditions" that nationalists claim to be very old are often in fact quite recent in origin and may even be "invented" (1983:1). In fact, the relative youth of the nation-state as a historical phenomenon virtually assures the novelty of national traditions. Once again we are confronted with the paradox that national cultures that claim to be old, and which draw the considerable power they hold from precisely this claim, are really quite new.

Hobsbawm and Ranger's argument, however, is flawed in one important respect. They make a distinction between "invented" traditions and "genuine" traditions, claiming for example that "where the old ways are alive, traditions need be neither renewed nor invented" (1983:8). This position rests on what is ultimately a false dichotomy between genuine and spurious traditions. As Handler and Linnekin (1984) have persuasively argued, all traditions, not just those that result from self-conscious political projects, must be understood as entirely symbolic constructions. The authenticity of a tradition "is always defined in the present"; it is "an assigned meaning rather than an objective quality." From this perspective tradition is "a process of interpretation, . . . a process that involves continual re-creation" (Handler and Linnekin 1984:286–87).

Many students of nationalism have remarked that the process of nation formation requires a collective remembering, the construction of a shared past, a shared history, that will unite people in a national community. As Ernest Gellner (1987:6, citing Ernest Renan) has pointed out, however, equally important are historical error, shared amnesia, and a collective forgetting. One simple, straightforward, and unambiguous national history must be written from the many complex and contradictory regional or ethnic histories that had previously been told. As citizens learn their national language, their national history, and their national folklore, they must forget their local dialects, their

---

[7] On the role of nationalist ideologies in the production of national cultures generally see R. G. Fox (1990). For studies of specific ethnographic cases see Borneman (1992), Handler (1988), Herzfeld (1982), Kapferer (1988), Kemper (1991), Layne (1994), McDonald (1989) and Verdery (1991).

village histories, and their regional folklores. As they remember the battles they fought together against their nation's enemies, they must forget the battles they fought against one another. And finally, as they try to remember what binds them together now, they must forget what separated them in the past.[8]

The process of nation formation, like many other social and cultural processes, is oppositional in character. A nation is defined through a process of exclusion; a self is defined in opposition to an other. The first and easiest task of nationalist movements is to stimulate "popular alienation from a foreign-dominated political order" (Geertz 1973c: 240), to convince people, in other words, of what they are not. Then, and only then, can national movements begin the far more difficult task of defining a collective subject, convincing people, that is, of what they are. Nationalist movements, therefore, are twofold in nature. First they define and reject a national other, then they define and create a national self.

With the rise of nationalism and the formation of nation-states, different cultures that had coexisted under multinational empires assume new significance. They become challenges to the homogeneous national culture of the new nation-state. In order to legitimate itself, the state needs to create a nation whose interests it will represent. In doing so the state necessarily excludes some people, since even if there did exist such a thing as a homogeneous national culture, it is very unlikely that all the people within the territorial boundaries of the state would share it. Thus any diversity of cultures, traditions, or identities that exists when a nation-state is formed, becomes, with the creation of a national culture, a threat to national unity. As the state creates the nation and welds by force if necessary a heterogeneous population into a unified body politic, some people, whose culture does not conform to the new national culture, will inevitably be left at the margins of the nation-state. At one level these people will be rejected and excluded, while at another they will be simultaneously assimilated and incorporated. It is precisely these people who eventually constitute the national minorities that are so threatening to the legitimacy of many nation-states.[9]

It is clear then that the very process of creating nations simultaneously creates national minorities. Movements of national separatism

---

[8] On Renan's comments concerning the importance of forgetting in the process of nation building see also Anderson (1983:15, 143; 1991:199–206).

[9] As Karakasidou (1992:131) points out, a limited degree of cultural diversity may survive the construction of a national culture. This is only possible, however, if these different cultures are defined as regional variants of one national culture and not as ethnic or national alternatives to it.

arise aimed at, or directed against, new states that claim a national homogeneity they have not yet created. What is more, they do so in the name of ethnic nationalism, precisely the same ideology in whose name the states they challenge were created. Peripheral ethnic groups, which have come to be defined as national minorities in the politicized climate that characterizes the formation of nation-states, reject the legitimacy of the state on the grounds that it is dominated by an alien group. Nationalism, by equating loyalty to the state with membership in the nation, transforms by definition members of national minorities into enemies of the state. These national minorities are potential nations themselves, and the separatist movements they engage in often lead to the creation of other nation-states, newer and even smaller still. Nationalisms spawn counternationalisms; nation-states contain within themselves the seeds of their own destruction. This is the dilemma nationalist movements confront. In order to protect their unique cultures and histories, they must create nation-states modeled precisely on those they struggled against. In doing so, however, they "lay the basis for the inner erosion" of the very cultures they seek to protect (Smith 1981:192).

As Maryon McDonald observes in *"We are not French!" Language, Culture and Identity in Brittany* (1989), the forces of modernization and urbanization that are thought to destroy minority languages and cultures are the very forces that actually create them, since it is the attempt to assimilate members of minority groups into national cultures that leads to their construction as national minorities in the first place. "The French government, in seeking to oppose minorities in the name of national unity, nurtures the very nightmare it wishes to dispel" (313). Ironically, then, a national minority, is "born disappearing" (104). Before it is threatened by the homogenizing forces of the nation-state, it does not exist anymore than the nation it defines itself in opposition to. What existed was not a national minority standing in opposition to a nation, but a complex tapestry of interwoven ethnic and regional cultures.

The existence of national minorities disproves the myth of national homogeneity by demonstrating the existence of "other" cultures within the nation-state. It shows that the complexities of multicultural and multilingual social life cannot easily be made to conform to the artificial dichotomies created by the borders of nation-states. Members of national minorities are exiles in their native land (Pellizzi 1988:154). The symbols that constitute their identity and give meaning to their lives are frequently appropriated by the nation-state in a way that excludes them. If members of national minorities seek to be accepted as full participants in the life of the nation-state, they must remember only the nation's history and forget their own. Their history is not part of the nation's history; it must be suppressed. Their culture is not part of the national culture; its existence must be denied.

If, however, members of national minorities choose to resist assimilation and retain, or more properly, construct, their own histories, cultures, and identities, they must do so without the vast array of facilities that are available to the state, such as national universities, state primary schools, standardized print languages, and ceremonies of national independence. The only means national minorities have to resist the cultural hegemony of nation-states are the oral and unofficial tools of resistance (jokes, folkore, and protests) described so well by James Scott in *Domination and the Arts of Resistance* (1990). As nationalist movements become better established, better organized, and better financed, they begin to acquire some of the capabilities initially available only to states. In this way the struggle of national minorities against nation-states becomes a more even contest.

The ultimate outcome of such struggles depends on a variety of factors: the quality of the leadership and the financial resources of the nationalist movement as well as the policies pursued by the state itself. These policies can range from genocide and ethnic cleansing at one extreme, through assimilation and acculturation, to the granting of some degree of political or cultural autonomy at the other. The international political situation may also have an important influence on the outcome of these nationalist struggles, particularly now at the end of the twentieth century when transnational organizations like the European Union and the United Nations are playing a more active role in world affairs.

The collapse of the Soviet Union and the breakup of Yugoslavia notwithstanding, because of the tremendous power of the state and the reluctance of the international community to interfere in the internal affairs of any one state, outright secession has not been a common result of nationalist movements (Brass 1976:240). Most often states are able to accommodate the more moderate demands such groups make for cultural and political autonomy, while at the same time resisting their more extreme demands for complete independence. As Milton Esman (1977:389) points out, however, the price states must pay to avoid disintegration is to abandon their assimilationist policies and renounce the ultimate goal of an ethnically homogeneous nation-state. In order to save the state, in other words, it is often necessary to sacrifice the nation.[10]

---

[10] On the threat posed by ethnic conflict to the security and stability of contemporary states, see Brass (1985), Horowitz (1985), and Tambiah (1989).

THE CONCEPT OF CULTURE IN NATIONALIST
AND ANTHROPOLOGICAL DISCOURSE

The concept of culture occupies a position of central importance in both the discourse of nationalism and the discourse of anthropology, as do other concepts such as race, ethnicity, tradition, continuity, and identity. Furthermore, the rise of anthropology as an academic discipline and the rise of nationalism as a political ideology have common historical origins in Europe of the late eighteenth and nineteenth centuries, a period often referred to as "the age of nationalism." A consequence of this shared genealogy is that anthropological studies of nationalism run the risk of being reduced to tautologies (Spencer 1990:288).

To avoid this risk, anthropologists must strive to maintain sufficient analytic distance between the nationalist discourse they study and the anthropological discourse in which they write. This task is further complicated by the existence of still other discourses dealing with the very same issues of culture and identity. These include the political discourse on ethnicity in multicultural societies like Canada and Australia, as well as that of international organizations such as the United Nations and the Conference on Security and Cooperation in Europe. This discourse occupies in a sense an intermediate position between the essentialism of nationalist ideologies and the ascriptivism of contemporary anthropology. All of these discourses are closely interelated; they draw on one another and shape one another in a variety of complex ways.

The most effective way for anthropologists to maintain the necessary analytic distance between their own anthropological discourse, on the one hand, and nationalist discourse, on the other, is to define the anthropological task as the deconstruction or dereification of the essentializing tendencies of nationalist conceptions of culture and identity. By demonstrating that culture and identity are socially and historically constructed, anthropologists can avoid unintentionally ratifying nationalist claims for the naturalness of national cultures and the innateness of national identities. Richard Handler (1985:174) suggests that anthropologists can accomplish this task by conducting what he describes as "destructive analysis" of national movements designed to challenge the commonsense notion of bounded, homogeneous cultures on which they are based. More specifically he suggests that anthropologists can avoid "buying into" nationalist ideologies by refraining from using terms such as "the Greek nation" or "the Macedonian nation," by not describing nations with metaphors of evolution, survival, and collective individuality, and by not presenting people as members of unified cultural entities.

Although I agree with Handler up to this point, I feel that in his admirable desire to establish the requisite analytic distance between anthropological and nationalist discourse he has failed to distinguish between the processes of reification and objectivation. According to Berger and Luckmann (1967:82–83), reification involves the apprehension of the products of human activity as if they were something other than human products, as if they were natural phenomena or the expression of divine will. Objectivation, on the other hand, implies simply that reality, which is in fact socially constructed, is nevertheless experienced as an external and objective fact. While nations are reified in nationalist discourse, they must be dereified in anthropological analysis. Nations, however, do exist both as human products and as objective social facts, and anthropological analysis must acknowledge this.

I disagree with Handler, therefore, when he encourages anthropologists to avoid using terms of self-designation or introducing studies of nationalism with historical narratives (1985:178). It is both possible and appropriate for anthropologists to use terms like "Greek" or "Macedonian," not to refer to people who share a common essence, but to refer to a demonstrably diverse group of people who nevertheless choose to adopt a common national identity. Similarly it is possible to write a historical narrative, not of the Greek or the Macedonian nation, but of Greek or Macedonian nationalism. It is possible, in other words, to write an account of the process by which the Greek or the Macedonian nation was socially constructed.

Anthropologists analyzing the process by which national cultures and identities are created must also be careful to avoid simply presenting an exposé in which the premises on which nationalist ideologies are based are undermined or dismissed as inaccurate, mistaken, or simply wrong (Badone 1992:809). In addition, anthropologists must not allow their analyses to be used by hostile governments or an unsympathetic public to undercut the cultural authority of minority groups or indigenous peoples by calling into question the authenticity of their cultures (Linnekin 1991:446). It is in this context that phrases like "the invention of tradition" (Hobsbawm and Ranger 1983) and "imagined communities" (Anderson 1983) must be used with care. Anthropologists need to stress that "invented" and "imagined" are to be understood in the sense of "constructed," "fashioned," or "created," not in the sense of "imaginary," "false," or "unreal."

Anthropologists, therefore, have two often conflicting responsibilities. On the one hand, they have an intellectual obligation to deconstruct the reifying tendencies of the nationalist ideologies they study.

On the other, they have an ethical responsibility to ensure that their "destructive" analyses are not used against groups of people whose cultural authenticity is legitimated by such ideologies. Anthropologists can meet these conflicting responsibilities by avoiding both the reifying language of nationalism and the rhetorical excesses inherent in the use of terms like "imagined" or "invented." They can also explicitly reject any interpretation of their work that reduces it to a simple ratification of some nationalist ideology, as well as any interpretation that implies that because cultural traditions are constructed they are therefore unauthentic or unreal.[11] In this way, anthropologists can affirm the right of minority groups and indigenous people living in states with assimilationist policies to construct and preserve their own distinct cultures and identities, but at the same time point out the tendency of many minority rights movements to assert the authenticity of their own cultures while denying the authenticity of others. After all, from an anthropological perspective all identities and cultures are both equally constructed and equally real.[12]

As Richard Handler (1988:8) points out, among the dominant metaphors used in nationalist discourse to describe national cultures are those of naturalness, homogeneity, boundedness, and continuity. National cultures are considered to be territorially based and mutually exclusive. Since a nation is portrayed metaphorically as a collective individual or a natural species, a national culture is something a nation possesses; it is a nation's property, and its existence "proves the existence of the nation itself" (Handler 1988:51). Just as nationalists lay claim to a clearly bounded national territory, they "construct an account of the unique culture and history that attaches to and emanates from the people who occupy it. It is at this point that disputes about the ownership of cultural property come into play" (154).

In their extreme form these disputes involve metaphorical or even literal attempts to treat some aspect of a nation's history or culture as a trademark, as something on which a copyright has been placed, marking it as "belonging" to one and only one nation. Attempts by one nation to appropriate some aspect of the history or culture of another may therefore be treated as seriously as threats to a nation's territorial integrity. For history and culture, like territory, are the objective manifestations of a nation's existence.[13]

---

[11] For a thoughtful discussion of these issues see Linnekin (1991) and Hanson (1991).

[12] This does not imply, however, that all nationalist histories are equally accurate. The fact that one nationalist history corresponds less closely to some "objective" or "impartial" historical record than another, does not mean that the culture or the identity legitimated by that history is any less "real."

[13] See Herzfeld (1991) for an excellent study dealing with the politics of culture and the disputed ownership of history.

Anthropologists have traditionally regarded cultures as discrete, bounded, and homogeneous units, just as nationalists have. More recently, however, anthropologists have begun to stress the unbounded, continuously changing, fluid, and permeable aspects of cultural reality. Eric Wolf, for example, rejects the notion of bounded and self-contained cultures, an idea he associates with the political project of nationalism. Instead, he suggests that a culture can be better seen as "a series of processes that construct, reconstruct, and dismantle cultural materials, in response to definite determinants" (1982:387). Wolf elaborates as follows:

> We can no longer think of societies as isolated and self-maintaining systems. Nor can we imagine cultures as integrated totalitites in which each part contributes to the maintenance of an organized, autonomous, and enduring whole. There are only cultural sets of practices and ideas, put into play by determinate human actors under determinate circumstances. In the course of action these cultural sets are forever assembled, dismantled, and reassembled. (390–91)

Similarly Drummond (1980) develops the concept of a "cultural continuum" in order to emphasize the importance of internal variation and difference in understanding cultural reality, particularly in the case of multiethnic societies. For Drummond culture is not an isolated, homogeneous, integrated system, but an "intersystem," a continuum of overlapping differences, characterized by heterogeneity and change. It is out of just such complex cultural reality that nationalist movements attempt to create territorially bounded culturally homogeneous nations.[14]

According to the logic of nationalism, because nations are equated with states and because states have unambiguous, clearly defined territorial borders, nations must have such borders as well. Complex cultural realities, however, know no such borders. While a particular village must be located on one side or the other of the border separating two sovereign states, the people who live in this village are likely to speak more than one language and participate in more than one culture. It would be a mistake, however, to assume that the inhabitants of this village speak the two national languages and participate in the two national cultures of the nation-states whose border the village lies near. The people of this village do not inhabit two homogeneous, bounded national cultures; they inhabit a cultural continuum, a cultural intersystem, in which cultural differences and similarities coexist in complex and constantly changing ways.

---

[14] For a more recent formulation of this critique of anthropological approaches to culture, see Clifford (1988).

This discussion of ethnic nationalism and the construction of national identities and cultures provides a theoretical framework for the
following analysis of the conflict between Greeks and Macedonians
over which group has the right to identify itself as Macedonian. This
dispute involves a variety of complex issues: competing claims to the
same identity, history, and territory; transnational disputes over the
human rights of the Macedonian minority in northern Greece and the
recognition of the Republic of Macedonia as a sovereign and independent state; as well as the construction and negotiation of national identities at the individual level by immigrants from northern Greece to
diaspora communities in multicultural societies like Canada and Australia.

I hope that this analysis will contribute not only to an understanding
of the Macedonian conflict in particular, but also to an understanding
of ethnic nationalism more generally. In this way it may offer some
insight into how ethnic nationalism can be prevented from destroying
the very societies and cultures it creates.

CHAPTER II

Conflicting Claims to Macedonian Identity and History

THE MACEDONIAN QUESTION has dominated Balkan history and politics for over a century. Competing claims to Macedonia put forward by Serbia, Bulgaria, and Greece led to the outbreak of the Balkan wars in 1912. Each state attempted to legitimize its territorial claims with arguments concerning the national consciousness, ethnic identity, linguistic affiliation, and religious loyalty of the inhabitants of the area. Since the present international boundaries in Macedonia were established in 1913, and particularly since the People's Republic of Macedonia became one of the federated states of Yugoslavia at the end of World War II, the Macedonian Question has focused on whether a distinct Macedonian nation actually exists and on whether there really are Macedonian minorities in Bulgaria and Greece (map 1). In the mid-1960s, during a period of political stability in the Balkans, Evangelos Kofos, a Greek historian who is employed as a special counselor to the Greek Foreign Ministry, wrote that the Macedonian Question could now be considered "a subject for the student of history rather than an issue for the policymaker" (1964:226). As recent events have shown, however, nothing has proved further from the truth.

By the early 1990s the Macedonian Question had once again become one of the dominant issues in Balkan politics. At meetings of the Conference on Security and Cooperation in Europe, Macedonians from northern Greece were charging the Greek government with violating their human rights, while the Republic of Macedonia, which had declared its independence from Yugoslavia in 1991, was struggling to gain international recognition from the European Community and the United Nations. In this heated dispute involving competing claims to Macedonian identity, Greeks and Macedonians in the Balkans and the diaspora each asserted that they, and they alone, have the right to call themselves Macedonians. This conflict took place at a variety of levels and in a variety of contexts. It involved politicians, scholars, journalists, and leaders of local ethnic organizations; it filled the pages of government press releases, academic publications, public relations pamphlets, and both national and local newspapers; and it provoked press conferences, academic seminars, and political demon-

Map 1. A map of Macedonia published in 1980 in the *Harvard Encyclopedia of American Ethnic Groups* indicating the areas where the Macedonian language is spoken

strations in Athens, Thessaloniki, Skopje, Brussels, New York, Toronto, and Melbourne.

In this chapter, I present brief accounts of the Greek and the Macedonian positions on the Macedonian Question. Both of these accounts are written in the voices and from the perspectives of Greek and Macedonian nationalists themselves. Neither represents my own anthropological point of view. By juxtaposing these two nationalist ideologies and the nationalist histories that legitimate them, I hope to show that in spite of the fact that they present diametrically opposed positions on virtually every issue, they are paradoxically very much alike in several important ways. They both portray their respective nations as natural, homogeneous, and bounded entities that possess unique and mutually exclusive identities, cultures, histories, and territories. They both lay claim to the same name, the same symbols, the same ancient heroes, even the same cities and towns.

In chapter 3, I present a third history of Macedonia, a history of the construction of Macedonian national identity written in my voice, from an anthropological perspective. In writing this third history I have attempted to step outside both Greek and Macedonian nationalist ideologies, to show how they both reify national identities and cultures and project them into the past in order to construct oversimplified, polarized nationalist histories in which everything is either black or white, Greek or Macedonian. In this way I hope to deconstruct both nationalist versions of Macedonian history, to depict the subtle shades of gray they both fail to capture. This third version of Macedonian history, then, is an exploration of the complex historical process by which Macedonian national identity has been constructed in the contested field of competing Balkan nationalisms.

"NO 'MACEDONIA' FOR THE SLAVS! MACEDONIA IS GREEK!" THE NEGATION OF MACEDONIAN IDENTITY IN GREEK NATIONALIST IDEOLOGY AND HISTORY

In February and March of 1992 in cities throughout Europe, North America, and Australia, hundreds of thousands of Greeks demonstrated against the recognition of the Republic of Macedonia by the European Community. Above their heads they carried blue and white signs proclaiming the Greekness of Macedonia: "Macedonia was, is, and always will be Greek!" "Macedonian History Is Greek History!" "Macedonia = Greece!" "Real Macedonians Are Greeks!" and "No Recognition of the Skopian Republic under the Hellenic Name 'Macedonia'!"[1]

The Greek position could not be more clear: Macedonia and everything associated with it are not only Greek; they are exclusively Greek and nothing else. As the president of Greece, Christos Sartzetakis, said during a visit to Australia in 1988, "We Macedonians are Greek precisely because we are Macedonians." Greece and Macedonia constitute such a perfect historical and cutural unity that the name "Macedonia" is, in the words of Stelios Papathemelis, former Socialist minister of Northern Greece, "an inalienable and eternal possession of Hellenism, a piece of its soul" (*Makedhoniki Foni* 1992, 2 [16]:9).

---

[1] The name "Skopian" is derived from "Skopje," the capital city of the Republic of Macedonia.

1. A demonstration held in Thessaloniki on February 14, 1992, to express Greek opposition to the recognition of the Republic of Macedonia by the European Community

In arguments over who has the right to identify themselves as Macedonians, the exact boundaries of the area known as Macedonia at various periods from antiquity to the present are often debated. From the Greek perspective the area known as Macedonia "in no sense constituted a unified entity" (Sakellariou 1983:484). Before the early 1990s a common Greek position was that "Macedonia" was purely a geographic term that referred to the inhabitants of a particular region in the Balkans regardless of their ethnic or national identity. It should not, therefore, be used to refer to a single ethnic group, and certainly not to refer exclusively to a group of Slavs. It should be used only in conjunction with an ethnic or national term. This would make it possible to distinguish between the different ethnic or national groups who inhabit the area—"Yugoslav-Macedonians," "Bulgarian-Macedonians," and "Greek-Macedonians." Similarly, because the "Republic of Skopje" (as the Republic of Macedonia is generally referred to in Greek sources) occupies only a part of the geographical area known as Macedonia, it has no right to name itself after the region as a whole. It has no more right to name itself the "Republic of Macedonia" than a country in Europe has the right to name itself the "Republic of Europe."

Since the early 1990s, however, when the "Republic of Skopje" began to seek recognition as an independent country under the name "Republic of Macedonia," the issue has become more sensitive, and the Greek position has changed. Many Greeks began to argue that the northern border of the "historical" Macedonia—the "real" Macedonia—lay approximately where the present border between Greece and the former Yugoslavia now lies. The "Republic of Skopje," therefore, lies almost completely outside the area that was known as Macedonia in antiquity and so has no right whatsoever to use the name "Macedonia." Only Greece does, since Macedonia is simply a region of Greece, like Crete, Thessaly, and the Peloponnesos.[2]

This claim reveals the fundamental propositions on which the Greek nationalist position on Macedonia is ultimately based: because Alexander the Great and the ancient Macedonians were Greek, and because ancient and modern Greece are linked in an unbroken line of racial and cultural continuity, only Greeks have the right to identify themselves as Macedonians. The theme of continuity is a pervasive aspect of Greek writing on Macedonia at both the scholarly and the popular level. Consider for example the volume *Macedonia: 4000 Years of Greek History and Civilization*, written by a group of well-known historians and archaeologists (most of whom are Greek), published in a lavish "coffee-table" format, and donated by the Pan-Macedonian Association of the United States and Canada (a Greek-Macedonian organization) to college and university libaries throughout North America. This book affirms Macedonia's "Hellenic character in ancient times," follows "Macedonian Hellenism's" struggle "for survival and national emancipation," and concludes with "the national liberation [of Macedonia] within the unified independent Greek state" (Sakellariou 1983:9).

From a Greek nationalist persective, then, since Macedonia and everything associated with it are Greek, the Slavs of southern Yugoslavia, who are descended from the Slavic tribes that settled in Macedonia in the sixth century A.D., a thousand years after the death of Alexander the Great, and who until 1944 called themselves "Bulgarians," have no right to identify themselves as Macedonians. They are generally referred to by Greeks as "Skopians," "so-called Macedonians," or "'Macedonians'" (i.e., Macedonians in quotation marks).[3] Papathemelis

---

[2] A parallel shift has occurred in the terminology used to refer to the Macedonian Question itself. In the early 1990s what had previously been called the "nonexistent Macedonian Question" came to be known as the "Skopian Question."

[3] An excellent example of the use of quotation marks to delegitimize Macedonian claims to Macedonian identity can be found in Kofos' (1964) study of the Macedonian Question. Kofos defines "Macedonians" as the name of an ancient "Hellenic people" and as a geographical term "used to denote the inhabitants of Macedonia irrespective of

in a speech presented at a conference in Melbourne in February 1988 referred to them as "a falsely named category of people who constitute the so-called ethnicity of Macedonians of the Skopian type."

The negation of Macedonian identity in Greek nationalist ideology focuses on three main issues: the existence of a Macedonian nation, a Macedonian language, and a Macedonian minority in Greece. The Greek position is that no such thing as a Macedonian nation exists. Since there has never been a Macedonian state, Greek nationalists argue, there cannot be a Macedonian nation.[4] The Macedonian nation is described as a "false" or "forged" nation. It is an "artificial creation," "fabrication," or "invention" of Tito, Yugoslavia's postwar Communist leader, who in 1944 "baptized" a "mosaic of nationalities" (Albanians, Serbs, Turks, Vlachs, Greeks, and Gypsies) and with no justification at all gave them the name "Macedonians." Tito took a geographical term and used it to name a new nationality. In doing so he appropriated all that was geographically Macedonian for the new "Macedonian nation." Unlike Greeks, then, who are born Greek, "the so-called Macedonians" were made; they were created by government decree.[5] In more extreme nationalist rhetoric the Macedonian nation is referred to as a "monstrosity," "a malignant growth" that Greece's allies, the Serbs, should "remove" from the Balkan scene (*Makedhoniki Foni* 1991, 1 [5]:5).

According to Greek nationalists, because the language spoken by the ancient Macedonians was Greek, the non-Greek Slavic language spoken in "Skopje" today cannot be called "the Macedonian language." It is generally referred to in Greek sources as "the linguistic idiom of Skopje." What is more, many Greeks argue, this "linguistic idiom" or "dialect" is not really a language at all. Before World War II the "so-called Macedonian language" was completely unknown. The language used by the Slavic speakers of Macedonia was "an idiomatic form of Bulgarian . . . with a very scanty vocabulary of no more than one thousand to one thousand five-hundred words" many of which were corrupt borrowings from Greek, Turkish, Vlach, and Albanian (*The Mace-*

---

their nationality." He defines " 'Macedonians' " (Macedonians in quotation marks) as "the name given by the Yugoslavs to the Slav inhabitants of upper Macedonia, in the attempt to invest them with a new national identity" (1964:xvi). On this use of quotation marks, see Mackridge (1985:348).

[4] In Greek sources the Republic of Macedonia, which until 1991 was one of the federated states of Yugoslavia, is never dignified with the designation "state." It is always referred to as a "ministate" or a "pseudostate."

[5] Kofos (1989:262), citing Anderson's work on "imagined communities," suggests that Macedonian national identity is "imagined," whereas Greek national identity is "real." This is a clear misuse of Anderson's work to serve the goals of nationalist historiography.

donian Affair n.d.:26). In the words of Nicholas Martis, a former conservative minister of Northern Greece, the "linguistic idiom of Skopje" was "a spoken collection of words, without syntax, without grammatical components, without spelling" (Popov and Radin 1989:46). In 1944 Tito artificially transformed this rural Slavic dialect into a national language and arbitrarily named it "the Macedonian language." As one Greek linguist put it, this language "is linked so closely to both Bulgarian and Serbian that according to linguistic principles it cannot constitute a language in its own right" (Andriotes 1957:6).

The official Greek position with regard to the ethnic composition of the population of Greece is that there are no ethnic or national minorities in Greece at all. Greece is in the fortunate position of being "a country with practically ideal ethnic, linguistic, and religious homogeneity and unity" (Angelopoulos 1979:129). The only exception to this claim of complete ethnic purity is the acknowledgment of the existence in eastern Thrace of what is carefully referred to as a Moslem "religious minority," as opposed to a Turkish "ethnic or national minority," which does not exist. There are no "Turks" in Greece, in other words, only "Moslem Greeks."

Similarly there are no Slavs in Greece, not to mention any "Macedonians." There is only a small group of "Slavophone Hellenes," or "bilingual Greeks" who speak both Greek and "a peculiar Slavic idiom," but who have a "Greek national consciousness" (Kofos 1964:226). As a sign at the "Rally for Greek Macedonia" held in Melbourne in February 1992, put it, "The only Slavs in Greece are tourists." What is often referred to as the "phantom Slavo-Macedonian minority" (Coufoudakis 1992:9) cannot exist by definition. For while there is a Greek minority in Albania "there is not nor can there be an Albanian minority in Albania. There cannot therefore be a Macedonian minority in Greece, since Macedonia constitutes Greece's northern state and all of its inhabitants are obviously Macedonian" (*Vergina* 1991, 1 [1]:2).

From the Greek nationalist perspective, the use of the name Macedonia by the "Slavs of Skopje" constitutes a "felony," an act of "plagiarism" against the Greek people. By calling themselves "Macedonians" these "Slavs of Skopje" are "stealing" or "hijacking" a Greek name; they are "embezzling" or "appropriating" Greek culture and heritage; they are "falsifying" Greek history. If "Skopje" is recognized as the "Republic of Macedonia," if "Slavs" are recognized as "Macedonians," then everything that is Macedonian, in particular the glorious accomplishments of Alexander the Great and the ancient Macedonians, will no longer be recognized as a part of Greek history and civilization, but will become the exlusive property of the Slavs. In the face of such a threat Greeks, especially Greek-Macedonians, are determined to de-

2. Two young Greek-Australians holding signs that
read, "The Only Slavs in Greece Are Tourists" at a
Greek demonstration in Melbourne held on February
22, 1992

fend their name from what they consider to be its "usurpation" and
consequent "monopolization" by foreigners.

The intensity of the Greek response to this threat can be felt at a
variety of levels, from official statements by representatives of the
Greek government to personal statements by individual Greek-Macedonians. Evangelos Kofos, who is himself a Greek-Macedonian, told a
reporter, "It is as if a robber came into my house and stole my most
precious jewels—my history, my culture, my identity" (*Boston Globe*,
January 5, 1993, p. 9). The director of the Office of Foreign Press in the
General Secretariat for Press and Information in Athens compared
Slavs who call themselves Macedonians to "likable donkeys" who happened to be born in the same manger in Bethlehem as Jesus Christ, and

who therefore claim to be descendants of Jesus Christ (*Neos Kosmos*, December 14, 1992, p. 2). Finally, a Greek high school teacher, addressing the Pan-Macedonian Association of Melbourne and Victoria in November 1991, opened his speech with an allegory about a poverty-stricken vagabond who decided to change his name to Onassis in order to lay claim to Onassis' enormous estate. He knocked at the door of the Onassis Foundation, identified himself as a descendant of Aristotle Onassis, and requested his inheritance, but all he received was the reputation for being a devious con man since the name on his birth certificate was Mr. Vagabond, not Mr. Onassis.

As the conflict between Greeks and Macedonians intensified in the early 1990s, Greek-Macedonians in Melbourne experienced anger, frustration, and pain because they felt that their identity as Macedonians was being threatened. One young man, a recent graduate of the University of Melbourne, described his feelings this way:

> I'm Macedonian. I was born in Macedonia. I'm Greek too, because Macedonia is part of Greece. I was raised with the glory of Greece. I'm proud of Alexander the Great. I have the feeling that I'm Macedonian, and that's a part of the feeling of being Greek. My blood boils when I see one of those Slavs dressed up as Alexander the Great at one of their demonstrations. That's a violation of the historical package that is sacred to Greece.

An older Greek-Macedonian professional described his feelings in similar terms.

> When I hear Skopians calling themselves Macedonians, it hurts so much it's indescribable. If I tell Bob Hawke [then prime minister of Australia] that I'm a Macedonian, he'll say "No you're not. You're a Greek." That's an insult; that hurts. The existence of that group takes away my identity. Why should we allow the Slavs the right to be ethnic Macedonians, while we can only be geographic Macedonians?

For many Greeks the use of the name "Macedonia" by the "Republic of Skopje" constitutes something even more serious than a usurpation of Greek history, culture, and identity; it implies that the parts of Macedonia that lie in other countries should also belong to the "Republic of Skopje." In other words, it literally implies territorial claims on Greek Macedonia and therefore constitutes a direct threat to the integrity of the Greek state. Greek commentators point to a variety of evidence to support their view that the "Republic of Skopje" has irredentist designs on Greek territory. For example, the "so-called Macedonians" can often be heard calling for a "free, united, and independent Macedonia" and for "freedom for their unliberated brothers oppressed by Greek rule." They circulate maps of a Greater Macedonia that includes all of Greek Macedonia, which they insist on calling "Aegean Macedonia," a name which itself constitutes a challenge to the legitimacy of Greek sovereignty over the area.

In addition, a new ultranationalist party in Skopje has adopted the name of what Greeks regard as a notorious anti-Greek terrorist organization active earlier this century, the Internal Macedonian Revolutionary Organization (VMRO). The president of this party has explicitly advocated the territorial unification of Macedonia. In an even more provocative gesture, for their new flag the "Skopians" have "stolen" one of the most powerful symbols of the Greekness of Macedonia, the sun or star of the ancient Macedonian kings, which adorned the tomb of Philip of Macedon and was found buried in Greek soil in the village of Vergina in Greek Macedonia. Finally, Greeks argue that Skopje's concern for the human rights of the nonexistent "Macedonian" minority in Greece is simply a cover for its unfulfilled irredentist claims on Greek Macedonia. An increasingly frequent response to these claims is the Greek counterclaim that Greece must protect the human rights of the oppressed "Greek minority of Skopje." A Greek consul in Melbourne went so far as to urge Greeks to liberate the part of Macedonia that is "under the domination of Skopje."[6]

The view of history on which the argument for the Greekness of Macedonia is ultimately based is quintessential nationalist history that reifies both the Greek nation and Greek culture and seeks to demonstrate the unbroken continuity of the Greek "race" and "Hellenism" from the dawn of history to the present. According to this interpretation of history Greeks, and more specifically Greek-Macedonians, not the "Slavs of Skopje," are the modern Macedonian descendants of Alexander the Great and the ancient Macedonians.

According to Greek nationalist historiography ever since Greek-speaking people settled in Macedonia early in the second millennium B.C., Macedonia has been an integral part of the Greek world.[7] Archaeological evidence clearly shows that throughout antiquity "there

[6] Support for the Greek position on the Macedonian Question, as I have outlined it here, is remarkably uniform and widespread. It unites Greeks of different generations, different political parties, as well as Greeks in Greece and in the diaspora. A few voices, however, have been raised in dissent. In May 1992, 169 intellectuals signed a petition criticizing the nationalist passions sweeping through Greece (see Karakasidou 1994). For important Greek scholarship that refutes many of the Greek nationalist claims concerning the Macedonian Question, see Lithoxoou (1992a, 1992b, 1993), Kostopoulos, Embeirikos, and Lithoxoou (1992), and Mouzelis (1994).

[7] The following summary of Greek nationalist historiography on Macedonia draws heavily on a booklet entitled *Macedonia: History and Politics* (*MHP*) put out in English and in Greek by the Center for Macedonians Abroad and the Society for Macedonian Studies. It was also published by the Ministry of Education and Religion for use in Greek schools both in Greece and in the diaspora.

was never any break (either cultural or linguistic) in the unity of the Macedonians with the other Greeks" (*MHP*:8). Ancient Macedonia was a Greek state with a Greek population, which spoke a dialect of ancient Greek, had Greek names, and worshiped the same twelve gods of Olympus as other ancient Greeks. In the fourth century B.C. Alexander the Great, a pupil of Aristotle (who was also a Macedonian), united the quarreling Greek city-states and then, as commander in chief of all the Greeks, spread Greek civilization throughout the known world. For this reason Alexander the Great has come to personify Macedonian Hellenism at its best.

Throughout the Roman and early Christian period the Greek population of Macedonia experienced no "ethnological adulteration" (*MHP*:9). In the sixth and seventh centuries A.D. Slavs, many of whom were later Hellenized, settled in the area. These Slavic invasions "were merely injections to the body of Macedonian history, and in no significant way altered the Hellenic character of the region" (*Makedhoniki Foni* 1992, 1 [1]:3). When a new group of invaders, the Bulgars, were linguistically assimilated by the Slavs and the two groups converted to Christianity, the medieval state of Bulgaria was formed (*MHP*:10). Then in the ninth century Cyril and Methodius, two Greek monks from Thessaloniki, developed the Cyrillic alphabet and spread both literacy and Christianity to the Slavs.[8]

The next few centuries of Macedonian history were characterized by conflict between the Byzantine Empire, a Greek empire whose capital was Constantinople, and the Bulgarian Empire, whose capital was Ohrid in western Macedonia. In 1014 the Bulgarian Emperor Samuel was defeated and thousands of his soldiers blinded by the Byzantine Emperor Basil II, who was known popularly as "Basil the Bulgar-slayer."[9] Then in the fifteenth century, Macedonia fell under Turkish rule when it became part of the Ottoman Empire.

During the Ottoman period, which lasted until 1913, the population of Macedonia consisted of three main groups: Moslems; Christian

---

[8] As many Greek commentators have been quick to point out, even Pope John Paul II, himself a Slav, has referred to Cyril and Methodius as Greeks and authorized the return of their remains from Rome to Thessaloniki, thereby "acknowledging that the Macedonian brothers from Thessaloniki, enlighteners of the Slavs, were Greek" (Mertzos 1987:428). One admirer of Cyril referred to him as "the greatest son of Macedonia since Alexander the Great" (*Makedhoniki Foni* 1992, 2 [14]:7). The view that Cyril and Methodius developed the Cyrillic alphabet is somewhat of an oversimplification. They are believed to have developed the Glagolitic alphabet, a precursor of the Cyrillic alphabet whose development is generally attributed to Clement of Ohrid.

[9] In *The Falsification of Macedonian History* (1983:97) Martis argues that if Samuel had been a "Macedonian," as the "Skopians" claim, then Basil would obviously have been called "Basil the Macedonian-slayer," not "Basil the Bulgar-slayer."

Slavs, who were primarily rural peasants living in the northern part of Macedonia; and Christian Greeks, who had come to occupy dominant positions in the economic, educational, and cultural life of the area. The affairs of the Orthodox Christian population of the empire were under the jurisdiction of the Greek patriarch in Constantinople.

> With the support and guidance of the Greek clergy, the Christian masses of Macedonia acquired a consciousness of their Greek identity.... Numerous Slav-speaking Christians sent their children to Greek schools, fought against the Ottoman Empire during the Greek War of Independence of 1821–28 and later took part, throughout the 19th century, in all the Greek risings in Macedonia, fighting for the unification of Macedonia with the free Greek state. (*MHP*:14)

With the establishment of an independent Bulgarian church known as the Exarchate in 1870, Greece and Bulgaria began to compete openly for the loyalty of the Slavic-speaking population of Macedonia, who had either a Greek or a Bulgarian national consciousness. In 1903 the Bulgarians of Macedonia rebelled against the Turks in what came to be known as the Ilinden Uprising. The Turks quickly suppressed the rebellion, but in the process many Greek cities and towns, such as Krushevo in central Macedonia, were destroyed. In the "Macedonian Struggle" that followed, "Macedonian-fighters," loyal Greeks who came from Macedonia as well as "free Greece," fought against Bulgarian terrorists and Turkish forces in order to preserve "the predominantly Greek character" of Macedonia (*MHP*:15).

The Macedonian Struggle reached its climax with the Balkan wars of 1912–13. In the First Balkan War Serbia, Bulgaria, and Greece easily drove the Ottoman forces out of Macedonia. In the Second Balkan War Bulgaria attacked Serbia and Greece, but was quickly defeated. With the signing of the Treaty of Bucharest on August 10, 1913, Serbia and Bulgaria were awarded the northern part of Macedonia (40 and 10 percent respectively). The southern half of Macedonia, the half which corresponded to the "historical" Macedonia of antiquity and which was now inhabited by Greek speakers and by Slav speakers with a Greek national consciousness, was awarded to Greece. With their victories in the two Balkan wars the Greeks had finally brought about the liberation of Macedonia from both the Turks and the Bulgarians.

The interwar Serbian (and later Yugoslav) goverment attempted quite unsuccessfully to "Serbianize" the Slavs of Yugoslav Macedonia, who generally defined themselves as Bulgarians, but who were officially referred to as South Serbs by the Yugoslav government. During World War II, Tito and the leaders of the Yugoslav Communist Party adopted a new policy toward the Slavs of Macedonia. They decided to

3. One of the most famous "Macedonian-fighters," Pavlos Melas, being honored at a memorial service sponsored by the Pan-Macedonian Association of Melbourne and Victoria

create a new nationality, the "Macedonian" nationality, and they established the "People's Republic of Macedonia" in what had previously been known as "southern Serbia" or "the Vardar Banovina." According to Greek nationalist historiography, it was at this time that the name "Macedonian" first began to be used to denote a specific ethnic or national group (Kofos 1989:243). The creation of a Macedonian nationality was, therefore, a "mutation experiment," a "surgical-type operation" or "face lift," in which the Slavs of Macedonia, "people with inadequately formed perceptions of identity," were "immunized with

'Macedonian' national ideology" (Kofos 1986:159, 163; 1989:250, 259). The political motivations behind this decision were obvious. Tito wanted to weaken Serbia, reverse the Bulgarian leanings of the Slavs of Yugoslav Macedonia, and lay the basis for the creation of a United Macedonia that would incorporate both Greek and Bulgarian Macedonia and become one of the states of the new Yugoslavia.

This process of artificially constructing a new nation, which had begun with the creation of a new state, continued with the creation of a new language and a new church, two important prerequisites for any new Balkan nation. In 1944 linguists in Skopje "invented" a separate Macedonian written language by engaging "in a massive campaign to rid the Slav-Macedonian dialect of all its Bulgarian features and replace them with Serbo-Croatian words" (*The Macedonian Affair*:27). In 1967 the Communists in Skopje succeeded in establishing an independent "Macedonian Orthodox Church" over the objections of the Serbian patriarch. According to Kofos (1986:160), this was an "ecclesiastical coup," which "broke all the canons of the Eastern Orthodox Church."

When Greek Macedonia was liberated in 1913, 43 percent of its population was Greek, 40 percent Moslem, and 10 percent Bulgarian (Angelopoulos 1979:123). During the next ten years the ethnic composition of the population of Greek Macedonia changed dramatically as a result of the upheaval of World War I and Greece's ill-fated Asia Minor campaign, which together led to a series of population exchanges carried out between Greece and Bulgaria and between Greece and Turkey. As a result, virtually all the "alien elements" were "eliminated" from Greek Macedonia, and Greece became "the most homogeneous state of the Balkans, if not of the entire Eastern Europe" (Kofos 1964:47). The Greek census of 1928 (Angelopoulos 1979:126) reported that out of a population of 6 million people in all of Greek Macedonia only 82,000 or 1.3 percent were "Slavophones," that is, Slav-speaking or bilingual inhabitants of Greek Macedonia who had a Greek national consciousness.

During World War II, when Bulgaria, an ally of Nazi Germany, occupied a large portion of Greek Macedonia, many of the Slav speakers in the area identified themselves as Bulgarians and collaborated with the Bulgarian forces in their persecution of the Greeks of Macedonia. Later in the war Yugoslav partisans organized "Slav-Macedonian" resistance units with "the hope of winning Greek Slav-speakers over to the 'Macedonian' ideology . . . and spreading propaganda for the idea of a 'Macedonian nation'" (*MHP*:26–27). During the Greek Civil War, which followed World War II, these "Slav-Macedonians" under the leadership of the Yugoslav Communists continued their efforts to separate Greek Macedonia from the rest of Greece, incorporate it into some kind of "autonomous Macedonia," and eventually bring it under Yugoslav control.

With the defeat of the Communist forces in 1949, 35,000 "Slav-Macedonian deserters" left Greece for Yugoslavia and other countries in eastern Europe. These people were "Slavophones who had been reared as Greeks and felt themselves to be Greeks. . . . [They] were neither Bulgarians nor 'Macedonians' of the Yugoslav type; they were merely a group of resentful Slav-speaking inhabitants from a remote part of Greece who . . . turned first toward the Bulgarians and later toward the Yugoslavs" (Kofos 1964:131). In one of the most tragic episodes of this period, generally referred to in Greek as the *pedhomazoma* (literally a "collecting of the children"), 28,000 Greek children were abducted by the Communists and settled against their will in the Communist countries of the Eastern bloc.[10]

At the end of the Civil War, then, "Greece was delivered of an alien-conscious minority which had actively threatened her security" (Kofos 1964:186). According to Greek nationalist historiography, therefore, there is no longer any Slav minority in Greece, just a small number of "Slavophone Hellenes" whose language is the only thing that distinguishes them from the rest of the Greek inhabitants of Macedonia. Today urbanization, an improved educational system, and a higher standard of living have greatly reduced the incidence of bilingualism. Some of the Greeks of northern Greece, however, do learn the Slav dialect "for reasons of commerce or tourism" (*The Macedonian Affair*:30).[11]

"MACEDONIANS EXIST AND THEY ARE NOT GREEK!" THE AFFIRMATION OF MACEDONIAN IDENTITY IN MACEDONIAN NATIONALIST IDEOLOGY AND HISTORY

In July 1992, the United Macedonians of Victoria published a small pamphlet calling for a boycott of Greek products to protest the Greek government's opposition to the international recognition of the Republic of Macedonia. This pamphlet opens with a straightforward summary of the Macedonian position on the Macedonian Question:

[10] On the *pedhomazoma*, see Baerentzen (1987).

[11] In addition to the works cited here, other sources that convey the content and tone of the Greek position on the Macedonian Question include the scholarly works of Konstantinos Vakalopoulos (1986, 1989), more popular works such as Vissoulis' *O Makedhonikos: Ellinismos* (Macedonian Hellenism) (1988) and Sarantis' *I sinomosia kata tis Makedhonias* (The conspiracy against Macedonia) (1984), and *Makedhoniki Zoi*, a monthly periodical published in Thessaloniki.

The Macedonians are an ethno-specific group with their own national individuality distinct from their neighbours the Serbians, Bulgarians, Greeks and Albanians. They have lived within a naturally defined territory on the Balkan Peninsula for over 4,000 years and are the descendants of the Ancient Macedonians and Alexander the Great.

A common language, traditions, customs and a national consciousness are shared by the Macedonians and have been preserved through a succession of invasions and centuries of foreign rule including Byzantium, Serbian, Bulgarian and the Ottoman Turks.

Macedonian nationalist ideology is dominated by two words: affirmation and recognition. Macedonians are committed to *affirming* their existence as a unique people with a unique history, culture, and identity, and to gaining *recognition* of this fact from international political organizations, the governments of individual countries, the academic community, and world public opinion. In their struggle for recognition Macedonians have had to confront competing claims to their very name and to the territory of Macedonia itself put forward by the Serbs, the Bulgarians, and the Greeks.

In asserting their "ethnospecificity" Macedonians in the Balkans and the diaspora insist that they are not Serbs, Yugoslavs, Bulgarians, or Greeks. In addition, they deny that there is any such thing as a Yugoslav-Macedonian, a Bulgarian-Macedonian, or a Greek-Macedonian. They reject these hyphenated terms as "divisive labels" indicative of a "partition mentality" that must be overcome. There are no Slav-Macedonians either, anymore than there are Slav-Russians or Slav-Poles. The use of such terms negates the existence of the Macedonians as a unique nation; it serves, in the words of a member of the Australian Macedonian Human Rights Committee, "the denationalizing aims of our Balkan masters" and "confirms the propaganda of those who practice genocide upon us."

A politically active Macedonian in Toronto, who was born in northern Greece, described what being Macedonian means to him.

> Our culture dates back to Alexander the Great and the brothers Cyril and Methodi. Unfortunately in 1913 we got partitioned. There goes our identity. Some people say we're really Greeks; some people say we're Bulgarians; but we're not. Our language is close to Bulgarian, but it's different. My father went to a Bulgarian school and learned Bulgarian. But when he spoke Bulgarian, I couldn't understand him. We are *druga nacija*—a different nationality. I don't identify as a Greek or as a Bulgarian or as a Serb. What the hell am I then? I have to be a Macedonian. What else can I be?
>
> After I came to Canada from Florina, I had everything I wanted—in my

work, in my family, everything. But I couldn't find myself. I felt like a bastard, an orphan. Something was missing. When I learned about Alexander the Great and Cyril and Methodi, when I learned about the Republic of Macedonia, I felt proud. Just the way a Greek feels about Greece or a Frenchman about France. I can go to the republic, take a deep breath, and shout all I want in Macedonian. That's me. I feel part of it. You wouldn't believe what that means to me . . . not to be embarrassed or ashamed . . . to be proud of my nationality.

Macedonians, like Greeks, are careful to distinguish between a geographic and an ethnic or national use of the term "Macedonian," but while Greeks argue that "Macedonian" cannot be used in an ethnic or national sense, Macedonians argue that it most certainly can. In the Articles of Association of the Macedonian Orthodox Community of Melbourne and Victoria, a Macedonian is defined as "a person by inheritance who speaks a Slavonic language coming from that area of Europe known as Macedonia whether such is part of Greece, Yugoslavia, Bulgaria, or Albania." In *Macedonia: A Brief Overview of Its History and People*, Michael Radin and Chris Popov, two leaders of the Macedonian human rights movement in Australia, state that in the nineteenth century the term "Macedonian" in an ethnic sense "was erroneously applied" to other ethnic groups in Macedonia, but that since then "it has been used to refer directly and exclusively to Macedonians of Slavonic descent." They add that Greeks and Bulgarians of Macedonia (whose ethnicity is Greek or Bulgarian) "may use the term as a regional or geographic indicator only" (Radin and Popov n.d. a:3).

Just as the Macedonian people have a long history as a distinct ethnic or national group, so Macedonia itself has a long history as a distinct geographical entity. Macedonia is a natural geographic unit whose boundaries ("clearly marked by nature over the course of several millennia") are the Shar Mountains to the north of Skopje, the river Mesta in the west, the Aegean Sea in the south, and the lakes of Ohrid and Prespa in the west. "The country arises amphitheatrically from Solun Bay on the Aegean seaboard," and its major cities include Skopje, Bitola, Prilep, Ohrid, Solun (Thessaloniki), which "lies in the heart of Macedonia," Lerin (Florina), Kostur (Kastoria), and Voden (Edhessa) (Radin and Popov n.d. a:1).[12] The existence of Macedonia as a single ethnographic and geographic entity came to an end with the tragic partition of 1913, when Macedonia was divided up among Serbia, Bulgaria, and Greece. These three parts of Macedonia are known respectively as Vardar, Pirin, and Aegean Macedonia.

---

[12] Of these cities, the first four are in the Republic of Macedonia, the last four are in Greece.

The Macedonians who inhabit Pirin and Aegean Macedonia (as well as those who inhabit the small part of western Macedonia now in Albania) have lost their historical status as a people and as a nation and have been reduced to the status of ethnic minorities. As such they have been subject to harsh policies of forced assimilation, denationalization, and cultural genocide by the governments of Albania, Bulgaria, and Greece. According to Macedonian sources there are about 50,000 Macedonians in Albania, 200,000 in Pirin Macedonia, and anywhere from 200,000 to 350,000 in Aegean Macedonia.[13]

In addition to affirming the ethnospecificity of the Macedonian nation and the existence of Macedonian minorities in Albania, Bulgaria, and Greece, Macedonian nationalists are concerned with affirming the existence of a unique Macedonian language. Radin and Popov (n.d. a:21), for example, while acknowledging the similarities between Macedonian and other South Slavic languages, point out that "there are marked distinctions of a grammatical, lexical, and phonetic nature, which set it [Macedonian] apart as a separate language." They also state that although the Macedonian literary language was "formally created and recognized in 1944 . . . it has a history and lineage dating back more than a millennium" (21). This is because Old Church Slavonic, the literary language developed by "the Macedonian educators" Cyril and Methodius in the ninth century, was based on the local Macedonian dialects of Solun (Thessaloniki). Old Church Slavonic was, therefore, an ancient form of the Macedonian language. International recognition of the existence of the Macedonian language is demonstrated by the fact that it is taught at prestigious universities in over twenty countries around the world (Vidoeski 1971).

As claims about the relationship between Old Church Slavonic and modern Macedonian suggest, the theme of continuity is an important theme in Macedonian nationalist ideology. Whereas Greek claims for the continuity of Greek culture from antiquity to the present are accepted almost unanimously by Greek nationalists, there are several different positions taken by Macedonians with regard to the issue of continuity in Macedonian culture.

According to the more extreme Macedonian nationalist position, modern Macedonians are not Slavs; they are the direct descendants of the ancient Macedonians, who were not Greeks. This claim is at least in part an attempt to refute the Greek claim that "Skopians" are Slavs and not Macedonians. According to extreme Macedonian nationalists "Slavism" is a destructive doctrine that "aims to eradicate Macedonism

---

[13] Some of the sources for these statistics are Popov and Radin (1989:17), Blagoev (1986:196), and Simovski (1978:472).

completely." If Macedonians are Slavs, then they "have no legal right to anything Macedonian"; they "legalize the robbery by the Greeks [of the ancient Macedonians]."[14] Macedonians should not allow the ancient Macedonians to be called Greeks anymore than they would allow themselves to be called Greeks. Thus a unique Macedonian people—neither Slavic nor Greek—has existed in Macedonia since antiquity and continues to exist there now. The most powerful symbols of the continuity of Macedonian culture are "Alexander the Macedonian," as he is referred to in Macedonian sources, and the sun of the ancient Macedonian kings, which in 1992 was chosen as the flag of the newly independent Republic of Macedonia.[15]

The more moderate Macedonian nationalist position, and the one generally adopted by educated Macedonians, is that Macedonians are Slavs and are, therefore, not descendants of the ancient Macedonians. Kiro Gligorov, the first president of the newly independent Republic of Macedonia endorsed this position in June 1992, when he said, "We do not have any relation to Alexander the Great. We are a Slavic people who arrived here [in Macedonia] in the sixth century" (*Neos Kosmos*, June 13, 1992, p. 3). Proponents of this more moderate position often go on to assert that the ancient Macedonians were not Greeks and that the Greek claim to continuity with the ancient Macedonians is, therefore, no more valid than the Macedonian claim.

A third position with regard to the issue of continuity in Macedonian culture is that the modern Macedonians are descendants of the people who came into being as a result of the "mixing" or "intermarriage" that took place in the ninth century between the invading Slavs and the indigenous ancient Macedonians.

Macedonian nationalist history is the history of the long, heroic struggle of the Macedonian people for freedom and independence. It is the history of the struggle of oppressed Macedonians to preserve their common national identity and culture in the face of the forced assimilation, denationalization, and cultural genocide that they experienced in all parts of Macedonia between the partition of 1913 and World War II, and which continues today in both Pirin and Aegean Macedonia. In the early 1990s Macedonians had two different views of the proper goals of the Macedonian nationalist struggle. They had two different views of the future, just as they had two different views of the past. The goal of more extreme Macedonian nationalists is the creation of a "free, united, and independent Macedonia" in which the parts of Macedonia "occupied" by Greece and Bulgaria will be "liberated" and all three regions

---

[14] These views were published in a Macedonian newspaper in Melbourne in 1986 and are cited in Kofos (1990:85).

[15] See the illustration on p. 165.

of Macedonia—Vardar, Pirin, and Aegean—will once again be reunited. Slogans at Macedonian political demonstrations proclaim, "Macedonia for the Macedonians!" and "Salonika belongs to Macedonia!" Others call for the United Nations to rescind the 1913 Treaty of Bucharest and to assist in the geographic unification of Macedonia.

Leaders of the Internal Macedonian Revolutionary Organization—Democratic Party of Macedonian National Unity (VMRO-DPMNE), the major nationalist party in the Republic of Macedonia, advocate the territorial unification of the Macedonian people. In Macedonian diaspora communities of Canada and Australia, one sees maps of a "United Macedonia" with the present international borders marked by strands of barbed wire or with Serbia, Bulgaria, and Greece shown as three wolves about to devour a bone of contention labeled Macedonia.[16] One can also find calendars decorated with photographs of Solun, Lerin, and Kostur. In the words of a Macedonian nationalist in Toronto, "The republic by itself is like a statue with its arms and its legs missing."

More moderate Macedonians realize the impossibility of redrawing international boundaries, recognize the inviolability of Bulgarian and Greek sovereignty, and explicitly renounce any territorial claims against Bulgaria and Greece. They do, however, demand that Bulgaria and Greece recognize the existence of Macedonian minorities within their borders and grant them their basic human rights. These more moderate Macedonians also express the hope that sometime in the future the Macedonian people might be able to achieve some kind of spiritual or cultural union in the context of a "united Europe," a "Europe without borders."

In response to the Greek nationalist argument that there is no Macedonian nation, language, or minority and that "Slavs" or "Skopians" have no right to the Macedonian name, Macedonians accuse Greeks of trying to negate Macedonian identity by monopolizing the name "Macedonia" and by misappropriating it to mean "Greek." They reject the idea that Greeks hold a copyright on the name Macedonia. Macedonian nationalists also dismiss the notion that Greeks and Greeks alone are the heirs of Alexander the Great and the ancient Macedonians, citing the work of Jacob Fallmerayer, the nineteenth-century German scholar who earned the undying enmity of Greeks for discrediting the romantic notion of the continuity of "the Greek race" by arguing that Greeks today are the descendants of Slavs and Albanians who settled in Greece in the Middle Ages.[17]

[16] See, for example, map 3 in chapter 6.

[17] It should be noted that serious scholars reject both Fallmerayer's thesis and the thesis of Greek racial continuity.

4. Two men dressed as Alexander the Great or ancient Macedonian warriors at a Macedonian demonstration calling for the recognition of the Republic of Macedonia held in Melbourne on February 1, 1992

Macedonians argue that while throughout history Macedonians have always been known as Macedonians, Greeks have changed their name many times. During the Roman period they were known as Achaeans; during the Byzantine period they were known as Romans. It was not until 1821 that they came to be known as Hellenes. Finally, Macedonians point out that many famous "Greeks" were not "Greeks" at all: Markos Botsaris, a hero of the Greek War of Independence, was an Albanian, and John Capodistrias, the first president of Greece, was a Venetian. When Greeks claim that Macedonians do not exist, Macedonians respond by claiming that it is Greeks, not Macedonians, who do not really exist.

Like Greek nationalist historiography, Macedonian nationalist historiography is concerned with demonstrating the continuity of the Macedonian people and their culture throughout history. While serious scholarly accounts of Macedonian history reject the claims of extreme nationalists that Macedonians today are the direct descendants of the ancient Macedonians, they almost always begin with some discussion of ancient Macedonia, nevertheless. They may simply point out that the origin and identity of the ancient Macedonians is unclear, or they may argue that the ancient Macedonians were definitely a non-Greek people. In either case Alexander the Great is such a powerful figure, so attractive a candidate for a famous ancestor of the Macedonian people, that he simply cannot be ignored.[18]

Thus a common Macedonian nationalist reading of ancient Macedonian history is that an indigenous, non-Greek Macedonian culture has always existed in the area and that the ancient Macedonian kingdom, which was not part of the world of the Greek city-states, actually constituted the first Macedonian state. Although the upper levels of Macedonian society were gradually Hellenized, Demosthenes and other Greeks continued to regard the Macedonians as barbarians. In the fourth century B.C. Alexander the Macedonian defeated the Greeks in battle, conquered the Greek city-states, and then spread the Macedonian name throughout the known world.

According to more moderate Macedonian accounts, the history of the present-day Macedonians begins in the sixth and seventh centuries A.D. when the ancient Macedonians were assimilated by the invading Slavs (Tashkovski 1976:57). In the ninth century two brothers Cyril and Methodius, Macedonian educators of Slavic origin from Solun, brought literacy and Christianity to the Slavs. This period marks the beginning of the Macedonian Orthodox Church. In 893 Clement and Naum, two disciples of Cyril and Methodius, founded the first Macedonian archbishopric in Ohrid. During the Macedonian Empire of Samuel, which is sometimes referred to as the first Macedonian state, the Archbishopric of Ohrid became one of the most important centers of Slavic culture in the Balkans. After the Greek emperor Basil II defeated Samuel in 1014, the Macedonian church in Ohrid fell under Greek control, where it remained until 1767, when it was abolished by officials of the Ottoman Empire under pressure from the Greek patriarch.[19]

The second half of the nineteenth century witnessed what Macedonian historians often call "a Macedonian national renaissance," a reawakening or revival of Macedonian culture, which had lain dormant for centuries. It was during this period of competing national movements in the Balkans that a small group of Macedonian intellectuals began to form organizations and publish newspapers and journals asserting the existence of a unique Macedonian language, culture, and

[18] See, for example, Andonovski (1978, 1979), Kofos (1994:14–22), Pribichevich (1982:37–64), and Tashkovski (1976:55).

[19] Attempting to explain why Samuel's "Slav-Macedonian" empire was called the "Bulgarian Empire," Tashkovski (1973:35) argues that at the time the term "Bulgarian" was not used to refer to an ethnic group but was only a "political label." On this period in Macedonian history, see also Dimevski (1973) and Panov (1972).

nation. It was also during this period that the first dictionaries, grammars, and textbooks of the Macedonian language were published in spite of strong opposition from Serbian, Bulgarian, and Greek officials. Among the most important figures of this Macedonian cultural renaissance were Ġorġi Pulevski, Grigor Prlichev, Kostantin and Dimitar Miladinov, and Krste Misirkov.

In 1875 Pulevski published a "Dictionary of Three Languages" (Macedonian, Albanian, and Turkish). In the introduction he wrote that "a nation is the term for a people who have the same origin, who speak the same language, . . . and who have the same customs, songs, and festivals. . . . Thus the Macedonians are a nation, and Macedonia is their fatherland."[20] Several years later he founded a Macedonian literary society in Sofia, which was quickly suppressed by the Bulgarian authorities. Prlichev (1830–93) has been called "the most talented figure and the most renowned poet of the Revival period of Macedonian literature" (Vishinski 1973:215), and his work has been described as "one of the most notable contributions to Macedonian literature of the nineteenth century" (Nurigiani 1972:154). The Miladinov brothers, "heroes of the Macedonian renaissance" (Polenakovič 1972:155), published an influential collection of Macedonian folksongs in 1861. As a result of their political activities they both died martyr's deaths in a Turkish prison in Constantinople.

Krste Misirkov, considered "the founder of the modern Macedonian literary language" (Nurigiani 1972:160–61) was an outspoken and unambiguous advocate of Macedonian linguistic and national separatism. In his book *On Macedonian Matters*, published in 1903 in Sofia and immediately supressed by the Bulgarians, Misirkov wrote, "I am a Macedonian. I write in the central Macedonian dialect, which from now on I shall always consider the Macedonian literary language." He not only advocated "completely separating our [Macedonian] interests from those of other Balkan states and independently continuing our own cultural and national development," but he also called for the "recognition of the Slavs in Macedonia as a separate nationality—Macedonians." He stated plainly and simply that the Macedonians are "a separate and independent Slav people" (Misirkov 1974:28, 34, 73, 182).

The national reawakening of the Macedonian people had political and military dimensions as well. After the establishment of the Bulgarian Exarchate in 1870 the Macedonian people became victims of the

---

[20] In citing this passage I have drawn on the translations of Lunt (1984:103) and Zografski (1973:236).

competing nationalist campaigns of Serbia, Bulgaria, and Greece, each of which sent priests, teachers, and bands of guerrilla fighters to terrorize the local Macedonian population and force these Macedonians to adopt a Serbian, Bulgarian, or Greek national identity. The founding of VMRO, the Internal Macedonian Revolutionary Organization, in 1893 by a small group of Macedonian patriots was a powerful affirmation of Macedonian identity and of the desire of the Macedonian people to achieve national independence and self-determination (Radin and Popov n.d.a:8). The rallying cry of VMRO was "Macedonia for the Macedonians."

One of the leaders of VMRO was Gotse Delchev, the father of the Macedonian revolution and the most powerful symbol of the dedication of the Macedonian people to the ideals of freedom and independence. On August 2, 1903, VMRO led the Macedonian peasantry in the Ilinden Uprising, named after the festival of the Prophet Elijah on which it began. This was one of the greatest events in the history of the Macedonian people. The high point of the Ilinden Revolution was the establishment of the Krushevo Republic in the town of Krushevo in central Macedonia. The leaders of the Krushevo Republic called on all the people of Macedonia, Moslems and Christians alike, to join them in fighting for an independent Macedonia. The Krushevo Republic was short-lived, however. Ten days after its liberation, the town of Krushevo was recaptured by the Turks. By November 1903 the Ilinden Uprising had been suppressed.

In 1913 at the conclusion of the Balkan wars a great tragedy occurred. Instead of becoming a free and independent country, Macedonia was partitioned and occupied by Serbia, Bulgaria, and Greece. In this way "the 'living body' of the Macedonian people" was divided (Minčev 1972:152), and the geographic and ethnographic unity of Macedonia, which had existed for over a millennium, was destroyed. From this point until the end of World War II Macedonians in all three regions of Macedonia were subject to violent campaigns of assimilation and denationalization whose goals were to deprive them of their true Macedonian identity and convince them that they were actually Serbs, Bulgarians, or Greeks.

There are two very different views of the postwar history of Vardar or Yugoslav Macedonia, a more moderate or pro-Yugoslav version, which dominated Macedonian historiography as long as Macedonia was part of Yugoslavia, and a more extreme nationalist version, which gained prominence after the breakup of Yugoslavia and the declaration of independence of the Republic of Macedonia in 1991. According to the more moderate view Tito and the leaders of the Yugoslav Commu-

5. A memorial service held on May 10, 1992, at the Macedonian Community Center in Melbourne for Gotse Delchev, the most important Macedonian national hero

nist Party are given credit for the creation of a Macedonian state within the context of a Yugoslav federation. August 2, 1944, when Macedonian independence was officially proclaimed at the first session of the Antifascist Assembly for the National Liberation of Macedonia (known as ASNOM), was "a second Ilinden," "a complete fulfillment of the ideals of the Krushevo Republic." The creation of the People's Republic of Macedonia constituted the "definitive recognition of the national individuality of the Macedonian people and of their sovereignty as a state on the basis of complete equality with the other peoples and nationalities of Yugoslavia" (Tashkovski 1976:123).[21]

According to this pro-Yugoslav version of Macedonian history, since 1944 Macedonians in Vardar Macedonia, the "free" or "liberated" part of Macedonia, have enjoyed almost complete cultural and political autonomy. This freedom has had particularly significant impact in the areas of language and religion. Shortly after independence Macedonian linguists began the process of codification and standardization

[21] September 8, 1991, when the Republic of Macedonia declared its independence from Yugoslavia, is often referred to as "a third Ilinden."

that led to the development of the Macedonian literary language. This process was continued by scholars at the Institute for the Macedonian Language and at the Cyril and Methodius University in Skopje. In the field of religion developments were slower because of the opposition of the Serbian Orthodox Church. In 1958 the Archbishopric of Ohrid was restored, and in 1967 the Macedonian Orthodox Church regained its full independence, exactly two hundred years after the Archbishopric of Ohrid had been abolished.

Revisionist Macedonian historians, influenced by the anti-Yugoslav sentiments that have emerged with increasing intensity in the early 1990s, argue that the policies of Yugoslavia, which they bitterly refer to as "Serboslavia," or "the prison of the Macedonian people," were simply a continuation of prewar Serbian oppression. According to a pamphlet put out by the United Macedonians of Victoria, as long as Macedonia was part of Yugoslavia, Macedonians were "a subjugated people under Serbian domination." Real Macedonian patriots were accused of being agents of Bulgaria and were harassed by UDBA, the Yugoslav secret police. In this view of Macedonian history Tito was a traitor to the Macedonian cause. The real hero of the early years of the Republic of Macedonia was Methodi Antonov Chento, the president of ASNOM, who was imprisoned by Tito for advocating complete independence for Macedonia.

When Aegean Macedonia was occupied by Greece in 1913 the "national structure" of its population was as follows: 28 percent Macedonian, 25 percent Turkish, and 21 percent Greek (Simovski 1978:457). The Greek government immediately began a violent campaign of assimilation and denationalization directed at the Macedonian population, whose existence the Greek government officially denied. The use of the Macedonian language was strictly forbidden, and all Macedonian names (both personal and place names) were replaced by Greek names. In addition, all evidence of the existence of Slavic literacy was destroyed with the desecration of churches, icons, and gravestones that bore inscriptions in Macedonian.

This process of forced Hellenization was accompanied by a deliberate attempt on the part of the Greek government to bring about drastic changes in the ethnic composition of the population of Aegean Macedonia through a combination of forced emigration and colonization. In a series of population exchanges between Greece and Bulgaria over 80,000 Macedonians were forced to emigrate from Aegean Macedonia to Bulgaria, while 23,000 Greeks from Bulgaria were settled in Aegean Macedonia. Similarly in the exchange of populations that took place between Greece and Turkey in 1923, 400,000 Turks were forced to leave

Greece for Turkey, while 1,200,000 Greeks from Asia Minor were settled in Greece. Of these "Asiatic Greeks," 640,000 were settled in Aegean Macedonia as part of a deliberate Greek policy of colonization of the area. By 1928 the Greek population of Aegean Macedonia had risen from 21 percent to 70 percent.[22]

Under the fascist Metaxas dictatorship of 1936–40, repression of Aegean Macedonians was particularly severe. They were fined, imprisoned, and even tortured just for speaking their own language or expressing in any way their national or cultural identity. Toward the end of World War II, Aegean Macedonians formed the Slav National Liberation Front (SNOF) in alliance with the Greek Communist forces in order to resist the fascist occupation of Macedonia by the Germans and the Bulgarians. During this period in the "liberated" areas of Greece under Communist control, Macedonians were free to publish newspapers, establish schools, and hold church services, all in the Macedonian language.

During the Civil War that followed, Aegean Macedonians continued their struggle for the creation of an autonomous Aegean Macedonia, which would ultimately become part of a united and independent Macedonia. But in 1949, with the defeat of the "democratic forces of Greece" by the "promonarchist bourgeois forces" of the Greek government, these hopes were dashed. Over the course of the Civil War thousands of Aegean Macedonians were killed, imprisoned, or had their land confiscated, and many Macedonian villages were completely destroyed. Fifty thousand Aegean Macedonians were forced to flee their homes and escape to Yugoslavia in order to avoid persecution. In one of the most tragic episodes of this period 28,000 Aegean Macedonian children, known as "child refugees" (*deca begalci*), were separated from their families and settled in eastern Europe and the Soviet Union in an attempt to save them from the terror, slaughter, and bombing inflicted on Aegean Macedonians by the Greek government.

In the decades that followed the Civil War, the Greek policies of forced assimilation and denationalization of the Aegean Macedonians continued. Macedonians experienced discrimination particularly in the fields of education and employment. These policies led to the large-scale emigration of Aegean Macedonians from Greece to Europe, Canada, and Australia. Today the Greek government continues to deny the existence of a Macedonian minority in Greece and refuses to grant Aegean Macedonians even the most basic linguistic or cultural rights.

[22] These statistics are drawn from Popov and Radin (1989:14), Radin and Popov (n.d. a:13), and Simovski (1978:462).

In spite of this, two or three hundred thousand Macedonians still live in Greece, concentrated in northwestern Aegean Macedonia in the regions of Kostur (Kastoria), Lerin (Florina), and Voden (Edhessa). They still speak Macedonian; they are still conscious of their identity as Macedonians and not Greeks; and they are still struggling to obtain their basic human rights.[23]

[23] A valuable source on Macedonian nationalist ideology and historiography is the periodical *Macedonian Review*, published since 1971 in Skopje. Other sources include Andonovski-Poljanski (1985), Apostolski and Polenakovich (1974), Nurigiani (1972), Pribichevich (1982), Ristovski (1983), and Tashkovski (1976). See also *Makedonija* and the *Macedonian Newsmagazine*, monthly periodicals published in Skopje. For an analysis of the ideological content of the secondary school textbooks recently adopted in the Republic of Macdonia, see Kofos (1994).

CHAPTER III

The Construction of a Macedonian
National Identity

THE HISTORY of the construction of a Macedonian national identity does not begin with Alexander the Great in the fourth century B.C. or with Saints Cyril and Methodius in the ninth century A.D., as Macedonian nationalist historians often claim. Nor does it begin with Tito and the establishment of the People's Republic of Macedonia in 1944 as Greek nationalist historians would have us believe. It begins in the nineteenth century with the first expressions of Macedonian ethnic nationalism on the part of a small number of intellectuals in places like Thessaloniki, Belgrade, Sophia, and St. Petersburg. This period marks the beginning of the process of "imagining" a Macedonian national community, the beginning of the construction of a Macedonian national identity and culture.

This third history of Macedonia depicts the complex historical process through which some of the Slavic-speaking people of Macedonia, and of Greek Macedonia in particular, developed a Macedonian national identity. This version of Macedonian history also offers important insights into the process by which national identities are constructed. It demonstrates that national identities are categories of ascription which are constantly subject to negotiation and change, that they often emerge in times of conflict, and that their construction involves a process of shared forgetting, as well as shared remembering. This third version of Macedonian history also confirms that national identities develop in opposition to categories of "others"—that people know who they *are not* before they know who they *are*. Finally, it suggests that nationalist policies of persecution and forced assimilation may actually create the very national minorities they are intended to eliminate.

"IN THE PAST WE HAVE EVEN CALLED
OURSELVES BULGARIANS"

Henry R. Wilkinson's study of the ethnographic cartography of Macedonia opens with an admission unlikely to be found in any nationalist account of the area. "Macedonia," he writes, "defies definition for a number of reasons. . . . History no more sets its seal upon the boundaries of Macedonia than does physical geography. . . . This region is distinctive not on account of any physical unity or common political experiences but rather on account of the complexity of the ethnic structure of its population" (1951:2–3). Indeed the diversity of the population of Macedonia in the nineteenth century was so well known that it inspired the French expression "Macédoine," meaning a salad of mixed fruits and vegetables.

Although most accounts of the "ethnic structure" of the population of Macedonia in this period agree that the main groups of people living there were Slavic-speaking Christians, Greek-speaking Christians, Turkish-speaking Moslems, Albanian-speaking Moslems, Vlachs, Jews, and Gypsies, they differ greatly with regard to the size of the various groups, the criteria used to define them, and the terms used to designate them. For these reasons, ethnographic maps and statistical data that attempt to assign precise locations and sizes to these different groups are a welter of confusion, hopelessly marred by inconsistencies and contradictions. As a result, while such material reveals a great deal about the ethnic and national categories employed by the people who compiled it, it reveals very little about the population of Macedonia itself.[1]

Some of the inconsistencies and contradictions in this material can be attributed to the fact that most of the early ethnographers of Macedonia were in the service of one nationalist camp or another. However, many of these inconsistencies and contradictions arose because these ethnographers imposed their *national* categories on people whose world was still organized in terms of linguistic, ethnic, and religious categories—people, in other words, for whom *national* categories held very little meaning. Consider, for example, the following list of groups classified as "Greek" by observers with a Greek nationalist perspective: Greek Moslems, Greek Orthodox Turks and Albanians, Hellenized Vlachs, Bulgarian Patriarchists, Bulgarian-speaking Greeks, and Greek Jews (Wilkinson 1951:316–17). Clearly proponents of other nationalist perspectives could place virtually all these people into different national categories with equal justification.

The population of the Ottoman Empire, which ruled Macedonia from the fourteenth century until 1913, was organized into communities or administrative units, known as *millets*, based on religion rather than on language or ethnicity. Being a Christian, a member of the Orthodox or *rum* millet, as opposed to being a Moslem, was the most

---

[1] See the wealth of ethnographic maps presented by Wilkinson (1951) and the statistical material analyzed by Larmeroux (1918) cited in Perry (1988:19).

important aspect of the identity of most of the inhabitants of Macedonia. Other important aspects of their identity were their status as members of a certain family, residents of a certain village or town, and members of a certain socioeconomic class.

Nationalist ideologies associated with the Enlightenment in western Europe began to penetrate the Balkans in the late eighteenth and early nineteenth centuries. This was the beginning of the age of nationalism in the Balkans, the period that marked the fateful transition from "the ecumenical community of Balkan Orthodoxy . . . to a still inchoate, inarticulate and uncertain world of modern linguistic nations" (Kitromilides 1989:151). An "imagined" community based on a shared Orthodox faith gradually broke up into several "imagined" communities based on a shared sense of national identity. Intellectuals throughout the Balkans began to articulate separate national identities based on a common language and a shared history. These nationalist ideologies spread and eventually reached even the most rural segment of the population of Macedonia.

In the early decades of the nineteenth century Greece, Serbia, and Romania emerged as independent states as a result of national revolts against Ottoman rule. These newly formed states then continued the process of nation building by cultivating a shared national identity with all the means at their disposal—the military, the civil service, and the educational system. In the Balkans one of the most important steps in the nation-building process has been the establishment of autocephalous national churches. In 1833, for example, the Church of Greece unilaterally and uncanonically proclaimed its independence from the patriarch of Constantinople. In this way, as Kitromilides (1989:180) points out, the Church of Greece set an example for other churches in the Balkans to follow.[2]

The establishment of an autocephalous Bulgarian church headed by an exarch in 1870 marked an intensification of the Macedonian Struggle, a three-way contest between Serbia, Bulgaria, and Greece over which country would gain control of the territory of Macedonia. Now Orthodox communities in Macedonia had the choice of affiliating with either the Greek patriarch, the Bulgarian exarch, or the Serbian Orthodox Church. By the first decade of the twentieth century all three of these new nation-states had fielded irregular bands of guerrilla fighters who attacked the Turks, fought each other, and terrorized the local population. In addition, through the construction of churches and schools and the assignment of priests and teachers these three coun-

---

[2] See Ramet (1988) for additional information on the various Balkan Orthodox churches and the role they have played in national politics.

tries conducted intense propaganda campaigns whose goal was to instill the "proper" sense of national identity in the Christian peasants of Macedonia in order to justify their claims to the territory these people inhabited.

In the attempt to incorporate the people of Macedonia into the "imagined" national communities represented by the Serbian, Bulgarian, and Greek states, terms of collective identity, which were in common use and which had no connotation of national identity whatsoever, experienced a form of semantic slippage and took on new national meanings. Thus *"rum,"* meaning "Orthodox Christian," a term that could refer to someone who spoke Albanian, Bulgarian, Turkish, or Greek, was reinterpreted by Greek nationalists to mean "Greek" in a national sense.[3] The term "Bulgarian," which had earlier been used to refer to all the Slavs of the Ottoman Empire (Friedman 1975:84), or as a virtual synonym for "peasant" without any political significance at all (Wilkinson 1951:149), came to mean "Bulgarian" in a national sense.

Similarly, the term "Greek," which was used in the early nineteenth century to refer to members of the Orthodox Christian merchant class regardless of their "ethnic origin" or the language they spoke, came to mean "Greek" in a national sense (Stoianovich 1960:311).[4] During the Ottoman period, therefore, terms like "Bulgarian" and "Greek" were not used to designate different ethnic or national groups; they were used to designate different sociocultural categories in what Hechter (1978) has called a system of "cultural division of labour." In this system of ethnic stratification the process of upward social mobility by which a Slavic-speaking peasant or a Vlach-speaking shepherd entered the merchant class was indistinguishable from the process of "Hellenization." When a farmer or a shepherd became a merchant, he was no longer a "Bulgarian" or a "Vlach"; he became a "Greek." During this time ethnicity was "the modality in which class [was] lived" (Hall et al. 1978:394).[5]

At the turn of the century, then, most of the inhabitants of Macedonia were illiterate peasants with no clearly developed sense of national identity at all. National identity was something that was imposed on

[3] As Kitromilides (1989:178) points out, "One of the greatest anachronisms of Balkan ... historiography has been the injection of national content into [the] traditional religious distinction [between Christian and Moslem]."

[4] See also Vakalopoulos (1989). This same process took place somewhat later in the case of the term "Macedonian." With the spread of Macedonian nationalist ideology in the twentieth century, a term that had been used with a primarily geographical meaning began to be used in an explicitly national sense.

[5] For a more detailed discussion of the relationship between ethnicity and class in the late Ottoman Empire, see Agelopoulos (1993), Van Boeschoten (1993a), and Vermeulen (1984).

them from the outside as a result of the three competing nationalist campaigns of Serbia, Bulgaria, and Greece. As Wilkinson points out (1951:178), any expression of national identity that was encountered among the Macedonian peasantry "was purely superficial, and owed its existence to religious or educational propaganda, or even to terrorism."

Factors that became increasingly important in the construction of collective categories of identity were whether a family or village was affiliated with the Greek Patriarchate or the Bulgarian Exarchate and whether they were Greek-speaking or Slavic-speaking. These factors of religious affiliation and language use were given a national interpretation by proponents of both Bulgarian and Greek nationalist ideologies. While Slavic-speaking Exarchists and Greek-speaking Patriarchists were easily claimed as "Bulgarians" and "Greeks" by their respective nationalist camps, the issue was much more complicated in the case of Slavic-speaking Patriarchists. They were claimed by both sides, by the Bulgarians on the basis of their language and by the Greeks on the basis of their religious affiliation.[6]

Many disinterested observers at the time concluded that the Slavic-speaking inhabitants of Macedonia were "Bulgarians" (R. King 1973:187) and that the term "Macedonian" was not used to identify people as belonging to a distinct "Macedonian" ethnic or national group. Rather "Macedonian" was either used in a general regional sense to designate all the inhabitants of Macedonia regardless of their ethnicity, or it was used more specifically to refer to the Slavic-speaking Christians living in the geographical area of Macedonia. If pressed to assert some other form of collective identity, these people may well have said they were "Bulgarians" (Perry 1988:19; Lunt 1959:20). There was also widespread agreement that the "Greek" population of Macedonia was concentrated in major urban centers throughout Macedonia as well as in rural areas in the southern portion of what is now Greek Macedonia. In the central and northern portion of what is now Yugoslav and Bulgarian Macedonia, the Slavic-speaking population predominated, with "Serbs" more numerous in the northwest and "Bulgarians" more numerous in the east. The part of Macedonia that lay on either side of the present northern border of Greek Macedonia and which was bitterly contested by Greece and Bulgaria was inhabited primarily by Slavic speakers.[7]

---

[6] Needless to say, the situation was further complicated by the fact that many people in Macedonia spoke two or more languages.

[7] See Brailsford (1971:87–88), Dakin (1966:17), Perry (1988:18–20), and Wilkinson (1951:192). This central zone can be described more precisely as the area lying between a line linking Kastoria and Serres in the south and a line linking Ohrid and Melnik in the north.

Sir Arthur Evans, a distinguished British archaeologist and ethnologist who traveled extensively in Macedonia at the turn of the century, described the population of Macedonia as follows: "There are no *Macedonians*. There are *Bulgars*." He went on to add that the Greek claim to Macedonia "is a dream" since "except for a narrow fringe to the south and some sporadic centres of no real magnitude in the interior of the province, the Greek element had no real hold on Macedonia" (Bulgarian Academy of Sciences 1978:540–41).

The British journalist H. N. Brailsford, a perceptive observer of conditions in Macedonia shortly after the Ilinden Uprising of 1903, offers many revealing insights into just how superficial a hold national categories had on the rural population of Macedonia. His observations also show very clearly the incredible facility with which villagers in Macedonia manipulated these categories in a constant process of negotiating identities in a manner designed to serve their interests most favorably. For example, Brailsford mentions a man who sent each of his three sons to a different school, one to be educated as a "Serb," one as a "Bulgarian," and one as a "Greek." He describes a village whose population was "Slav in blood and speech," but which belonged "to the Greek [i.e. Patriarchist] party and took no share in the Bulgarian movement" (1971:160). He describes another village that had been "Greek" four years earlier, but which recently became "Bulgarian" because the Bulgarians had sent the village a teacher *and* a priest, while the Greeks had only sent a teacher. In this way, Brailsford observes wryly, "the legend that Alexander the Great was a Greek goes out by one road, and the rival myth that Alexander was a Bulgarian comes in by the other." Brailsford adds that he once heard "a witty French consul declare that with a fund of a million francs he would undertake to make all Macedonia French" (103).

Commenting on the role of the Orthodox clergy in these nationalist struggles, Brailsford reports that one Bulgarian bishop advised certain villages to transfer their allegiance to the Greek church in order to "distract the suspicions of the authorities." He also points out that the Greek bishop of Florina had to address his flock in Turkish since they were all "Bulgarians" even though Florina was considered a Greek town because it was loyal to the Patriarch (1971:167, 197). Finally, commenting on the Greek policy of trying to prove that Macedonia is Greek by exterminating all the Bulgarians, Brailsford writes that "the worst of this practical ethnography is that it leaves so many corpses to testify to the contrary thesis" (218).

Before 1870 the literate Slavic-speaking inhabitants of Macedonia and Bulgaria were engaged in a common struggle against Greek cultural and linguistic domination in the Balkans. During this period the Slavs of Macedonia called their language Bulgarian. They hoped to create a single Macedo-Bulgarian literary language based on some kind of compromise among the various dialects of Macedonia and Bulgaria (Friedman 1993). It was not until after the establishment of the Bulgarian Exarchate and the increasing attempts by the Bulgarian intellegentsia to impose an eastern Bulgarian–based standard language on the people of Macedonia that efforts to establish a single Macedo-Bulgarian literary language were abandoned and the first signs of Macedonian linguistic separatism appeared. This is the period when dictionaries, grammars, and textbooks began to be published in what was specifically referred to as the "Slavo-Macedonian" or "Macedonian" language. In 1892 the Kostur (Kastoria) parish school council adopted the proposal of a group of teachers "to eliminate both Bulgarian and Greek and introduce Macedonian as the language of instruction in the town school" (Andonovski 1985a, cited in Friedman 1993). However, the Greek bishop and the Turkish governor of the city prevented this from taking place.[8]

The careers of some of the important literary figures in Macedonia in the nineteenth century illustrate the degree to which the different languages and cultures of the Balkans had not yet become separated into bounded, mutually exclusive national spheres. They also poignantly reveal the dilemmas these writers faced as a result of the conflicting nationalist pressures that had begun to converge on Macedonia at this time.

Grigor Prlichev, who was born in Ohrid in western Macedonia in 1830, gained his reputation as a famous poet when his poem *The Bandit*, written in Greek, won a prize in Athens in 1860. He was described as a "second Homer." When Greek officials offered him a scholarship to study in western Europe, however, he turned it down. He realized that even though he loved Greek literature, he was not Greek. Shortly thereafter he left Greece for Macedonia and never wrote in Greek again.

After spending five months in Constantinople learning "the Slav language," Prlichev returned to Ohrid where he was imprisoned by the Greek bishop for opposing the use of the Greek language in the schools and churches of Macedonia. His translation of the *Iliad* into the local Slavic language of Ohrid was dismissed by Bulgarian critics, who said he had a poor knowledge of Bulgarian. Prlichev himself wrote, "In Greek I sang like a swan; now in Slavic I cannot even sing like a donkey." Even though he described himself once as "slain by the Bulgari-

---

[8] On the history of the Macedonian language and the relationship between the development of the Macedonian literary language and Macedonian nationalism, see De Bray (1980), Friedman (1975, 1985, 1986, 1993), and Lunt (1952, 1959, 1984).

ans," toward the end of his life, when he decided to write his autobiography, he chose to write it in Bulgarian.[9]

The brothers Kostantin and Dimitar Miladinov confronted similar challenges. Dimitar was born in Struga on Lake Ohrid in 1810. He received a Greek education and taught Greek there until a visiting Russian scholar encouraged him to teach in his own language. As Dimitar became more interested in his native Slavic language, he developed a Bulgarian national consciousness (De Bray 1980:139). His younger brother Kostantin, after completing his studies in Athens and Moscow, returned to Struga to work with his brother on a collection of folksongs in the local Slavic language. "I shall have these songs . . . published," Dimitar wrote, "so that they can always be sung, because these cursed Greeks will Graecize us and we shall no longer count for anything" (Nurigiani 1972:129).

Unable to find a publisher for his collection in Moscow, Kostantin finally obtained the sponsorship of a Croat bishop and patron of South Slavic culture in Zagreb. After Kostantin transcribed the six hundred songs he and his brother had collected in western Macedonia into the Cyrilic alphabet from the Greek alphabet in which they had originally recorded them, seventy-seven songs from eastern Bulgaria collected by a Bulgarian folklorist were added, and the total collection was finally published in Zagreb in 1861 under the title *Bulgarian Folk Songs* (Bulgarian Academy of Sciences 1978:182).

Finally, Krste Misirkov, who had clearly developed a strong sense of his own personal national identity as a Macedonian and who outspokenly and unambiguously called for Macedonian linguistic and national separatism, acknowledged that a Macedonian national identity was a relatively recent historical development. In *On Macedonian Matters*, published in 1903, Misirkov, referring to himself and other Slavs of Macedonia in the first person plural, admits repeatedly that "our fathers, grandfathers, and great-grandfathers have always been called Bulgarians" and that "in the past we have even called ourselves Bulgarians" (1974:27, 150). He describes "the emergence of the Macedonians as a separate Slav people" as a "perfectly normal historical process which is quite in keeping with the process by which the Bulgarian, Croatian and Serbian peoples emerged from the South Slav group" (153).[10]

---

[9] This account of Prlichev's career is based on the following sources: De Bray (1980:140), Nurigiani (1972:144–59), and Stalev and Kabrovski (1991:103–7).

[10] Bulgarian nationalist historians, who regard Misirkov as a Serb-inspired traitor, attempt to undermine Misirkov's central position in the Macedonian nationalist canon by pointing out that when he taught in a Bulgarian school in Romania in 1918 he identified himself as a Bulgarian and that, like Prlichev, he chose to write his memoirs in Bulgarian (Lunt 1984:107–8).

The political and military leaders of the Slavs of Macedonia at the turn of the century seem not to have heard Misirkov's call for a separate Macedonian national identity; they continued to identify themselves in a national sense as Bulgarians rather than Macedonians. The political goals of the Internal Macedonian Revolutionary Organization (VMRO) were the liberation of Macedonia from the Ottoman Empire and the establishment of an autonomous Macedonia, but VMRO's leadership of the revolutionary movement in Macedonia was challenged by the formation of the Supreme Macedonian Committee in Sofia, whose ultimate goal was the annexation of Macedonia by Bulgaria.

In spite of these political differences, both groups, including those who advocated an independent Macedonian state and opposed the idea of a Greater Bulgaria, never seem to have doubted "the predominantly Bulgarian character of the population of Macedonia" (MacDermott 1978:85).[11] Even Gotse Delchev, the famous Macedonian revolutionary leader, whose nom de guerre was Ahil (Achilles), refers to "the Slavs of Macedonia as 'Bulgarians' in an offhanded manner without seeming to indicate that such a designation was a point of contention" (Perry 1988:23). In his correspondence Gotse Delchev often states clearly and simply, "We are Bulgarians" (MacDermott 1978: 192, 273).

After the failure of the Ilinden Uprising, the struggle for Macedonia continued. In the period leading up to the Balkan wars of 1912–13, Serbia became increasingly involved in what had until then been primarily a conflict between Bulgaria and Greece. In their attempt to achieve the "ethnographic reclamation" of Macedonia (Wilkinson 1951:316–17), the Serbs first had to refute the Bulgarian claims that Macedonia belonged to Bulgaria because the Slavs of Macedonia were Bulgarians. The Serbian position, which was effectively articulated by Jovan Cvijić, one of the most respected human geographers of the Balkans at the time, was that the Slavs of Macedonia were a transitional group located linguistically and culturally somewhere between the Bulgarians and the Serbs. Cvijić gave this group the neutral name of "Macedo-Slavs." According to the Serbs, because the "Macedo-Slavs" did not exhibit any permanent national consciousness, they should be considered "incipient Serbs" (Wilkinson 1951:258).

In 1909 Cvijić published the first map to depict "Macedo-Slavs" as a distinct ethnic group. His later ethnographic maps were extremely influential and were used as the basis for most postwar maps of the Bal-

---

[11] See also Crampton (1983:236), who says that while VMRO refused to commit itself to the Bulgarian state, it "did not dissociate itself in any way from Bulgarian culture."

kans in both Europe and the United States. Through Cvijić's maps, then, the existence of a group of "Macedo-Slavs" became widely accepted, as did the right of the newly created Kingdom of Serbs, Croats, and Slovenes (later Yugoslavia) to retain a large portion of Macedonian territory after World War I (Wilkinson 1951:148–203).[12]

At the end of World War I there were very few historians or ethnographers who claimed that a separate Macedonian nation existed. It seems most likely that at this time most of the Slavs of Macedonia, especially those in rural areas, had not yet developed a firm sense of national identity at all. In a revealing passage from *Life in the Tomb*, Stratis Myrivilis' novel about life on the Balkan front during World War I, a Slavic-speaking family from a village in Vardar Macedonia is described as wanting to be neither "Boulgar," "S'rrp," nor "Grrts" (1977:182). Significantly, there is no positive statement of what they *do* want to be, no assertion of any nationality that they *do* identify with. Of those Slavs who had developed some sense of national identity the majority probably considered themselves to be Bulgarians, although, as R. King (1973:217) points out, they were aware of differences between themselves and the inhabitants of Bulgaria.

MACEDONIANS IN YUGOSLAVIA AND BULGARIA

Throughout the interwar period the official Serbian (and later Yugoslav) position was that the Slavs of Macedonia were "South Serbs." Macedonia was referred to as "South Serbia," and the language spoken there was considered a dialect of Serbian. Serbo-Croatian was the only language permitted in public life (Barker 1950:10, 22; Friedman 1993; Lunt 1959).

The question as to whether a Macedonian nation actually existed in the 1940s when the Communist Party of Yugoslavia decided to recognize one is difficult to answer. Some observers argue that even at this time it was doubtful whether the Slavs of Macedonia considered themselves to be a nationality separate from the Bulgarians (Palmer and King 1971:199–200). Another observer wrote in 1950 that "the feeling of being Macedonians, and nothing but Macedonians, seems to be a sentiment of fairly recent growth, and even today is not very deep-rooted" (Barker 1950:10). Finally, Wilkinson quotes someone from northern Macedonia who at the end of World War II said, "We have experienced enough of both the Serbs and the Bulgarians. Happy was

[12] The first Greek map to recognize the existence of "Macedo-Slavs" was published in 1918 (Wilkinson 1951:192).

the day when we were rid of both." Wilkinson concludes that "the *Macedo-Slavs*, whatever might have been their origins, had arrived at a state in their national development when identification with either the Serbs or Bulgarians was no longer possible in theory or in practice" (1951:299–300).

Whether a Macedonian nation actually existed at the time or not, it is perfectly clear that the Communist Party of Yugoslavia had important political reasons for declaring that one did exist and for fostering its development through a concerted process of nation building, employing all the means at the disposal of the Yugoslav state. In any event, what is important to remember is that the dichotomy between states creating nations and nations creating states is ultimately false. The processes of state formation and nation formation coexist in a dialectical relationship. Together they result in the creation of new nation-states in which the bonds of race, ethnicity, language, and religion, which constitute the nation, are raised to the level of political principles that define the state.

By recognizing the existence of a separate Macedonian nation, the Communist Party of Yugoslavia was able to gain control of Vardar Macedonia and justify retaining it as part of the Yugoslav federation (Palmer and King 1971:199). In order to accomplish this it was necessary to eliminate the sense of Bulgarian national identity shared by many inhabitants of the area, for according to the doctrine of national self-determination, if in fact the inhabitants of Vardar Macedonia were Bulgarians, then the land they inhabited should be part of Bulgaria. Since this was clearly not in the interests of Yugoslavia, and since the previous policy of Serbianization had failed, the only alternative was to recognize the Slavs of Macedonia as neither Bulgarians nor Serbs, but as something else—as Macedonians. Recognizing the Macedonian nation and establishing the People's Republic of Macedonia to serve as its national state was the most effective way for Yugoslav officials to integrate Vardar Macedonia securely into the Federal Republic of Yugoslavia. Another motive behind the Communist Party of Yugoslavia's decision to recognize the existence of a separate Macedonian nation was the desire to extend Yugoslav control over Bulgarian and Greek Macedonia as well.[13]

The decision of the Yugoslav Communists to grant Macedonia a significant degree of autonomy in the cultural sphere was a great impetus to the development of a Macedonian national identity. The establishment of standard literary Macedonian as the official language of the

---

[13] See Andonov-Poljanski (1985, 2:607, 635), Barker (1950:117), and Jelavich (1983, 2:321).

Republic of Macedonia in 1944 was a major contribution to the construction of a distinct Macedonian nationality. It was also regarded by the Yugoslav government as an important "bulwark against Bulgarian irridentism" (Palmer and King 1971:154). Before this period the different dialects of Macedonian were part of a single linguistic continuum that stretched from central Yugoslavia in the northwest, where Serbian was spoken, down into northern Greece and on to the Black Sea coast of Bulgaria in the east, where Bulgarian was spoken. At no point along this continuum could a line be drawn between mutually unintelligible dialects. People living in adjacent areas were able to understand each other, but as the distance between them increased so did the differences between dialects. While Macedonian dialects had few unique traits, they did exhibit combinations of traits that were different from both Serbian and Bulgarian (Lunt 1952:6).

The new Macedonian literary language was based on the west-central Macedonian dialect for two important reasons. It was this dialect that had the most speakers and was the most different from both Serbian and Bulgarian (Palmer and King 1971:155). This was also the dialect that Krste Misirkov had suggested as the basis for a Macedonian literary language in 1903. The language planners involved in the codification of standard literary Macedonian in 1944, however, were working in complete ignorance of Misirkov's work, since most copies of *On Macedonian Matters* had been confiscated and destroyed by the Bulgarian police in Sofia shortly after the book was published (Friedman 1975:91). The decision to establish Macedonian as the official language of the Republic of Macedonia in 1944, therefore, "confirmed what was already *de facto* practice. It did not create a language out of the air, rather it granted recognition to a literary language whose modern development began in the 19th century" (Friedman 1985:35).

Sociolinguists agree that in such situations the decision as to whether a particular variety of speech constitutes a language or a dialect is always based on political, rather than linguistic criteria (Trudgill 1974:15). A language, in other words, can be defined "as a dialect with an army and a navy" (Nash 1989:6). It is clear, therefore, that whatever may have been the situation in 1944, in the fifty years since then a new South Slavic literary language has come into being, the Macedonian language, and its existence has been accepted by scholars throughout the world.[14] These linguistic developments have played an important

---

[14] In the words of Horace Lunt, a distinguished Slavic linguist, Bulgarian scholars who argue that the concept of a Macedonian language was unknown before World War II or who continue to claim that a Macedonian language does not exist "look not only dishonest, but silly," while Greek scholars who make similar claims are displaying " 'arrogant ignorance' of their Slavic neighbors" (1984:110, 120).

part in the larger nation-building process that continued to occur in the Republic of Macedonia after its establishment in 1944.

Before World War II the Bulgarian government had always considered the inhabitants of Bulgarian or Pirin Macedonia to be Bulgarians. Most of the population had probably always considered themselves Bulgarians as well (Palmer and King 1971:197). With the establishment of the People's Republic of Macedonia in 1944, the Bulgarian Communist Party recognized the existence of a Macedonian nation with the hope that should Macedonia become independent it might eventually come under Bulgarian control.

As part of a policy to foster the develpment of a Macedonian national consciousness among the inhabitants of the Republic of Macedonia, the Bulgarian government in 1946 presented the remains of Gotse Delchev, the leader of the Ilinden Uprising, to the government of the Republic of Macedonia. These remains, which had been buried in a church near Serres, where Delchev died in 1903, and which had been taken to Sofia when Serres came under Greek control in 1913, were now transferred from Sofia to Skopje for reburial there. Shortly thereafter 3,500 volumes from the ethnological collection of the Scientific Institute of Macedonia in Sofia were sent to Skopje as well (Kofos 1964:160). Both these events were important symbolic steps in the construction and consolidation of a distinctive Macedonian national identity and culture.

Soon, however, Bulgarian policy shifted, and the Bulgarian government reverted to a more nationalist stance. In 1948 use of the Macedonian language was forbidden in Pirin Macedonia, and by 1958 the Bulgarian Communist Party had again adopted the position that Macedonians were Bulgarians and that neither a Macedonian nation or language existed.[15] Since then Bulgarian scholars have regularly accused Macedonians of attempting to appropriate Bulgarian national heroes and Bulgarian national culture.

The Macedonian Question is still a sensitive topic in Bulgaria. The official position of the Bulgarian government is that no Macedonian minority exists in Bulgaria. According to a recent Helsinki Watch report, however, there are several thousand Bulgarian citizens who have a Macedonian national identity, most of them living in southwestern Bulgaria. Two organizations are concerned with defending the human rights of the Macedonian minority in Bulgaria. Neither of them, however, has been allowed to register by the Bulgarian courts on the

---

[15] According to Palmer and King (1971:188), this intense Bulgarian campaign to deny the existence of a Macedonian nation "was the major factor in bringing about the establishment of the Macedonian Orthodox Church in 1958." See also Pavlowich (1988:341).

grounds that they are separatist organizations that threaten the territorial integrity of the Bulgarian state. Members of these organizations have complained of a variety of human rights violations, including the inability to hold meetings and the confiscation of their passports.[16]

"REAL GREEKS HAVE PARENTS WHO SPEAK GREEK, NOT SOME SLAVIC LANGUAGE"

With the signing of the Treaty of Bucharest at the end of the Balkan wars in 1913, the southern half of Macedonia came under Greek rule. At this point the Greek government began a policy of Hellenization whose goal was to assimilate the ethnically diverse inhabitants of the area and integrate them into the Greek state whose citizens they had recently become. Between 1913 and 1928 the Slavic names of hundreds of villages and towns were Hellenized by a Committee for the Changing of Names, which was charged by the Greek government with "the elimination of all the names which pollute and disfigure the appearance of our beautiful fatherland and which provide an opportunity for hostile peoples to draw conclusions that are unfavorable for the Greek nation" (Lithoxoou 1992b:55). In 1927 the Greek government issued a directive calling for the destruction of all Slavic inscriptions in churches and forbidding church services from being held in a Slavic language. Finally, in 1936 a law was passed ordering that all Slavic personal names, both first and last, be Hellenized (Human Rights Watch/ Helsinki 1994b:6–7). Jovan Filipov, therefore, became Yannis Filippidis, and Lena Stoikov became Eleni Stoikou.

After the exchanges of population that took place at the end of World War I between Greece and Bulgaria and between Greece and Turkey, the percentage of "Greeks" in Greek Macedonia increased, from 43 percent in 1912 to 86 percent in 1926 (Clogg 1979:121). It has been estimated that between 1913 and 1928 approximately 87,000 Slavic-speaking people left Greek Macedonia to be resettled in Bulgaria, while 600,000 refugees from Asia Minor and Bulgaria, classified as "Greeks" because they were Orthodox Christian or spoke Greek, were settled by the Greek government in this area (Rossos 1991:28). The ethnic composition of the eastern and central areas of Greek Macedonia was affected much more by these exchanges of population than the area of western Macedonia, particularly the regions of Florina, Kastoria, and Edhessa,

---

[16] See Human Rights Watch/Helsinki (1991) and United States Department of State (1994:815–25).

where large numbers of Slavic-speaking people continued to live. According to the Kalfov-Politis Protocol signed by Greece and Bulgaria in September 1924, Greece agreed to place its "Bulgarian" minority under the protection of the League of Nations. However, because of objections raised by the Serbian government, which considered the Slavic-speaking inhabitants of Macedonia to be Serbs, and because many Greeks considered the Slavic-speaking people of Greek Macedonia to be Greeks, the Greek parliament in February 1925 refused to ratify the protocol (Kofos 1964:48–49).

In May 1925, the Department for the Education of Foreign-Speakers in the Greek Ministry of Education published the *Abecedar*, described by Greek writers at the time as a primer for "the children of Slav speakers in Greece . . . printed in the Latin script and compiled in the Macedonian dialect" (Andonovski 1976:67). The Greek government submitted this primer to the League of Nations as proof that it had fulfilled its obligations toward its Slavic-speaking minority. The Bulgarians and the Serbs objected vehemently to the publication of the *Abecedar* because it had not been written in Bulgarian or Serbian and because it had not been printed in the Cyrillic alphabet. Although some copies of the *Abecedar* reached villages in Greek Macedonia, it was never actually used in schools there. In one village threats from the local police chief led people to throw their copies of the *Abecedar* into a nearby lake. Residents of another village were called together by their mayor to hear a man who had studied Bulgarian in an Exarchate school sometime before 1913 denounce the *Abecedar* (which he was unable to read since it was printed in the Latin alphabet) as "not written in the language of the Macedonians" (Andonovski 1976:68).[17]

The goal of the Greek government's assimilationist policies in Greek Macedonia were to impose a sense of Greek national identity on the diverse inhabitants of the area, most of whom still identified themselves primarily in regional and ethnic terms. During the interwar period the important ethnic categories that organized social and economic life in rural parts of northern Greece were popularly referred to in Greek as "races" (*ratses* or *files*). Members of the largest of these groups were known as "locals" (*dopii*) or "local Macedonians" (*dopii*

---

[17] It seems clear that the *Abecedar* was printed in the Latin alphabet precisely to insure that it would be rejected by all parties concerned. In that way it would not contribute to the development of ties between the Slavic-speaking people of northern Greece and either Serbia or Bulgaria. Needless to say, Greek nationalist histories of the period do not mention the existence of the *Abecedar* at all, while their Macedonian counterparts seize on it as proof not only that a separate Macedonian language and people existed in northern Greece in 1925, but that this was actually acknowledged by the Greek government as well. See also Andonovski (1985b).

Makedhones). This group was made up primarily of Slavic speakers in the northern portions of Greek-Macedonia and of Greek speakers in the southern portions. Another important ethnic group comprised the "refugees" (*prosfiyes*), people who had come from Asia Minor and Thrace in 1922 in the exchange of populations between Greece and Turkey. In addition, there were the Vlachs (descendants of transhumant shepherds, who speak a language closely related to Romanian and who identify themselves in their own language as Arumani), the Arvanites (who speak a dialect of Albanian), and people from southern Greece (who were sent by the Greek government to work in the "New Lands" of northern Greece as civil servants, teachers, police, and military officials), as well as smaller numbers of Gypsies and Jews. These were the categories of people that the Greek government's policy of Hellenization attempted to subsume under the national category "Greek" and incorporate fully into the Greek nation-state.

In general this policy was quite successful. The refugees, the Vlachs, the Arvanites, and the Greek-speaking local Macedonians readily developed a sense of Greek national identity. For a portion of the Slavic-speaking local Macedonians, however, particularly in the western Macedonian districts of Florina, Kastoria, and Edhessa (whose Slavic names are Lerin, Kostur, and Voden, respectively), this process of Hellenization was much less successful. As a result many of these people did not develop a Greek national identity, but came to identify themselves in a national sense as Macedonians, not as Greeks. The partial failure of this assimilationist policy can be attributed to a large degree to the class conflict that existed between the Slavic-speaking local Macedonians, who were primarily poor farmers in small, rural villages, and members of the other ethnic groups, who often had more land and who, as a result, could more easily enter the urban middle class.[18]

Clear evidence for the failure of the Greek government to impose a Greek national identity on many of the Slavic-speaking local Macedonians in western Macedonia is contained in various internal Greek government documents from the 1930s. In 1930 the prefect of Florina estimated that Slavic-speaking local Macedonians constituted 61 percent of the population of his district and that of these 81 percent were "lacking a Greek national consciousness" (Mavrogordatos 1983:247). Police records and other local government documents, which have recently been published by Dimitris Lithoxoou of the Minority Rights

---

[18] In many cases land bought by local Macedonians from the Turks who had left Greek Macedonia during the exchange of populations in 1922 was declared by the Greek government to be state property and was subsequently distributed to the refugees from Asia Minor (Van Boeschoten 1993a).

Committee in Athens, also demonstrate that a significant number of these Slavic-speaking local Macedonians had developed a distinct identity, not as Greeks, but as Bulgarians or Macedonians. For example, a 1932 report prepared by the prefect of Florina states that of the 80,000 Slavic speakers in the districts of Florina and Kastoria (more than double the number listed in the census of 1928) slightly more than half had "declared Slavic political views" (*dhedhilomena slavika fronimata*) and were "sympathetic to Bulgarism." Equally revealing is a 1934 letter from a police lieutenant to the prefect of Florina that identifies the village of Boufi as "a center of anti-Greek propaganda" where young children know how to read and write the Bulgarian language, where young men sing the Bulgarian national anthem, and where a Macedonian-Bulgarian émigré organization in the United States (the Macedonian Political Organization) has great influence. Not only did many of these people call themselves Macedonians and not Greeks, but they called their language Macedonian and not Bulgarian (Lithoxoou 1992a, 1992b, 1993).[19]

Under the right-wing dictatorship of Ioannis Metaxas, which preceded the outbreak of World War II, the Slavic-speaking population of Greek Macedonia was treated very harshly. People in Florina, Toronto, and Melbourne, who in the 1990s had a Macedonian and not a Greek national identity, recall this period in their lives with particular bitterness. This was the time when many of them finally came to the conclusion that they were Macedonians and not Greeks. A story many Macedonians tell in order to convey the quality of their lives under the Metaxas regime describes an old man riding into Lerin (Florina) to sell garlic and onions at the weekly market. When he says "čukš" to his donkey so that it will stop, he is arrested by a Greek policeman and charged with speaking "Bulgarian." To avoid paying a fine of several hundred drachmas, he has to spend the night in jail. Then, before his release, he is forced to drink castor oil to help purge "the Bulgarian poisons" from his system.

John Markov, a member of the Macedonian community in Melbourne, remembers the Metaxas period as a turning point in his life. Throughout his childhood in a village near Lerin, John's father always told him, "We are not Greek." When John entered Greek elementary school, he didn't know a word of Greek. A few years later, he said, he and some friends were secretly learning how to read and write "Bul-

[19] Official court documents recording sales of land by Slavic-speaking local Macedonians who did not know Greek and who therefore required an interpreter indicate that during the interwar period this language was referred to variously as "the local Slavicizing [*Slavophanes*] idiom" (1937), "the Macedonian linguistic idiom" (1924), and simply "Macedonian" (1930).

garian, or Macedonian as you can call it now." A classmate found one of their notebooks and showed it to their teacher, who notified the police. When the police blindfolded the boy and threatened to shoot him, he told them the notebook belonged to John. The police grabbed John and began hitting him. They knocked him down in the snow and called him a "bloody Bulgarian." Right then and there he took an oath. He said to himself, "I won't tell them anything; I'll hate them forever. May God strike me dead if I ever betray my people! I'll work for my people for the rest of my life." Two years later, in 1939, he left Greece for Australia, where he has been active in Macedonian organizations ever since.

During World War II and the Greek Civil War that followed, the Slavic-speaking inhabitants of Greek Macedonia, many of whom had probably still not developed a strong sense of national identity, were confronted with a stark choice. Years of constant conflict and violence—invasion, foreign occupation, armed resistance, and civil war—had led to a situation where ethnic identities had been politicized and transformed into sharply polarized and mutually exclusive national identities. People who had previously identified themselves primarily as local Macedonians in an ethnic rather than a national sense, and who probably spoke both Greek and their local Slavic language, were forced under very difficult circumstances to adopt a national identity and become Greeks, Bulgarians, or Macedonians.

When the Bulgarians occupied eastern Macedonia in 1941, they began a campaign to win the loyalty of the Slavic-speaking inhabitants of Greek Macedonia and to instill in them a Bulgarian national identity. While some of these people did greet the Bulgarians as liberators, particularly in eastern and central Macedonia, this campaign was less successful in German-occupied western Macedonia.[20] Many of the Slavic speakers who did declare themselves to be Bulgarian were forced to flee across the border to Bulgaria with the retreating Bulgarian army in 1944. Resistance to the German occupation in western Macedonia was organized by the Greek Communist Party, which hoped to win the support of the Slavic-speaking inhabitants of the area by promising them equal rights in a future "people's democracy." Yugoslav Communists encouraged the formation of "Slav-Macedonian" resistance units in Greek Macedonia as part of their efforts to construct a Macedonian national identity among the Slavic-speaking population of Macedonia and gain control over at least part of Greek Macedonia. Given the large number of Slavic speakers who were joining the resistance forces, the Greek Communist Party agreed to the formation of such units.

[20] On the development of national identity in eastern Greek Macedonia, see Cowan (1990:39–49) and Karakasidou (1992).

In areas controlled by the resistance forces, schools were established, newspapers were published, and church services were held, all in the "Slav-Macedonian" language. By 1948, 11,000 children and adults had studied "Slav-Macedonian" in schools operated by SNOF, the Slav National Liberation Front (Kofos 1964:171). This marked an intensification of the process begun during the interwar period through which a "Slav-Macedonian" or "Macedonian" national identity developed among the Slavic-speaking inhabitants of northern Greece. It was at this point that many Slavic speakers who had previously thought of themselves as local Macedonians in a regional or ethnic sense began to refer to themselves as "Slav-Macedonians" or "Macedonians" in a national sense. This was also a time when an increasing number of Slavic-speaking people began to refer to their language as Macedonian, rather than simply as "our language" or "the old language."[21]

Throughout the Greek Civil War the importance of the Slav-Macedonian contribution to the Communist cause continued to increase. According to Greek sources, by the end of the Civil War 30 percent of the Communist-led "Democratic Army" was made up of "Slav-Macedonians," the majority of whom favored some form of autonomy for Macedonia after the war (Kofos 1964:176). These same sources also estimate that at this time more than half of the "Slavophones of Greek Macedonia exhibited a Slav conscience" (Kofos 1964:131).

There were of course many Slavic-speaking inhabitants of Greek Macedonia who had already developed a *Greek* national identity, or who did so at this time. The majority of these people fought with the Greek army against the Communists during the Civil War. In this way a strong link was established between national identity, on the one hand, and political orientation, on the other. Slavic-speaking people who did *not* identify themselves as Greeks tended to support the Communists during the Civil War, whether they were ideologically committed to communism or not. In the process they developed a Macedonian national identity, if they had not already done so earlier. Slavic-speaking people who *did* identify themselves as Greeks generally supported the Greek government and fought against the Communists. In the process their national identity as Greeks was forcefully affirmed.

[21] According to a confidential report submitted to the Foreign Office at the end of World War II by Captain P. H. Evans, a British intelligence officer, the district of Florina was "predominantly a SLAV region not a GREEK one," where Greek was regarded "as almost a foreign language" and the Greeks were "distrusted as something alien." Evans emphasizes that "the inhabitants of the area, just as they are not GREEKS, are also not BULGARIANS or SERBS or CROATS. They are MACEDONIANS" (Rossos 1991:293–94). See also Rossos (1994).

Like the Metaxas dictatorship a decade earlier, the Civil War was a crucial period in the formation of a Macedonian national identity for many people. Looking back on this period Macedonians from northern Greece cannot forget what they experienced at the hands of the Greek authorities. For these people the inability to forget these experiences has played an important part in the construction and maintenance of a Macedonian, rather than a Greek, national identity.[22] Macedonians living today in northern Greece, Canada, and Australia remember seeing their parents and grandparents being beaten by Greek soldiers for singing Macedonian songs or being humiliated by having to learn Greek at night school. They remember growing up alone because their fathers had fled to Yugoslavia and their mothers were in jail.

Angelo Papadopoulos, a Macedonian who emigrated to Melbourne from a village near Florina, remembered his grandfather's last words to his father as his father was about to leave for the mountains to join the Macedonian resistance forces, "You are my only son, but you must die for your mother tongue, for Macedonia." Vangel Rozakis, another Macedonian living in Melbourne who was originally from the Florina area, talked bitterly about his experiences during the Civil War at a Macedonian dance, which was held a few weeks after the referendum on Macedonian independence in September 1991.

> We've been fighting for our freedom for two thousand years. With the referendum we finally broke our chains. The more you suppress a people, the more they assert their identity. People are like tobacco seeds: there can be a drought for thirty or forty years, but when the moisture comes, the seeds will begin to grow.
>
> The hell we've seen, especially from the Greek side. We'll have nightmares till we die. The Macedonian people went through a mincing machine and came out a people who fight for freedom.
>
> My grandfather was arrested because he was a Macedonian. He was sixty years old, and he didn't speak Greek. He didn't know anything about politics either. He went to jail for four years because he wouldn't sign a paper saying he was Greek. I'll never forgive the Greeks for that. Every family here has dropped a tear from the Greek government. My wife saw a Greek soldier cut open a woman who was eight months pregnant and put her baby on the end of his bayonet. That's what makes the nightmares come. Where was the UN? Where was Europe?
>
> I remember sitting with my friends for three days in a dirt hole with no food and no water. The Greek soldiers had machine guns; they were just waiting for orders from Athens to kill us. They dropped a bomb on

---

[22] See chapter 1, note 8, on the role of collective forgetting in the construction of national identities.

my godfather's house and killed eleven members of his family. It wasn't their nation; it wasn't their people. We were Macedonians. They did it so they could bring Greeks from Asia Minor to take our land.

During the 1940s, then, the Slavic-speaking inhabitants of northern Greece, who had to a large extent shared a common regional or ethnic identity, were split into two hostile and opposed groups with different national identities—Greek and Macedonian. At the end of the Civil War many of those who had come to identify themselves as Macedonians left Greece and settled in the Republic of Macedonia in Yugoslavia and in other countries of eastern Europe. Eventually many of them emigrated to Canada or Australia for economic reasons or in order to be reunited with their families.

In Greece the decades following the Civil War were marked by a powerful legacy of hostility, bitterness, and distrust. According to the Greek census of 1951, which was the last to request information concerning "mother tongue," 42,000 Slavic-speaking people remained in Greek Macedonia after the Civil War (Kofos 1964:187). The majority of them had probably developed a Greek national identity. Many of them, however, particularly those who had supported the Communists during the Civil War, had not. Since the public assertion of a non-Greek identity was not possible at this time, members of this group generally adopted a Greek national identity in public, while in private they maintained that they were Macedonians and not Greeks. "After all," they said, "real Greeks have parents who speak Greek, not some Slavic language."[23]

During this period these Slavic-speaking people who knew they were not Greek—these Macedonians—were severely persecuted. They were accused of being "Communists," on the one hand, and "Slavs" or "Bulgarians," on the other. They were considered "enemies of the state" because of their politics and because of their ethnic or national identity. On both counts they were not "real Greeks"; they were not full members of the Greek nation.

The persecution of the Macedonians in Greece took on two particularly egregious forms: the administration of language oaths and the confiscation of property. In the late 1950s the inhabitants of several villages in the districts of Florina, Kastoria, and Edhessa were forced to

---

[23] In 1952 the nomarch of Florina told an American diplomat in Thessaloniki that "70% of the Slav-speaking population of the districts of Florina and Kastoria are patriotic Greeks and strong nationalists while 30% would welcome allegiance to a foreign Slav government." A year later a Greek specialist on Macedonia told an American diplomat that the 60,000 Slavic-speaking people left in Greek Macedonia "were practically all potentially unreliable, *Macedonian* and/or Bulgarian in loyalty" (Iatrides 1993:6, 10; emphasis in the original).

take oaths in which they swore never again to speak "the local Slavic idiom," but to speak only Greek. According to one newspaper account the "simple" residents of Atrapos, a village "whose Greekness was beyond doubt" (but whose old name, a Slavic name, was Krpešina) took "the heroic decision to expel from their speech" this "local Slavic idiom" and in the future speak only Greek, a language "as pure as the crystal clear water of their village." After the raising of the Greek flag to the accompaniment of the Greek national anthem, the people of Atrapos in the presence of church, government, and military officials raised their right hands and repeating the words of their village president took the following oath:

> I promise before God and men and the official authorities of the state that from this day on I shall cease speaking the Slavic idiom, which only gives grounds for misunderstanding to the enemies of our country, the Bulgarians, and that I will speak everywhere and always the official language of my fatherland, the Greek language, in which the Holy Gospel of Jesus Christ is written.[24]

In the late 1940s and early 1950s several laws were passed according to which the property of people who had lost their Greek citizenship because they had fought with the Communists during the Civil War or had left the country illegally could be confiscated without compensation, even if it was occupied by members of their families who had remained in Greece. According to some estimates two-thirds of the 22,000 political refugees to whom these laws applied were Macedonians. These same laws also made provision for the removal from border territories of people who were dangerous to the state and for their replacement with "colonists" from other parts of Greece who had "a healthy national consciousness" (Blagoev 1986:186).

These "colonists" were often settled at government expense on land that had been confiscated from the political refugees who had left Greece. The colonization of the border areas of Greek Macedonia was considered necessary both for demographic reasons and for reasons of national security. The twin processes of confiscation and colonization continued through the 1950s and well into the 1960s. The impact of these laws could still be felt in the 1990s as political refugees, many of them Macedonians, tried unsuccessfully to return to Greece and regain the property they abandoned when they fled north after the Civil War (Blagoev 1986:190).

---

[24] This account is from the Athenian newspaper *Sfera* (September 1, 1959). For similar accounts see *Elliniki Foni* (August 8, 1959), *Foni tis Kastorias* (October 4, 1959), and Pribichevich (1982:246).

During the military dictatorship that ruled Greece from 1967 to 1974 many Macedonians were interned or imprisoned. With the return of democracy, the more coercive forms of harassment and persecution stopped, but the general policies of denying the existence of a Macedonian minority in Greece and attempting to assimilate Macedonians into mainstream Greek society continued. Macedonians in northern Greece, particularly those who actively sought to maintain or express their Macedonian identity, continued to experience discrimination, especially in the fields of education and employment.

Since 1950 the poverty and underdevelopment that have long characterized many rural areas of northern Greece have resulted in serious depopulation through internal migration to urban centers in Greece, as well as through external migration to western Europe, North America, and Australia. Given the fact that the majority of the Macedonian-speaking inhabitants of Greek Macedonia live in rural areas, and given the discrimination they have experienced at the hands of the Greek state, it is not surpising that they have emigrated from this area in particularly large numbers.[25]

For obvious reasons it is difficult to estimate the number of Macedonian-speaking people who remain in northern Greece today. For equally obvious reasons it is even more difficult to estimate how many of these people have a Macedonian, as opposed to a Greek, national identity. According to the report on Greece in the United States Department of State's *Country Reports on Human Rights Practices for 1990* (1991:1172), there are between 20,000 and 50,000 Macedonian-speaking people in all of Greek Macedonia. In a recent report to the European Commission entitled "Minority Languages in Northern Greece," Van Boeschoten (1993b) estimates that in the district of Florina and the neighboring region of Aridhea alone there are approximately 18,000 Macedonian-speaking inhabitants out of a total population of 60,000 people. Some of these Macedonian speakers, perhaps 10,000 or more, have a Macedonian national identity. Since the mid-1980s a small group of Macedonians in Florina and Aridhea has become politically active and begun to demand human rights for the Macedonian minority in northern Greece.

[25] Between 1966 and 1972 Greek Macedonia lost 165,000 inhabitants from a total population of under 2 million. The population of the districts of Florina and Kastoria, which suffered a great deal of damage during the Civil War and which have the greatest concentration of Slavic-speaking people in northern Greece, dropped from 156,000 in 1941 to 116,000 in 1951, and then to 105,000 in 1981 (Sakellariou 1983:510, 516).

CHAPTER IV

Transnational National Communities

UNTIL recently studies of ethnic nationalism have focused primarily on the relationships between ethnic minorities and nation-states. It is no longer possible, however, to understand ethnic and national conflicts in terms of these units of analysis alone. Now with diaspora communities and international organizations playing important roles in nationalist struggles throughout the world, ethnic nationalism must be approached from a more global perspective. Current work on the phenomenon of globalization offers a valuable perspective from which to analyze the new forms taken by national conflicts like the Macedonian Question. Globalization theory shifts our attention away from distinct national societies and cultures and directs it toward consideration of the process by which "the world has become a single place." It leads us to examine how "the world-as-a-whole" is organized (Robertson 1987:30).[1]

In contrast to the expectations of many, the process of globalization has not meant the end of nationalism. It has not brought about the demise of nation-states or the obsolescence of the national identities associated with them, nor has it led to the development of one homogeneous global culture. The European Union and the United Nations have not replaced Greece or Macedonia as important foci of collective identity. Instead, Greeks and Macedonians in the Balkans as well as in the diaspora have begun to carry out their nationalist stuggles on a global scale. The globalization of culture involves the simultaneous and contradictory processes of cultural integration and cultural disintegration (Featherstone 1990b:1). A "United Europe" is coming into being, Yugoslavia is breaking apart, and nationalist conflict between Greeks and Macedonians has spread from the Balkans to Canada and Australia.

In this era of globalization, national communities are being "imag-

---

[1] On the concept of globalization see also Featherstone (1990a) and A. King (1991). As Gregory Jusdanis (n.d. and personal communication) has pointed out, however, it is important not to overemphasize the novelty of these trends toward transnationalism and globalization. See Braudel (1972) and McNeill (1986). The Greek case, and the Jewish case as well, demonstrate that diaspora communities have a long history of active participation in the nationalist struggles of their homelands.

ined" in a new way (Anderson 1983). We are witnessing the construction of *transnational* national communities. The "primordial sentiments" of region, ethnicity, language, and religion have become globalized (Appadurai 1990), spreading throughout the world to unite vast networks of people who remain loyal to a national homeland they no longer inhabit. National communities are not being replaced by transnational ones; they are being constructed on a transnational scale.

Two important developments have made possible the emergence of transnational national communities as major forces in world political affairs in the second half of the twentieth century. The internationalization of labor and the waves of labor migration that took place in the decades following World War II have led to the creation of large diaspora communities scattered throughout the world. These communities consist of people who have left their homeland, either voluntarily or by force, and who have an awareness of constituting a minority immigrant community in the host country in which they have settled. In addition, recent improvements in the fields of communication and transportation now enable diaspora communities to remain much more deeply involved in the national struggles of their homelands than they ever could before. Although members of diaspora communities no longer inhabit their national homelands, these homelands still play an important role in shaping their sense of collective identity. People of the diaspora continue to be members of the nations whose homelands they have left behind.[2]

Diaspora communities are able to maintain their ties to their homelands and to participate in the construction of transnational national communities in a variety of ways. New satellite telecommunications networks, the ease and speed of intercontinental air travel, and the accessibility of new technologies such as electronic mail, fax machines, video equipment, and personal computers all make it possible for national societies, cultures, and identities to transcend the spatial limits of national boundaries and spread throughout the world in what Appadurai has called "global cultural flows" of people, money, information, and images (1990).

In addition these global cultural flows have enabled local communities and identities to retain their meaning and power in the face of the threats posed by the forces of deterritorialization and globalization. A depopulated village in northern Greece with only a few hundred in-

---

[2] On diasporas generally, see the new journal *Diaspora: A Journal of Transnational Studies*; on the role played by diasporas in international politics more specifically, see Sheffer (1986). For a valuable discussion of transnationalism, see Schiller, Basch, and Blanc-Szanton (1992).

habitants may have thriving émigré communities of several thousand living in Canada and Australia. Village associations whose organizational structure parallels that of local village governments, celebrate village festivals with dances, picnics, and barbecues in Toronto and Melbourne. Members of diaspora communities maintain contact with relatives in villages in their homelands through regular phone calls and frequent visits; they watch videotapes of village weddings in their living rooms in Toronto and Melbourne; they contribute money to support schools, churches, and athletic teams in the villages of their birth; and they keep informed of political developments in their homelands through ethnic media, which often reproduce material directly from sources in the national capital.

In this way the centrifugal forces that have fragmented territorially based nations and created diaspora communities around the world have been offset by the centripetal effect of these global cultural flows. The deterritorialization of national communities has not meant the death of nationalism, by any means. It has meant the creation of complex transnational networks in which the problems of cultural reproduction for diaspora communities abroad have become tied to the politics of ethnic nationalism at home (Appadurai 1990:11).

Diaspora communities that have been established in pluralistic Western democracies like the United States, Canada, and Australia are particularly well situated to play an active role in the construction of transnational national communities. The multicultural policies that have been adopted to one degree or another in these host countries have encouraged immigrants to continue to define themselves in terms of their ethnic or national origin. They have also made it possible for the home countries of these immigrants to become actively involved in the educational and religious activities of the diaspora. Members of these diasporas who have experienced significant upward social mobility possess the educational, occupational, and financial resources that enable them to make important contributions to the national struggles of their homelands. Finally, the democratic nature of the host countries' political systems means that they will be sensitive to lobbying efforts conducted by diaspora communities on their homelands' behalf. Well-organized and politically mobilized diaspora communities can, therefore, play an important part in a triadic set of relationships involving diaspora communities themselves, their host countries, and their homelands (Esman 1986:349).

"Exile is the nursery of nationality" (Acton 1967:146, cited in Anderson 1994:315), and the "long-distance nationalism" (Anderson 1994: 326) nurtured there has become a significant force in today's global world.

HOMELANDS AND DIASPORAS

The homelands that lie at the symbolic center of transnational national communities are "inventions"; they are products of the imagination of deterritorialized groups (Appadurai 1990:11). Myths of return and evocative systems of imagery involving parents, birth, roots, and soil all contribute to the power homelands exert over the lives of people scattered in diaspora communities throughout the world (Malkki 1992). When the homeland of a nation is a state in which that nation is dominant, then the homeland will also be the literal center of the network of global cultural flows through which the transnational national community is constructed and maintained. If, however, the homeland is located in a state or states dominated by other nations, then the hub of the transnational national community may be displaced or decentered and come to be located in the diaspora itself.

Greeks of the diaspora generally refer to Greece, their homeland, as the "fatherland," or in a more powerful, if somewhat mixed, metaphor, as the "mother fatherland" (*mitera patridha*). It is also frequently referred to as "our national center" (*to ethniko mas kendro*). Greece is a well-established nation-state with an area of some fifty-thousand square miles and a population of just over ten million. In Michael Herzfeld's apt phrase (1987) Greece is located "on the margins of Europe," enjoying economic and political ties to western Europe as a member of NATO and the European Union, as well as cultural and historical ties to the Balkans and the eastern Mediterranean as a result of the dominant position of the Orthodox Church in Greek society and the legacy of four hundred years of Ottoman rule. Although in comparison with many other Balkan states, Greece is relatively free of large ethnic or national minorities whose demands threaten its stability, Greece does contain within its borders several different minority groups, which vary greatly in terms of their size and the degree to which they have been assimilated into mainstream Greek society.[3]

Within the larger Greek transnational community there is a smaller transnational community of Greek-Macedonians. Greek Macedonia, their homeland, with an area of 13,000 square miles and a population

---

[3] In addition to the Macedonian minority, these include relatively small groups such as the Jews (Molho 1991), the Roma (Gypsies) (Messing 1981), and the Bulgarian-speaking Moslem Pomaks (Sarides 1985); large but fairly well assimilated groups such as the Vlachs (Balamaci 1989, 1991; Schein 1975; and Winnifrith 1987), and the Arvanites; and, finally, the large, unassimilated, and politically mobilized Turkish minority of Thrace (Human Rights Watch/Helsinki 1990; United States Department of State 1990, 1991). For a general discussion of ethnic minorities in Greece, see Keefe et al. (1977), Poulton (1993:173–92), and Siguan (1990).

of just over two million, suffered a disproportionate share of the destruction and depopulation experienced in Greece during World War II and the Civil War that followed. As a result, for several decades thereafter Macedonia remained one of the more underdeveloped parts of Greece. Through both internal and external migration the rural population of Greek Macedonia decreased significantly during the 1960s and early 1970s. This trend, however, has been largely reversed with government-sponsored programs of economic development and modernization that were undertaken in the 1970s and 1980s.

Strictly speaking the sense of community shared by Greek-Macedonians cannot be considered a national community because it does not exist in contrast to, or in conflict with, the Greek national community. It is rather a subcategory, a part, of the Greek national community. Being Greek-Macedonian, in other words, is a regional, or perhaps even an ethnic identity, rather than a national one. Nevertheless, one can almost speak of a Greek-Macedonian "nationalism," whose symbols are easy to identify. Greek Macedonia has its own "capital" city, Thessaloniki, which is frequently referred to as the "co-capital" (*simbrotevousa*) of Greece. It also has its own "national" heroes: the ancient Macedonians and the heroes of the Macedonian Struggle. And since the Macedonian Question became one of the dominant "national issues" facing Greece in 1991, Greek Macedonia has virtually acquired its own national flag (the gold sun or star of Vergina) and its own national anthem—"Famous Macedonia, the land of Alexander, you drove out the barbarians, and now you are free"—both of which featured prominently in demonstrations asserting the Greekness of Macedonia that took place in the early 1990s in cities throughout the world.

The situation with regard to the homeland of the Macedonians is somewhat more complex. The geographical region of Macedonia, the symbolic center or homeland of the Macedonian transnational community, is generally referred to as a "fatherland" (*tatkovina*), or as a "native land" (*roden kraj*). In Macedonian patriotic songs Macedonia is often portrayed as a mother crying for her children who live scattered around the world in Europe, Canada, the United States, and Australia.

Until recently, however, there has been no sovereign or independent state to serve as the literal center of the Macedonian transnational community. Although the People's (later Socialist) Republic of Macedonia was a Macedonian state in the sense that Macedonian was the official language and Macedonians the dominant ethnic group, it was, nevertheless, part of the Federal Republic of Yugoslavia, a multinational state whose existence depended in large part on suppressing, or at least muting, the nationalist sentiments of its constituent nations. In the interest, therefore, of maintaining good relations among the nations of Yugoslavia, as well as between Yugoslavia and its Balkan neighbors, particularly Bulgaria and Greece, the Yugoslav federal government in Belgrade placed strict limits on the expression of Macedonian nationalism.

Since declaring its independence in September 1991, the Republic of Macedonia, with an area of ten thousand square miles and a population of two million, has enjoyed a very fragile existence as a multiparty democracy. Because of Greek objections to its use of the name "Macedonia," it was the last of the former Yugoslav republics to gain widespread international recognition as an independent state. In addition, its economy, which was the weakest of the former Yugoslav republics to begin with, has been devastated by the international boycott of Serbia to the north and the blockade of the republic by Greece to the south. Finally, the stability of the new Republic of Macedonia has also been challenged from within by the fact that over one-fifth of its citizens are members of a large Albanian minority, which openly supports the creation of an autonomous Albanian state.

The Macedonian homeland, the symbolic center of the Macedonian transnational community, does not coincide with the territory of the new Republic of Macedonia, which Macedonians themselves refer to as Vardar Macedonia and which was known more generally as Yugoslav Macedonia. The Macedonian homeland also includes Bulgarian and Greek Macedonia, which Macedonians refer to as Pirin and Aegean Macedonia respectively. Because Macedonians in these areas are members of unrecognized and often persecuted ethnic minorities, they live as exiles in their native land (Pellizzi 1988). Although they live in their national homeland, in other words, they experience it in many respects as a foreign place. Paradoxically the Macedonians of Bulgarian and Greek Macedonia, who have never left their homeland, are less free to express their identity and their culture than Macedonians who have emigrated abroad and live now in multicultural societies like Canada and Australia.[4]

[4] Some authors (Landau 1986) would include the Macedonians of Greece and Bulgaria as part of the Macedonian diaspora. I agree with Esman (1986:333), however, when he argues that "ethnic groups whose minority status results not from migration, but from conquest, annexation, or arbitrary boundary arrangements" differ from diaspora groups and should be treated separately. This approach preserves migration as an essential feature of the diaspora experience and avoids equating a national homeland (the entire geographical region of Macedonia) with the state in which a nation is the dominant group (the Republic of Macedonia itself). From a Macedonian perspective Aegean Macedonia is part of a larger Macedonian homeland, even if it is not part of the Macedonian state. As such it is the target of the irredentist aspirations of extreme Macedonian nationalists in a way that the places inhabited by Macedonian diaspora communities—Toronto and Melbourne, for example—are not.

Although national homelands lie at the symbolic center of transnational national communities, this does not mean that diaspora communities should be considered peripheral to these communities in any way. The geographical displacement of diaspora communities, the physical distance that separates them from their national homelands, grows less and less significant as the world becomes "a single place" through the processes of transnationalization and globalization. Greeks and Macedonians of the diaspora, often living side by side in suburbs of Toronto and Melbourne, just as they once did in villages in northern Greece, participate actively in the conflict over Macedonian identity that dominates the politics of their homelands.

The Greek diaspora, which was in large part responsible for the creation of the Greek nation-state in the early nineteenth century (Jusdanis 1991:209), and which today, according to some Greek estimates, consists of four million Greeks throughout the world (*Neos Kosmos*, August 6, 1992), has played a crucial role in both the Cyprus conflict and the Macedonian Question, two of the most important "national issues" that have confronted Greece in the international political arena during the second half of the twentieth century. Important Greek diaspora communities that have been active in international politics on behalf of their homeland include those in Europe, Canada, the United States, and Australia. Greek diaspora communities in Europe are made up of large numbers of Greeks who emigrated to urban centers in western Europe in the 1960s to work as *Gastarbeiter*, or guest workers, in the large factories of Luxembourg, Belgium, Switzerland, and West Germany.[5]

Greek-Americans constitute the largest Greek community outside of Greece. According to the 1990 United States census slightly over a million Americans identified themselves as being of Greek ancestry. There were two periods when Greek immigrants entered the United States in particularly large numbers: between 1890 and 1920 (when 368,000 Greeks arrived in the United States) and then again in the 1960s and 1970s (when 142,000 did). Many of these Greek immigrants opened small businesses in the cities of the northeastern and north-central states. Since World War II second-generation Greeks have ranked among the highest of all American ethnic groups in educational achievement and in per capita income.[6]

[5] In 1965 alone over 150,000 Greeks emigrated to western Europe (Keefe et al. 1977:80). According to Papadimitriou (1978), in 1975 there were 238,000 Greeks living in northern and western Europe.

[6] This account draws on Saloutos (1980). Other important sources on the Greek-American community are Moskos (1989), Papaioannou (1985), Saloutos (1964), and Scourby (1984).

Emigration from Greece to Canada in the early twentieth century took place on a relatively small scale in comparison with emigration from Greece to the United States. By 1912 fewer than 6,000 Greeks had settled in Canada. After World War II, when the Canadian government adopted much more liberal imigration policies, Greece became one of the most important sources of immigrants for Canada. Between 1945 and 1971 over 107,000 Greeks settled in Canada. During the 1950s and 1960s the number of Greek churches and community organizations increased greatly, so that by 1975 there were over ninety such organizations located primarily in Toronto and Montreal. In the 1991 Canadian census, 191,000 people identified themselves as of Greek ethnic origin.[7]

Many of the early Greek migrants to Australia settled in the goldfields of New South Wales and Victoria in the middle of the nineteenth century. By the end of World War II, however, only 12,000 Greeks had emigrated to Australia. Many of these early immigrants were self-employed and ran their own small businesses. With the opening of an Australian Migration Office in Athens in 1952 and the Australian government's establishment of an assisted-migration program, the number of Greek migrants to Australia increased dramatically. Between 1959 and 1982 160,000 Greeks arrived in Australia. The great majority of them found work in the factories of the industrialized cities of the eastern states, Melbourne and Sydney in particular. According to an estimate prepared for the Australian Bicentenary in 1988, there were 323,000 people of Greek ethnic origin in Australia (Jupp 1988:124). One Greek-Macedonian organization estimated that of these, 55,000 were Greek-Macedonians.[8]

The precise size of Macedonian diaspora communities around the world is extremely difficult to estimate for several reasons. If census data in their host countries employ the category "country of origin," Macedonians (who come from Yugoslavia, Bulgaria, or Greece) are rendered invisible.[9] Even census data that employ categories of "ancestry," "ethnic origin," or "mother tongue" are unreliable for estimating the size of Macedonian diaspora communities because many people who identify themselves as Macedonians in private identify themselves as "Yugoslavs," "Bulgarians," or "Greeks" in official contexts. The reasons why this occurs include fear, illiteracy, and confusion.

In spite of these difficulties it is clear that the Macedonian diaspora

[7] On the Greeks of Canada, see Chimbos (1980).

[8] On the Greek community in Australia, see Bottomley (1979, 1992), Jupp (1988:507–33), Loukakis (1981), Price (1975), and Tamis (1994).

[9] This is an example of what has been called "genocide by census redefinition" (Geertz 1973d:275). See also Anderson (1991:164–70) and Urla (1993).

is much smaller than its Greek counterpart. With one important exception, however, the Macedonian diaspora has been equally involved in the transnational conflict with Greece over the Macedonian Question since it reemerged as a controversial issue in the late 1980s. There are Macedonian diaspora communities in the large cities of western Europe, particularly in Germany, Belgium, and Sweden. There are also Macedonian communities in eastern Europe, in countries such as Poland, Romania, and the former Czechoslovakia, as a result of the settlement of Aegean Macedonian refugees there after the Greek Civil War.

Macedonians in the United States have not participated in the present phase of the Macedonian conflict anywhere near as actively as Macedonians in Canada and Australia. This is because the largest number of Slavic-speaking immmigrants from Macedonia came to the United States during the first decade of the twentieth century, at which time they identified themselves either as Bulgarians or as Macedonian-Bulgarians. It has been estimated that between 1903 and 1906, 50,000 people who identified themselves in this way entered the United States. According to this source, approximately the same number of Bulgarians or Macedonian-Bulgarians still lived in the United States in 1980 (Thernstrom 1980:690–91). The majority of these immigrants settled in the industrial centers of the Midwest where they formed parishes affiliated with the Bulgarian Orthodox Church. The most important organization established by these Macedonian-Bulgarians was the Macedonian Political Organization founded in Fort Wayne, Indiana, in 1922.[10] The MPO, as it is known, publishes a newspaper in Bulgarian called the *Macedonian Tribune* and generally promotes the view that Macedonians are Bulgarians. For this reason the MPO is not considered a Macedonian organization by many Macedonians in Canada and Australia, nor has it played an important role in the Macedonian transnational community during the recent conflict.

Since 1960, when Yugoslav emigration policies were liberalized, most of the immigrants from Macedonia to the United States have come from Yugoslavia and have had a strong sense of Macedonian national identity. They have founded their own churches in affiliation with the Macedonian Orthodox Church of Skopje, as well as their own cultural, sporting, and political organizations, all of which are concerned with preserving a uniquely Macedonian national identity. These organizations (some of which have maintained good relation-

---

[10] In 1952 this organization changed its name to the Macedonian Patriotic Organization.

ships with the Republic of Macedonia and some of which advocate a more extreme and irridentist form of Macedonian nationalism) have succeeded in instilling a distinctly Macedonian national identity in some of the older immigrants from Macedonia who had previously adopted a more Bulgarian orientation. In 1980 there were between 25,000 and 30,000 people who identified themselves as of Macedonian ancestry in the United States (Thernstrom 1980:691).

In contrast to the United States, Canada received only a small number of immigrants from Macedonia in the early twentieth century. As a result the Macedonian-Bulgarian community there has not been anywhere near as influential as it has in the United States. When Canada adopted less restrictive immigration policies in 1947 in an attempt to promote population growth and economic development, large numbers of Slavic-speaking inhabitants of Greek Macedonia were trying to emigrate in order to escape the poverty and destruction caused by World War II and the Greek Civil War. While many of these immigrants identified themselves as Greeks, many others, particularly after they decided to remain permanently in Canada, openly asserted their Macedonian identity.

In the early 1960s with the arrival of large numbers of Macedonians from Yugoslavia a strong Macedonian-Canadian community began to develop. One of the most important organizations in the Macedonian community of Canada was the United Macedonians, founded in Toronto in 1958. In the 1970s an increasing number of Macedonian organizations sought to depoliticize community life by deemphasizing the links between the community and the Republic of Macedonia in Yugoslavia and by stressing the common culture and identity shared by all Macedonians in Canada. Although only 21,000 people identified themselves as of Macedonian ethnic origin on the 1991 Canadian census, one estimate places the number of Macedonians in Canada in the 100,000–120,000 range (Vasiliadis 1989:307, 316).[11]

The history of emigration from Macedonia to Australia is very similar to the history of emigration from Macedonia to Canada. In the early twentieth century men from Macedonia came to Australia as *pečalbari*, workers who left home temporarily in order to earn enough money to build a house or buy additional farmland when they returned to their villages. Many of these men eventually decided to remain in Australia permanently and brought their families there to live with them. Nevertheless, the number of immigrants to Australia from Macedonia before World War II was quite small.[12]

[11] On the early history of the Macedonian community in Toronto, see Petroff (1995).

[12] According to Hill (1988:686) by 1947 there were only 1,300 Macedonians in all of Australia.

In the late 1950s many migrants from Greek Macedonia began arriving in Australia. This included many Aegean Macedonians who had been displaced by the Civil War and had settled originally in eastern Europe before emigrating to Australia. In the 1960s large numbers of Macedonians from Yugoslavia began to emigrate to Australia, just as they had to Canada. These immigrants, who had a strong sense of their Macedonian national identity, settled in the suburbs of large industrial cities and gradually established a variety of Macedonian institutions and organizations that included churches, political organizations, cultural societies, village associations, and soccer teams. According to an estimate prepared for the Australian Bicentenary, in 1988 there were 75,000 people of Macedonian ethnic origin in Australia. Approximately two-thirds of them had come from Yugoslavia and one-third from Greece (Jupp 1988:123–24).[13]

THE CONSTRUCTION OF A GREEK-MACEDONIAN TRANSNATIONAL COMMUNITY

Greeks and Macedonians, both in their overlapping Balkan homelands and in the diaspora, form two transnational national communities that are engaged in what could be described, following Featherstone (1990b:10), as a "global cultural war" over which group has the right to identify itself as Macedonian. These communities, while similar in many ways, exhibit several important differences with regard to how they have been constructed and how they are organized, differences that in turn have a direct bearing on how the global conflict over Macedonian identity has been carried out.

The Greek transnational national community is generally referred to simply as the "*omoyenia*," a cognate of the English "homogeneous," which literally means "[people of] the same [i.e., Greek] birth, origin, or descent [*yenos*]." It can be translated more freely as "the Greek people," "the Greek race," or "the Greek nation." The Greek transnational national community is also referred to as "worldwide Hellenism" (*apandahou ellinismos*). As such it consists of both "expatriate Hellenism" (*apodhimos ellinismos*), or "Greeks abroad," and Greeks living in their "native land" (*yenetira*).

This notion of a "world Hellenism" as "a reified nationality," or "a physical population" (Herzfeld 1987:200) that transcends the territorial

---

[13] There are of course higher and lower figures that could be cited. In the 1986 census approximately 42,000 Australians declared they were of Macedonian ancestry. Hill (1988:691) estimates that there may be 100,000 Australians of Macedonian descent. For further information on the Macedonians of Australia, see Hill (1989).

boundaries of the Greek state, was expressed vividly in a lecture given by a Greek economist teaching at a Canadian university during an international conference on Greeks in the English-speaking diaspora held in Melbourne in March 1992. He compared Hellenism to a beautiful butterfly whose body was Greece and whose wings, "its most precious asset which keeps it alive and aloft," were the diaspora. He went on to call for a "Great Greece of World Hellenism," in which Greeks abroad would be represented in the Greek parliament, which is after all, as he pointed out, the Parliament of Greeks, not the Parliament of Greece (Triantis 1992). An article entitled "Greece of the Five Continents," published in *Makedhoniki Zoi* (Macedonian life), a periodical for Greek Macedonians of the diaspora, also conveys the idea of a nation that is at once deterritorialized and worldwide in scope, created by a kind of nonterritorial, cultural irridentism that occurs as the influence of ancient Greek culture and of modern Greek emigrants spreads throughout the world (Menounos 1992).

The value of the Greek diaspora in assisting the Greek state when it is challenged on vital "national issues," such as the Cyprus conflict or the Macedonian Question, is repeatedly stressed by Greek politicians at all levels. In speeches calling on Greek communities in Canada and Australia to speak out against the "falsification" of Macedonian history by the "Slavs," Constantine Karamanlis, then president of Greece, described "overseas Greeks" as "the largest and most powerful weapon which Hellenism possesses" (Martis 1983:118). Similarly the Greek consul in Melbourne stated in a 1991 radio interview that Australia was the first line of defense in the battle for Macedonia.

The Greek government plays an important role in constructing and maintaining the links that unite Greek diaspora communities with the homeland. Through its embassies and consulates it provides administrative and financial support for diaspora organizations and activities throughout the world. Consular officials responsible for public relations and educational affairs are closely involved in planning community cultural events and coordinating community political activities. Another avenue though which the Greek government interacts with Greek diaspora communities around the world is the General Secretariat for Greeks Abroad, which was established in 1982 as part of the Ministry for Culture. In the early 1990s the General Secretariat for Greeks Abroad was considering a proposal to establish a "Parliament of Greeks Abroad."

There are various diaspora organizations in the United States, Canada, and Australia that participate actively in the life of the Greek transnational national community. These include local parishes of the

Greek Orthodox Church, Greek educational institutions, Greek welfare societies, and Greek athletic teams. Also important are organizations based on place of origin in Greece such as the Cretan Brotherhood of Melbourne or the Pan-Pontian Association of Melbourne and Victoria. In addition there are organizations based on place of residence in the host country such as the Hellenic Canadian Community of Guelph and the Greek Community of Metropolitan Toronto. Finally there are more general cultural organizations such as the American Hellenic Educational and Progressive Association (AHEPA) and the Greek Orthodox Youth Association (GOYA), as well as political lobbying groups such as the United Hellenic American Congress, which was formed in 1975 after the Turkish invasion of Cyprus to promote the interests of Greece in the United States.

Ties linking Greek diaspora communities, their host countries, and their homeland are affirmed both symbolically and in actual practice by the establishment of "sister city" relationships between the cities in the host countries where members of the Greek diaspora live and cities in their homeland where they were born. By 1993 the city of Thessaloniki, the "capital" of Greek Macedonia, had established "sister city" relationships with sixteen cities around the world. In the mid-1980s, when the Macedonian Question had again emerged as a sensitive issue, Toronto and Melbourne became sister cities of Thessaloniki, while Scarborough (one of the satellite cities that makes up Metropolitan Toronto) became a sister city of Florina. These sister city arrangements provide a framework in which a multitude of cultural exchanges are able to take place. A continuous stream of musicians, folk-dance groups, and archaeological exhibits from Greece flows through diaspora communities in cities with large Greek populations. A focus for such events is often the celebration of an ethnic festival such as "Greek Month" in Toronto or the "Antipodes Festival" in Melbourne. Occasionally specific reference is made to the valuable role these sister city relationships play in promoting the Greek position on the Macedonian Question in places like Toronto and Melbourne, which are hotbeds of anti-Greek propaganda from "Skopje."

These networks which link the Greek diaspora and the Greek homeland also exist in the academic world. Exchange agreements have been established between York University in Toronto and the University of Thessaloniki, for example, through which scholars from Greece who specialize in one of the "national issues" facing the country are often invited to present lectures on these topics to Greek communities abroad. The most impressive contexts in which academics participate in these transnational national networks are the many conferences held in cities with large Greek diaspora communities, which bring together scholars from Greece, Greek scholars of the diaspora, and non-Greek scholars to discuss some aspect of Greek history or culture.

In 1988, for example, the Australian Institute of Macedonian Studies organized the First International Congress on Macedonian Studies; in 1989 the Pan-Macedonian Association of America and Canada sponsored a conference at Columbia University in New York entitled "Macedonia: History, Culture, and Art"; and in 1992 the Hellenic Studies Forum held an "international seminar" in Melbourne entitled "Greeks in English Speaking Countries." Present at such conferences as honored guests, and sometimes even as conference participants, are political figures from Greece, from the Greek diaspora community, and from the host country. Their presence testifies to the important role these conferences play in the construction and maintenance of a Greek transnational national community.

The transnational community of Greek-Macedonians, collectively referred to as "Macedonian Hellenism," can be seen as a microcosm of the larger community of "world Hellenism." The Center for Macedonians Abroad in Thessaloniki serves the Greek-Macedonian diaspora just as the Secretariat for Greeks Abroad serves the entire Greek diaspora. In its efforts to promote the Greek perspective on the Macedonian Question and mobilize the Greek-Macedonian diaspora through a program of education and public relations, the Center for Macedonians Abroad is assisted by official government agencies such as the Ministry of Macedonia-Thrace (formerly the Ministry of Northern Greece), as well as by scholarly organizations such as the Society for Macedonian Studies and the Institute for Balkan Studies, which are both located in Thessaloniki.

An important vehicle for maintaining the transnational community of Greek Macedonians is the "monthly illustrated magazine" *Makedhoniki Zoi*, which was described by one of its editors as "the most vital and enduring link between the children of Macedonia living in foreign lands and the Mother Fatherland" (August 1990, p. 7). *Makedhoniki Zoi* has been published in Thessaloniki since 1966 and is read by Greek-Macedonians in Greece and the diaspora. The majority of articles are written in Greek, but it also has a small "English Supplement." Many issues open with a short editorial in support of the Greek position on the Macedonian Question. The articles that follow deal with recent political and cultural events taking place in Greek Macedonia, with important people and events in the history of Greek Macedonia, and with various aspects of Greek-Macedonian folklore. At the end of each issue are short articles written by correspondents in Europe, the

6. The cover of the May 1994 issue of *Makedhoniki Zoi* showing Greek demonstrators opposed to the recognition of the Republic of Macedonia marching along the waterfront toward the White Tower, one of the most famous landmarks in Thessaloniki

PANMACEDONIAN ASSOCIATION
OF MELBOURNE AND VICTORIA

ΠΑΜΜΑΚΕΔΟΝΙΚΗ ΕΝΩΣΗ
ΜΕΛΒΟΥΡΝΗΣ ΚΑΙ ΒΙΚΤΩΡΙΑΣ

ΘΕΣΣΑΛΟΝΙΚΗ

ATHENS

«ΔΗΜΗΤΡΙΑ» 1990
21 ΟΚΤΩΒΡΙΟΥ —
11 ΝΟΕΜΒΡΙΟΥ

"DIMITRIA" 1990
21 OCTOBER —
11 NOVEMBER

CANBERRA
MELBOURNE

7. The official logo of the Dimitria Festival held every year in Melbourne to celebrate the Greek-Macedonian transnational community

United States, Canada, and Australia about the activities of Greek-Macedonian communities of the diaspora.

In addition to the diaspora organizations mentioned thus far, there are several whose specific purpose is to promote the Greek position on the Macedonian issue. They include groups such as the Committee for the Truth about Macedonia in Toronto and the Australian Institute of Macedonian Studies and the Macedonian Academic Society in Melbourne. There are also specifically Macedonian cultural events celebrated by Greek-Macedonian communities in the diaspora. The most important of these is the Dimitria Festival, which was "revived" by the Tourist Board of Thessaloniki in 1966 and is now celebrated in Thessaloniki and in major cities of the Greek-Macedonian diaspora throughout the world. According to its organizers the Dimitria Festival is a continuation of the festival of the same name, which was celebrated in Thessaloniki in the Byzantine period in honor of Saint Dimitrios, the patron saint of the city.

The Dimitria Festival held in Melbourne in 1992 was sponsored by the Pan-Macedonian Association of Melbourne and Victoria. It featured lectures on topics such as the archaeological treasures of Vergina, and "The City of Florina: Bastion of Hellenism," as well as a concert of traditional Greek folk dances entitled "Glimpses of Our Roots," and a memorial service for Pavlos Melas, the most famous Greek hero of the Macedonian Struggle. The official logo of the festival, which was printed on plastic bags distributed by Greek businesses throughout Melbourne, depicted maps of Greece and Australia linked by two arms (with the Greek and the Australian flags on the sleeves) joined in a handshake at the center.

The most important organizations in the transnational community of Greek-Macedonians, however, are without a doubt the various Pan-Macedonian Associations that exist in Greek-Macedonian diaspora communities in the United States, Canada, and Australia, as well as in Greek Macedonia itself. At the transnational level there exists a worldwide Confederation of Pan-Macedonian Associations and Federations. There are also organizations active at the national level, such as the Pan-Macedonian Federation of Australia and the Pan-Macedonian Association of America and Canada, as well as organizations active at the state or provincial level, such as the Pan-Macedonian Association of Melbourne and Victoria, or the Pan-Macedonian Association of Ontario. These organizations, in turn, have as member organizations societies and clubs that represent individual cities, regions, and villages in Greek Macedonia, such as the White Tower Association of Thessaloniki, the Philanthropic Association of Edhessa and Surrounding Villages, and the Association of Papayanni of Florina. The important role these organizations play in promoting Greek national interests is indicated by the fact that the Academy of Athens in 1992 honored the Pan-Macedonian Association of America and Canada for the work it had done in combatting "anti-Greek propaganda" on the Macedonian Question, work that included establishing a branch of the Pan-Macedonian Association Library at New York University, setting up a public relations office in Washington, D.C., and buying expensive advertisements in the *New York Times* for the purpose of "enlightening" American public opinion on the Macedonian Question (*Makedhoniki Zoi*, May 1993, p. 50).

The climax of the activities of all these organizations, and a powerful expression of the transnational community of Greek-Macedonians, is the World Convention of Pan-Macedonian Associations, which takes place every year in Thessaloniki and other sites in Greek Macedonia. One of the purposes of the Fifth World Convention of Pan-Macedonian Associations held in the summer of 1989 was "to defend the Truth about Macedonian History, and to demonstrate to friends and foes alike that Macedonians living abroad have not forgotten their place of origin or their obligation to defend the sacred land of Macedonia." The convention also gave Greek-Macedonians of the diaspora an opportunity to experience "the immense *appreciation* and *love* the people of Greece harbor for them."

After attending a service at the church of Saint Dimitrios in Thessaloniki, participants in the convention attended opening ceremonies at the Society for Macedonian Studies, where they were addressed by Christos Sartzetakis, then president of Greece, who told them that they "have always been the embodied proof of the indestructible historical truth that Macedonia was, is, and will remain, only Greek." Other speakers at the opening ceremonies included the minister of Macedonia-Thrace, the mayor of Thessaloniki, a member of the Australian parliament, and Gerry Weiner, the secretary of state of Canada and minister of multiculturalism and citizenship, who in an interview after the convention expressed the Canadian government's support for the Greek position on the Macedonian Question saying: "There is only one Macedonia, and it is Greece." The opening ceremonies ended with a slide presentation by Dimitris Pandermalis, professor of archaeology at the University of Thessaloniki, on ancient Macedonia.

The convention then moved to a large tourist resort by the sea on the peninsula of Halkidiki near Thessaloniki for several days of business meetings and one "scholarly day devoted to the history of Macedonia," which included presentations by members of the Australian Institute of Macedonian Studies, two former ministers of Northern Greece, and Evangelos Kofos, a historian employed by the Greek Ministry of Foreign Affairs. This portion of the convention ended with the passage of several resolutions denouncing attempts "to falsify the Hellenic identity of the Macedonians and alienate their age-old cultural heritage." The convention concluded with a three-day excursion through western Macedonia during which participants visited the archaeological sites of Pella and Vergina and the cities of Kastoria and Florina, where local officials welcomed them with elaborate receptions. The emotional high point of this excursion was a pilgrimage to the birthplaces of several heroes of the Macedonian Struggle, where wreaths were laid at memorials that had been erected in their honor. In this way "the contemporary Macedonian-fighters" of Pan-Macedonian Associations from around the world were able to renew their ties to the sacred places and the sacred past of their homeland. They were also able to reaffirm their commitment to the transnational community of Greek-Macedonians.[14]

THE CONSTRUCTION OF A MACEDONIAN
TRANSNATIONAL COMMUNITY

The Macedonian transnational community, unlike its Greek counterpart, has not had, and still does not have, a strong independent nation-state at its center to play a leadership role in organizing its activities throughout the world. When the Republic of Macedonia was one of the federated states of Yugoslavia, important aspects of the relationships between Macedonians of the diaspora and their homeland were handled through Yugoslav embassies and consulates, which many Macedonians regarded with suspicion because of the Yugoslav government's hostility to any overt expression of Macedonian nationalism. Given the desire of the Yugoslav government to promote a Yugoslav national identity and its desire to maintain good relationships with its Balkan neighbors, particularly Bulgaria and Greece, Yugoslav embassies and consulates were not in a strong position to serve as vehicles for the construction and maintenance of a Macedonian transnational national community. In fact from the mid-1950s until the late 1980s the Yugoslav government did nothing to encourage the development of any sense of Macedonian national identity that transcended the borders of the Republic of Macedonia and included Macedonians of Bulgaria or Greece.

Even the newly independent Republic of Macedonia has not been in a strong position to support the Macedonian transnational national

---

[14] This account of the Fifth World Convention of Pan-Macedonian Associations is based on an article in *Makedhonia* (Fall 1989).

community either financially or organizationally, given the disastrous state of its economy and the fact that it does not have embassies or consulates in many countries, since it is not widely recognized internationally. As a result, the Macedonian transnational community is decentered; the leadership role in the international conflict between Greeks and Macedonians has been displaced from the "national center," the Republic of Macedonia, to the Macedonian diaspora in Canada and Australia.[15]

The most important organizations through which the Republic of Macedonia has maintained contact with Macedonians of the diaspora, both before and after the breakup of Yugoslavia, are the Macedonian Orthodox Church and the Queen Bee of Emigrants from Macedonia (*Matica na Iselenicite ot Makedonija*), a center for Macedonians abroad whose name effectively conveys the image of the national homeland as a powerful mother who keeps her diaspora children working busily to promote her interests. Since 1954 this organization, whose goals are comparable with those of the General Secretariat for Greeks Abroad and the Greek Center for Macedonians Abroad, has published an "illustrated magazine" *Makedonija*, which promotes the Macedonian perspective on the Macedonian Question with both a format and a content that are remarkably similar to those of its Greek counterpart *Makedhoniki Zoi*. Issues of *Makedonija* generally include articles on recent political, economic, and cultural events in the republic, on Macedonian history and folklore, as well as on the activities of Macedonian communities in the diaspora. Articles documenting the discrimination experienced by Aegean Macedonians at the hands of the Greek government are featured prominently, as are articles describing the activities of Macedonian human rights groups around the world on their behalf. These articles are accompanied by photographs of well-known tourist sites in "Aegean Macedonia," such as "the White Tower of Solun" and "the waterfalls of Voden," places in northern Greece whose photographs are also featured prominently in the Greek magazine *Makedhoniki Zoi*, but which are referred to there by their Greek names: "the White Tower of Thessaloniki," and "the waterfalls of Edhessa."

The referendum on Macedonian independence held on September 8,

---

[15] I am certainly not suggesting here that Macedonian nationalism is a spontaneous, grass-roots phenomenon, whereas Greek nationalism is an artificial product of the Greek state. Such a position would be as mistaken as the often heard Greek claim that all Macedonian nationalists are "agents of Skopje." On both the Macedonian and the Greek sides of the Macedonian Question there exist popular nationalist sentiments as well as government exploitation and manipulation. I am simply pointing out a difference in the resources available to the states that lie at the center of the two transnational national communities.

МАКЕДОНИЈА

ИЛУСТРИРАНО СПИСАНИЕ НА МАТИЦАТА НА ИСЕЛЕНИЦИТЕ ОД МАКЕДОНИЈА   Број 482 VI 1993

8. The cover of the June 1993 issue of *Makedonija* showing the "sun of Macedonia" at the head of a Macedonian demonstration held in Sydney on May 9, 1993

1992, offers some revealing insights into attempts by the government of the Republic of Macedonia to construct a transnational national community of Macedonians, which parallel those of the General Secretariat for Greeks Abroad. Not only were citizens of the republic who had become permanent residents of other countries allowed to vote in the referendum; "ethnic Macedonians" (people who identified themselves as Macedonians, even if they were not citizens of the republic, but citizens of Greece, Canada, or Australia) were allowed to vote as well. At Macedonian Orthodox churches, Macedonian cultural centers, and Yugoslav consulates in Australia, where voting in the referendum took place, citizens of the republic received "official" black ballots, while ethnic Macedonians who were not citizens of the republic received "unofficial" red ballots. Their votes were counted separately; they constituted an expression of "moral support" for the establishment of a sovereign and independent Macedonian state. Nevertheless, by extending the privileges enjoyed by the citizens of a state to people who identify themselves as members of an ethnic or national group, this unusual voting practice conflated the categories of nationality and citizenship, nation and state, and contributed powerfully to the construction of a transnational national community of Macedonians who identify with the newly emerged Republic of Macedonia.

Communities of the Macedonian diaspora have formed much the same range of organizations as communities of the Greek diaspora. Local parishes of the Macedonian Orthodox Church, welfare organizations, and athletic teams are important features of Macedonian communities throughout the world. There are also a large number of Macedonian "cultural and artistic societies" with names such as Cyril and Methodius, Gotse Deltchev, and Ilinden, which are devoted to preserving Macedonian culture. There are many associations based on village or region of origin in the homeland, such as the Skopje Club, the Ohrid Society, and the Macedonian Benefit Society: Prespa, all of which can be found in Toronto, as well as organizations based on place of residence in the diaspora such as the Macedonian Orthodox Community of Melbourne and Victoria, and the Macedonian Community of Western Australia. Finally, there are general umbrella organizations that try to coordinate all the various activities of the individual Macedonian groups, such as the Canadian Macedonian Federation and the Federation of Macedonian Associations of Victoria.

Given the relative weakness of the Republic of Macedonia in comparison to the Greek state, the Macedonian diaspora has had to play more of a leadership role in the international conflict between Greece and Macedonia than the Greek diaspora. Organizations that have attempted to fill this role include the United Macedonians, which promotes the national unity of Macedonians from all three parts of Macedonia in an explicitly irredentist manner, as well as more moderate organizations specifically concerned with the human rights of the Macedonians in Bulgaria and Greece, such as the Australian-Macedonian Human Rights Committee and the Macedonian Canadian Human Rights Committee. In the early 1990s, when the Republic of Macedonia was struggling to gain international recognition from both the European Community and the United Nations, John Bitove, a wealthy member of the Macedonian community of Toronto, founded an International Macedonian Lobby to assist in this effort. As a result, former advisors of two United States presidents and one Canadian prime minister were hired to lobby foreign governments, as well as the European Community and the United Nations, to recognize the Republic of Macedonia as a sovereign and independent state.

At this time Bitove, together with leaders of the Macedonian human rights community in Australia, formed a World Macedonian Congress, modeled after the Jewish World Congress, to promote the interests of the Republic of Macedonia and the Macedonian people throughout the world. Bitove's organization, which enjoyed the full support of President Kiro Gligorov and the moderate government of the Republic of Macedonia, was soon challenged by a rival World Macedonian Congress, formed by people associated with VMRO-DPMNE, the largest opposition party in the republic whose platform is extremely nationalistic. Both congresses held their first meeting in the Republic of Macedonia in August 1993.

One of the major accomplishments of the international Macedonian lobbying effort was the establishment of the Macedonian Information and Liaison Service (MILS), based at first in Brussels and later in Skopje, to provide worldwide distribution of news on Macedonia. Within a short time a competing news service was formed—the Macedonian Information Centre (MIC). Soon the reports of both these news services were being posted daily on MAK-NEWS, an electronic mailing list available over the international computer network, Internet.

The transnational conflict between Greeks and Macedonians has entered the world of electronic communication in other ways as well. In May 1993, when Macedonians attempted to create a discussion group under the name "social.culture.makedonija" or "talk.politics.macedonia," they were prevented from doing so because in the voting required under Internet rules they were outvoted 20 to 1 by Greek Internet users. By 1994, however, both Macedonian and Greek perspectives on the Macedonian Question were being aired on "alt.news.macedonia" and "soc.culture.greek," two unmoderated interactive news groups, which are available to the public over the Internet, as well as on "Make-don" and "Hellas," two moderated discussion groups available by subscription only.

Macedonian diaspora communities have attempted to create ties between cities in their homelands where they were born and cities in their host countries where they live through the establishment of sister city relationships, just as Greek diaspora communities have. However, while Greek Macedonian diaspora communities have been able to link Thessaloniki, the "capital" of Greek Macedonia, with major international cities like Toronto and Melbourne, Macedonian diaspora communities have had to settle for establishing ties between Skopje, the capital of the Republic of Macedonia, and the Borough of East York in metropolitan Toronto, and between Bitola, the second largest city in the republic, and Rockdale, a district in the city of Sydney. The larger and more influential Greek diaspora communities have obviously succeeded in establishing more impressive ties between their host countries and their homelands than the Macedonian diaspora communities have.

Macedonians of the diaspora hold many folk festivals and other cultural events, and they have organized a wide variety of literary societies and drama groups. Educational institutions, academic organizations, and scholarly conferences, however, have not figured anywhere near as prominently in the Macedonian diaspora as they have in the Greek diaspora for several reasons. Not only is the Macedonian diaspora significantly smaller than its Greek counterpart, but it does not contain as many well-educated or professional members. Furthermore, the great prestige accorded the language and civilization of ancient Greece within Western academic circles simply cannot be matched by anything in the study of Macedonian or South Slavic culture more generally.

The Macedonian transnational community has proved extremely difficult to construct and maintain for several reasons. Whereas the Greek transnational community consists almost entirely of Greeks in the national homeland (which is essentially identical to the Greek state) together with economic migrants from the Greek state who make up the Greek diaspora, the Macedonian transnational community is more complex because it is composed of a much more diverse group of people. In addition to Macedonians in the republic and emigrants from the republic who have settled abroad (all Vardar Macedonians), the Macedonian transnational community consists of Aegean and Pirin Macedonians in Greece and Bulgaria, who live as unrecognized minorities in states of other nations, as well as Aegean Macedonians of the diaspora, many of whom are doubly displaced, having first fled their homeland in northern Greece to settle in eastern Europe and then having emigrated to Canada or Australia.

Many of these Aegean Macedonians have had virtually no contact with the Republic of Macedonia, the only state that could possibly serve as their national homeland. In addition, many of them are not allowed by the Greek government to return to their real homeland—their villages in northern Greece—because they identify themselves as Macedonians and not Greeks. Those who *are* able to return to the villages of their birth often experience them not as a homeland but as a foreign land. Having been raised in Canada or Australia as Macedonians, not as Greeks, they speak Macedonian, not Greek, and yet they return to their birthplaces to find Greek, not Macedonian, villages. They return as strangers to the villages where they were born.

Leaders of Macedonian organizations in the diaspora are critical of what they call "the partition mentality," an attitude they attribute to many Macedonians and which they hold responsible for the difficulties Macedonian communities often have working together toward a common goal. This phrase implies that the fragmentation and lack of unity exhibited by Macedonian diaspora communities today has its origins in the "partitioning" of Macedonia accomplished by the Treaty of Bucharest in 1913. It is certainly true that the construction of a Macedonian national identity has been rendered more difficult by the fact that Slavic-speaking people living in different parts of Macedonia have been subject to the assimilationist policies of three different states. For this reason many of these people have come to identify themselves as Yugoslavs, Bulgarians, or Greeks. As we shall see in Chapters VII and VIII, there are people from the same villages, even the same families, who have adopted different national identities.

The situation, however, is even more complex than this. Even people who participate in the transnational Macedonian community, people who identify themselves first and foremost as Macedonians (as opposed to Yugoslavs, Bulgarians, or Greeks), are split into three distinct regional groups. It has been difficult for Vardar Macedonians from Yugoslavia, Pirin Macedonians from Bulgaria, and Aegean Macedonians from Greece to construct a shared national identity because until very recently at least there has never been a state that has attempted to create such an identity. On the contrary, the governments of Greece, Bulgaria, and (to a lesser extent) Yugoslavia have actively opposed such a process.[16]

---

[16] On the internal divisions of the Macedonian community in Toronto, see Kramer (1993).

Many Macedonians in Melbourne, both Vardar and Aegean Macedonians, say that before they came to Australia they had no idea there
were people like themselves, fellow Macedonians, *"naši"* ("our people"), on the other side of the border between Yugoslavia and Greece.
People who define themselves now as Aegean Macedonians say that
while they were growing up in northern Greece they thought that the
only people who lived north of the border "in Serbia," as they put it,
were "Serbians." Conversely, Vardar Macedonians thought that the
only people living across the border to the south were "Greeks." It was
not until they settled in Canada and Australia that they realized they
shared a common language and a common culture with people from
the other side of the border. Only with that realization did Vardar and
Aegean Macedonians of the diaspora begin the process of constructing
a common Macedonian national identity.

This process was itself not without difficulties, for in many ways
Vardar and Aegean Macedonians did *not* share a common language or
culture. Some Aegean Macedonians, who spoke only the local Macedonian dialects of the villages of their birth, said they could not understand educated Vardar Macedonians, who spoke standard literary
Macedonian; they thought they were speaking Serbian. Conversely
Vardar Macedonians sometimes pointed out that Aegean Macedonians
served guests coffee and water together, the way Greeks did, or that
bands from Aegean Macedonia played Macedonian music "in a Greek
style" with a bouzouki, which everyone knows is a Greek instrument.
When conflicts between them arose, Aegean Macedonians would call
Vardar Macedonians "Yugoslavs" or "Serbs," while Vardar Macedonians would call Aegean Macedonians "Greek lovers" (*Grkomani*). As a
Vardar Macedonian high school student in Melbourne put it, "Sometimes *Egej* [Aegean Macedonian] kids say they're Greek, sometimes
they say they're Maso. My parents say they're two-faced." In contexts
where a common Macedonian identity is being stressed, such comments are attributed to "a partition mentality" and criticized as de-
visive and destructive.

In many cases immigrants to large cities in Canada and Australia
from Vardar Macedonia settled in different residential areas from immigrants from Aegean Macedonia. As a result, the two communities
often have separate churches, separate social organizations, and separate community centers. In Melbourne, for example, the majority of
Vardar Macedonians live in the western part of the city, whereas
most Aegean Macedonians live in the northern suburbs. It was not
until the mid-1980s, when serious efforts began to be made to construct
one unified Macedonian transnational community, that the two communities came together under one umbrella organization, the Federa-

tion of Macedonian Associations of Victoria. When the Yugoslav consul in Melbourne (a Macedonian who supported the Yugoslav government's official position that a Macedonian nation existed only within the borders of Yugoslavia) learned of these developments, he asked community leaders "Do you think you will unify Macedonia here in Australia?"

A revealing expression of the difficulty of constructing a unified Macedonian transnational community from such a diverse group of people occurred in the summer of 1992 during the visit to Melbourne of Christos Sideropoulos, one of the leaders of the movement for Macedonian human rights in Greece. The purpose of his visit was to raise money from the Aegean Macedonian community of Melbourne for the work of the Committee for Macedonian Human Rights in northern Greece, as well as to strengthen the ties between the Aegean Macedonians in Australia and those in Greece. After meeting with Australian government officials in the Ministry of Foreign Affairs and in the Office of Multicultural Affairs, Sideropoulos spoke to a small group of Aegean Macedonians at a dinner held at a restaurant in the northern suburbs of the city.

Sideropoulos criticized Aegean Macedonians in Australia for engaging in petty leadership disputes and for lacking a greater sense of focus and unity. He said they needed to fight peacefully to convince the world that Macedonians exist. "We need a common language in order to be united, or else we're lost," he said. Sideropoulos clearly intended that his reference to a "common language" be taken figuratively. Taken literally, however, this comment revealed a bitter irony. Because he had never had the opportunity to learn Macedonian properly while growing up in Greece, Sideropoulos was speaking Greek. Several members of the audience, who had grown up in Australia speaking Macedonian and English, could not understand the language he was speaking.

The formation of the Association of Child Refugees from Aegean Macedonia represents an attempt by Aegean Macedonians who left their homes at the end of the Greek Civil War in 1948 to construct a transnational community. The association was founded in 1986 at the initiative of Aegean Macedonians in Canada. It is headquartered in Skopje and has branches in Romania, Poland, the former Czechoslovakia, Canada, and Australia. The goals of the association include publicizing the plight of the "child refugees," lobbying for their right to return to their homeland in Greece, and protesting more generally the discrimination Aegean Macedonians have experienced at the hands of the Greek government.

The unofficial anthem of Aegean Macedonians, which can be heard at virtually all their social and political gatherings, is "Where Are You,

Children of Macedonia?" (*Kade ste Makedončinja?*), a song written by a Vardar Macedonian in Australia, who had known nothing about the experiences of the "child refugees" until he learned about them from members of the Macedonian community in Adelaide. The song's refrain laments the tragic separation of the "child refugees" from their homeland:

> Where are you, children of Macedonia?
> Where are you? Where have you gone?
> Mother Aegean Macedonia is crying sadly.
> Macedonia is crying for you.

After winning first prize at the music festival of Valandovo in the republic in 1987, *"Kade ste Makedončinja?"* was banned because the Yugoslav government did not want to risk damaging its relationship with Greece. Through the efforts of the Association of Child Refugees in Skopje the ban was lifted, and the song was heard on the radio again for the first time during the First International Reunion of Child Refugees of Aegean Macedonia held in Skopje in the summer of 1988, forty years after the tragic exodus of Aegean Macedonians from their homeland in northern Greece.

Although the Yugoslav government opposed holding this reunion in the republic, pressure from the European Community, Canada, and Australia persuaded Yugoslav authorities to allow the gathering to take place. The reunion was attended by several thousand Aegean Macedonian "child refugees" from all around the world. After the reunion about a hundred of the participants set off on an excursion to visit the villages of their birth in Greece.[17] When they arrived at the Greek border, however, they were stopped. Many of them, even Canadian and Australian citizens traveling with Canadian and Australian passports, were not allowed to enter Greece. Some had their passports stamped "invalid"; others had them stamped with both an entry and an exit stamp. One of the "child refugees" was addressed by a Greek official with the Greek version of his name. When he corrected the official and gave the Macedonian form of his name, his passport was stamped "invalid." Another man, who had been born in Greece, was refused permission to enter Greece, while his wife, who had been born in Czechoslovakia, and his daughter, who had been born in Canada, were given permission to enter the country.[18]

---

[17] Some of these villages no longer exist. They were destroyed during the Greek Civil War and never rebuilt.

[18] When asked about such instances, Greek officials either refuse to discuss the issue or attempt to justify such decisions with general references to the seditious acts committed by the Communist resistance during the Greek Civil War.

The Pan-Macedonian Association and the Association of Child Refugees from Aegean Macedonia are similar organizations in many ways. They are both diaspora organizations concerned with counteracting the effects of alienation and dislocation experienced by emigrants from northern Greece. They attempt to construct transnational communities by creating ties among diaspora groups in different countries and even more importantly between diaspora communities and their homelands. What is more, they both have branches in some of the same large cities of Canada and Australia, and their members come from the same villages and towns in northern Greece.

Since the mid-1980s, however, these two groups of people have found themselves on opposite sides of a global cultural war being conducted between Greeks and Macedonians over which group has the right to identify itself as Macedonian. Inhabitants of the same villages and towns in northern Greece and emigrants from these villages and towns who have settled in Europe, Canada, and Australia have become polarized into two different transnational communities. They are either Greeks, or they are Macedonians; they are either Greek-Macedonians (Macedonians who *are* Greeks) or Aegean Macedonians (Macedonians who are *not* Greeks).

The different relationships these two groups have been able to establish with their homeland in northern Greece are dramatically expressed in the contrast between the Fifth World Convention of Pan-Macedonian Associations and the First International Reunion of Child Refugees from Aegean Macedonia. Members of the Pan-Macedonian Associations were given a warm, official welcome by the Greek state; they were honored as "modern day Macedonian-fighters" and as defenders of the Greekness of Macedonia. They were able to make an emotional pilgrimage to the villages where they had been born. Members of the Association of Child Refugees from Aegean Macedonia, however, were refused permission to enter Greece. They were stopped at the border and denied the right to return to the villages of their birth. They were treated like enemies of the Greek state because they deny that they are members of the Greek nation; they are cut off from their homeland because they identify themselves as Macedonians and not as Greeks. Such is the impact of ethnic nationalism on diaspora communities in a transnational world.

CHAPTER V

The Macedonian Human Rights Movement

UNTIL the fall of 1991, when the Republic of Macedonia declared its independence and began its campaign to gain international recognition as a sovereign state, the Macedonian minority of northern Greece was the primary focus of the "global cultural war" (Featherstone 1990b:10) taking place between Greeks and Macedonians. Since the mid-1980s a small group of Macedonians in northern Greece, with the support of Aegean Macedonian diaspora communities in Canada and Australia, has been actively campaigning to persuade the Greek government and the international community to recognize the existence of a Macedonian minority in Greece and to guarantee them their basic human rights. The existence of a Macedonian human rights movement effectively refutes the Greek government's claims that there are no Macedonians in Greece, only "Slavophone Hellenes with a Greek national consciousness."

An analysis of this global cultural war between Greeks and Macedonians must not only take into account the growth of transnational national communities; it must also consider the increasingly important role played in world affairs by international organizations like the United Nations, the European Union, the World Bank, and the Non-aligned Movement. Each of these organizations constitutes an international forum in which nationalist conflicts can be raised, monitored, and even arbitrated. It is to these organizations that nations and states must increasingly turn when they seek international recognition, legitimacy, and support.

The culture that pervades these organizations is the culture of international business, law, and diplomacy. This "third culture" (Useem, Useem, and Donaghue 1963), in which transnational communication at virtually all official levels takes place, has as its central values universalist concepts, ultimately western European in origin, of individual equality, personal freedom, and human rights.[1] It is ironic that the organizations espousing these values, which are so fundamen-

---

[1] Texts in which these values have been articulated include the Universal Declaration of Human Rights adopted by the General Assembly of the United Nations in 1948 and the European Convention for the Protection of Human Rights and Fundamental Freedoms adopted by the Council of Europe in 1950.

tally at odds with nationalist principles, were originally established by nation-states and have come to exert a significant degree of control over the external and internal affairs of these states. It is one of the paradoxes of the global world of the late twentieth century that national conflicts are being contested on a transnational level. Relationships between nation-states and the national minorities, within their borders are no longer the private, internal affairs of state they once were. Now they frequently involve not only diaspora communities of both the dominant national group and the national minority, but various international economic, political, and human rights organizations, as well.

The net effect of these developments on specific nationalist conflicts is often quite dramatic. Nation-states are being challenged simultaneously from above and below—from without and within—by international organizations, on the one hand, and by national minorities, on the other. National minorities struggling for recognition and human rights from the nation-states they inhabit attempt to mobilize the support of diaspora communities abroad. National minorities also seek to shift the balance of power in their favor and away from the nation-states they are struggling against by appealing to international organizations that are committed to human rights and cultural pluralism. It is not surprising that these organizations often prove more responsive to the concerns of national minorities than the governments of nation-states with their commitment to nationalist ideologies of purity and homogeneity.[2]

NATIONALIST IDEOLOGY, EUROPE, AND
MINORITY RIGHTS IN GREECE

In nationalist ideologies, national identity is reified and essentialized; it is defined, not as something situational, which is constantly constructed and negotiated, but as something innate and permanent, which constitutes a natural or spiritual essence often identified with a person's blood or soul. When the ideal of national self-determination is realized, the community of people who share a common national identity and who therefore constitute a nation are joined as citizens of the same sovereign state and live together in a homogeneous cultural community within the territorial boundaries of that state.

[2] For further discussion of these issues, see Hall (1991), Robertson (1987), and Wallerstein (1991). Gupta (1992) examines the way Third World nations have attempted to strengthen their position in the world system by joining together to form the Nonaligned Movement.

From a Greek nationalist perspective Greece is just such a nation-state. Members of the Greek nation, or *ethnos*, are said to be Greek because they are "Greek by birth" or because "Greek blood" flows in their veins. In order to be considered full members of the Greek nation people must also demonstrate their loyalty to the Greek state, with which the Greek nation is identified, by being "Greek in spirit" (*ellinopsihi*) or "nationally minded" (*ethnikofrones*).[3]

One of the major consequences of the nationalist identification of the Greek nation with the Greek state is that people who are not considered full members of the Greek nation are also not considered full citizens of the Greek state. For this reason people who do not speak Greek, who are not Orthodox Christians, or who simply do not identify themselves as Greek pose a threat to the concept of a pure, homogeneous Greek nation, and therefore to the security of the Greek state, as well. In order to defend the integrity of the Greek nation-state the existence of such people must be denied; they must be externalized, portrayed as somehow "other" or foreign. This process of exteriorization is illustrated by the medical imagery with which George Papadopoulos, leader of the military junta that ruled Greece from 1967 to 1974, described the enemies of Greece: they were "cancerous growths" that needed to be surgically removed in order to restore the health of Greek society.[4]

Another way in which people who do not identify themselves as members of the Greek nation can be labeled enemies of the Greek state and exteriorized is by defining them as agents of a foreign country. Thus Macedonian human rights activists in northern Greece are frequently described as "agents of Skopje." One Greek commentator referred to the relationship between the "nonexistent" Macedonian minority in Greece and the government of the Republic of Macedonia as an "umbilical cord" (Valinakis 1990:75), an image that vividly portrays the "alien" Macedonian minority as a biological extension of its national homeland, its "mother," the Republic of Macedonia.

In nationalist ideology not only is the state identified with the nation, but the sovereign territory of the state is considered to be the property of the nation. An acknowledgment of the existence of a national minority within the territory of the state is, therefore, tantamount to an ad-

---

[3] On the concept of the *ethnos* in Greek nationalist ideology, see Herzfeld (1987), Just (1989), and Tsaousis (1983).

[4] Compare Papadopoulos' image of enemies of the Greek state as "cancerous growths" with Kofos' image of the creation of Macedonian national identity as a "mutation experiment" discussed in Chapter II. In both cases images of medical pathology are used to describe "foreign" ideologies (communism, on the one hand; Macedonian nationalism, on the other) that are perceived as a threat to the Greek state.

mission that the area inhabited by that minority is not the legitimate property of the state. As a result, requests by leaders of national minorities for recognition are often regarded by members of the dominant group as a threat not only to the homogeneity of the nation, but also to the territorial integrity of the state.

In Greece, as in other nation-states where nationalism is the fundamental legitimating principle, any criticism of the nationalist policies of the Greek government constitutes "antinational" or "anti-Greek" activity. Although it is a general characteristic of nationalism that claims of the nation-state take precedence over claims to individual human rights, this is particularly true in Greece. Whereas the democracies of western Europe have been able to develop political cultures and legal philosophies that guarantee the protection of the individual from the state and prevent some of the more extreme violations of human rights, in Greece such liberal principles of individual rights and freedoms have never developed. Instead, the emergence of a strong centralized state together with a long tradition of authoritarianism has led to a situation in which the state is the protector of the social whole, of which the individual is only a part. As a result, individual human rights exist only if they are concretely specified in law and "only to the extent that they do not conflict with the more highly valued interests of the state" (Pollis 1987a:151; 1987b:600–601).

In this context it is not surprising that the role of the judiciary in Greece has always been to defend the interests of the Greek state and to legitimate whatever poltical regime was in power, rather than to protect the rights of individuals against attempts by the state to restrict individual freedoms. As instruments of the state, Greek courts have tended to legitimate even repressive regimes like the military dictatorship that came to power in 1967. As Adamantia Pollis has convincingly argued, on many occasions since World War II Greek courts have "legalized" gross violations of fundamental democratic rights that were guaranteed in the Greek constitution and, in that way, reaffirmed "the primacy of the state over and above any ideological commitment to freedom and democracy" (1987b:604). The fact that there are no individual human rights except those specifically granted by the Greek state, taken in conjunction with the general tendency of the courts to adopt narrow legalistic approaches, has meant that abstract constitutional provisions involving general moral concepts are not given legal standing. This has frequently led Greek courts to sanction "severe restrictions on freedom of speech, freedom of communications, and the right of assembly" (1987b:604).

The violation of individual human rights in Greece is often justified by an appeal to nationalist ideology, by the need to defend the purity of the Greek nation or the territorial sovereignty of the Greek state. This is particularly true when the people whose rights are being violated are not "really" Greek. An obvious example of the institutionalization of discrimination against Greek citizens who are not members of the Greek nation is contained in Article 19 of the Greek citizenship code, which distinguishes between Greek citizens who are of Greek nationality and those who are not. Only the latter may be deprived of their Greek citizenship if they are found to have left Greece with no intention of returning. The majority of people who have lost their Greek citizenship as a result of this measure are members of the Turkish and the Macedonian minorities of northern Greece.

There are several other examples that illustrate the degree to which the individual human rights of Greek citizens, particularly those who do not define themselves as ethnically or nationally Greek, are subordinated to the primacy of the Greek nation as it is embodied in the Greek state. According to Article 25 of the Greek constitution of 1975 the state has the right to require all citizens "to fulfill the duty of social and national solidarity." Given the central place that the ideal of national purity and homogeneity occupies in Greek nationalist ideology, it is not surprising that the existence of Greek citizens who are not ethnically or nationally Greek poses by definition a threat to national solidarity, as does the mere assertion by others that such people exist. Article 25 of the Greek constitution also states that the "abusive exercise of rights is not permitted." These measures provide constitutional grounds for acts of legislation and court decisions that significantly restrict the human rights of individual Greek citizens. More specifically, they have been, and are being, used to limit individual human rights, such as freedom of religion, freedom of expression, freedom of association, and freedom of movement, all of which are provided for in principle by the Greek constitution, but which in practice are violated in the case of people who belong to religious, ethnic, or national minorities.[5]

In addition to the Macedonian minority of northern Greece, there are two other minority groups which are discriminated against in significant ways because they threaten the notion of a religiously, linguistically, and nationally homogeneous Greek state: the Jehovah's Witnesses and the Turkish minority of Thrace. Since Orthodox Christianity is an essential component of Greek national identity, people who are not Orthodox Christians cannot be fully Greek. Although the Greek constitution officially prohibits discrimination against religious minor-

---

[5] These articles of the Greek constitution are discussed in greater detail in Pollis (1987b, 1992).

ities, Jehovah's Witnesses in Greece are denied a variety of religious rights on the grounds that they do not constitute a "known" religion: they do not have the right to proselytize, to establish houses of worship, or to refuse military service as conscientious objectors.[6]

The only minority formally recognized by the Greek government is a "religious minority," the "Moslem minority" of Thrace, whose existence is referred to in the 1923 Treaty of Lausanne. The majority of the approximately 120,000 Moslems in Greece are ethnic Turks, but there are also small numbers of Bulgarian-speaking Pomaks and Roma (Gypsies) who are Moslems as well (United States Department of State 1993:794). Although the Greek government insists that the religious rights of this "Moslem minority" are fully protected, the existence of a Turkish ethnic minority in Greece is officially denied. Just as there are no Macedonians in Greece, only "Slavophone Greeks," so there are no Turks in Greece, only "Moslem Greeks." Such terminology maintains the fiction that the people referred to in this way are "really" Greeks— Greeks who simply speak a different language or adhere to a different religion.

The Greek Supreme Court has upheld lower court rulings forbidding the use of the word "Turkish" in the name of local cultural and social organizations. In addition, Ahmet Sadik, an ethnic Turk and former member of the Greek parliament, has been arrested and convicted "on charges of 'fomenting discord' by insisting on the Turkish identity of the Moslem minority" (United States Department of State 1990:1167).[7] More generally the Turks of Greek Thrace have experienced significant restrictions in their rights to freedom of movement, freedom of association, and freedom of expression.[8]

In the present era of globalization, in which nation-states are becoming integrated into various transnational organizations, the relation-

---

[6] For additional information on the situation of Jehovah's Witnesses in Greece, see Pollis (1992) and the entry on Greece in recent volumes of the United States Department of State's *Country Reports on Human Rights Practices*.

[7] The following exchange between Ahmet Faikoglu, another Turkish member of the Greek parliament, and the president of the parliament took place on the parliament floor in November 1990:

> FAIKOGLU: "We are Greek citizens, but we are another race [*fili*]. . . . We are
> Turks. . . ."
> PRESIDENT: "You cannot say you are Turks. . . ."
> FAIKOGLU: "We are Turks, Mr. President. Yes, I say it. I say that we are Turks. . . .
> We are Turks with Greek citizenship. . . ."
> PRESIDENT: "My dear colleague, sir, you are Greeks."
> (*Eleftherotypia*, November 17, 1990)

[8] For additional information on the Turkish minority in Greece, see Poulton (1993:182– 88) and Human Rights Watch/Helsinki (1990).

ships between national minorities and the states they inhabit have begun to change. The increasing involvement of diaspora communities, their host countries, and transnational organizations in what had previously been the internal affairs of states, has given ethnic minorities greater power in their struggle for human rights. One aspect of this process of globalization that is having an important impact on the status of minority groups in Greece is the gradual integration of Greece into Europe.

Although Greece has long been regarded as being situated on the "margins of Europe" (Herzfeld 1987) in large part because of the legacy of four hundred years of Ottoman occupation, it is now in the process of becoming increasingly "Europeanized." Greece joined the North Atlantic Treaty Organization in 1951 and became a full member of the European Community in 1981. Now, as the long-awaited emergence of "a united Europe" approaches, Greece is under even greater pressure to conform as fully as possible to a wide variety of economic, political, social, and cultural practices that characterize the liberal democracies of western Europe.

One of the most serious conflicts that have arisen during this process of Europeanization has been the conflict between Greek nationalist ideology, with its commitment to a pure and homogeneous nation-state, on the one hand, and the more pluralistic values of the European Union, which emphasize the importance of preserving the fundamental human rights of religious, linguistic, ethnic, and national minorities, on the other. It is becoming very difficult to preserve a static, organic conception of Greek national identity, one in which religion, nationality, and citizenship all coincide, at a time when the European Union is assuming greater power over the social and political affairs of its member countries (Pollis 1992:191).

More specifically, although Greece ratified the European Convention for the Protection of Human Rights and Fundamental Freedoms in 1963, it has largely ignored the convention's provisions. When the Council of Europe concluded that Greece under the junta was guilty of violating the convention, its military rulers considered these findings "an infringement of the state's sovereignty." After the fall of the dictatorship in 1974, Greece again ratified the convention. In addition, the new Greek constitution of 1975 states that such international conventions supersede contrary provisions of domestic law. Finally, in 1985 Greece ratified a protocol to the convention allowing individuals to petition the European Commission on Human Rights concerning alleged violations of their human rights (Pollis 1987b:599; 1992:178).

While in many respects Greece's general commitment to the protection of individual rights has conformed to European standards, there is one major exception. With regard to the rights of religious and national minorities serious violations have occurred. In such cases Greek courts have usually just ignored the convention when ruling on the constitutionality of particular legislation, or else they have argued that certain provisions of the convention do not apply, given the uniqueness of the Greek case. Greek violations of the European Convention on Human Rights, especially with regard to the rights of religious and national minorities, are primarily responsible for the failure of Greece to conform to European standards concerning individual human rights (Pollis 1992:172; 178).

Only recently have Greek citizens who belong to religious or national minorities begun to appear before the European Commission on Human Rights charging the Greek government with violations of their human rights. This is in large part because of the requirement that individuals exhaust all domestic remedies before presenting a petition to the commission. Several cases involving Jehovah's Witnesses who have been found guilty of proselytism in Greek courts are presently pending before the commission (Pollis 1992:184). In addition, a decision of the Greek Supreme Court upholding a lower-court ruling that the use of the word "Turkish" in the name of cultural organizations is illegal has been appealed to the European Parliament (United States Department of State 1990:1138). Macedonians too, as we shall see, have begun to approach various international human rights organizations with charges that their human rights are being violated by the Greek state.

As these examples illustrate all too clearly, in order for Greece to become more completely integrated into the European Union it must adopt additional measures to protect the human rights of members of its religious and national minorities. In order to do so, it must modify the static and organic conception of a pure and homogeneous Greek nation that has dominated Greek nationalist thinking for so long. Only when this nationalist myth has been abandoned, can an essentialist and absolutist notion of Greek national identity be replaced with a more diverse and pluralistic one.

The challenge to the traditional conception of Greek national identity posed by Greece's need to conform to European standards of individual human rights will, one would hope, lead to the development of a new sense of Greek national identity, a more situational, layered, and pluralistic one—one in which being Turkish or Macedonian, on the one hand, and being Greek, on the other, would not be mutually exclusive. Then it would be possible for a Greek national identity to coexist not only with more localized ethnic or regional identities, but also with transnational identities as well. Only when Jehovah's Witnesses are fully Greek even though they are not Orthodox Christians, only when Macedonians and Turks can enjoy all the rights of Greek citizens even though they are not "Greeks by birth," will Greek practices be fully in accord with European ideals concerning the human rights of religous, ethnic, and national minorities.

THE MACEDONIAN MINORITY IN NORTHERN GREECE

The district of Florina is located in the northwestern corner of Greek Macedonia, where the international borders of Albania, the former Yugoslavia, and Greece come together in the middle of the blue waters of Great Prespa Lake. It is a "border area" often referred to in nationalist contexts as a "bulwark of Hellenism," a region of high, rugged mountains and small, enclosed valleys. Florina is also one of the poorer, more isolated, and more underdeveloped parts of Greece, a place where the legacy of bitterness and destruction from the Greek Civil War is still very strongly felt. As a consequence the region has experienced severe depopulation. A majority of the inhabitants of many villages in the area has emigrated to Europe, North America, and Australia. Only recently has the Greek government attempted to reverse several decades of neglect with efforts to improve the infrastructure of the area and develop its potential for tourism. Nevertheless, there is still very little industry in the region, and over half the population remains employed in the agricultural sector of the economy.

In the district of Florina, as in other parts of Macedonia, the most important categories people use to classify one another are ethnic categories. Of the 53,000 inhabitants of the district of Florina the largest group, 65 percent according to one Greek estimate, refer to themselves as "locals," or "local Macedonians."[9] In addition to Greek, most of these local Macedonians speak Macedonian. They often refer to this "other" language not as "Macedonian," but rather as "our language" (*ta dhika mas* in Greek or *naše* in Macedonian) or "the local language." These are the people Greek scholars refer to as "bilingual" or "Slavic-speaking Greeks."[10] The majority of these local Macedonians have been fully Hellenized and have a Greek national identity. They say that they are Macedonians *and* Greeks; they are Greek-Macedonians. Some, however, do *not* have a Greek national identity. They have a

[9] See *Ethnikos Kiryx* (April 9, 1992, p. 11) and Van Boeschoten (1993b).

[10] In the northern portion of Greek Macedonia (in the districts of Kastoria, Florina, Edhessa, Kilkis, Serres, and Dhrama), most local Macedonians speak Macedonian and Greek, but in the more southern areas (Grevena, Kozani, and Halkidhiki) they speak only Greek.

Macedonian national identity; they say that they are Macedonians and *not* Greeks.

The next most important ethnic group in the Florina area are the refugees from Asia Minor, who settled in the area after the exchange of populations between Greece and Turkey in 1922. These people, who are generally referred to simply as "refugees," speak Greek, have a strong sense of Greek national identity, and constitute 25 to 30 percent of the population (Van Boeschoten 1993b).[11] Another important ethnic group in the Florina area are the Vlachs, descendants of transhumant shepherds, who speak a language closely related to Romanian as well as Greek. Many Vlachs were settled in the Florina area in the 1950s after the Greek Civil War. Most have developed a Greek national identity. There is also a small group of Arvanites, who speak a dialect of Albanian and who, like the Vlachs, have developed a strong sense of Greek national identity. Finally, there are the Greeks from central and southern Greece who have come to the area since it became part of the Greek state in 1913. More than half the villages in the district of Florina are inhabited by local Macedonians. There are also many villages inhabited by members of more than one ethnic group, as well as some villages inhabited exclusively by refugees. In addition there are a small number of villages inhabited by Vlachs or Arvanites.

As Van Boeschoten (1990) has pointed out, in the Florina region, as in other parts of Macedonia, society is highly stratified along ethnic lines. The different ethnic groups in the area have unequal access to land, education, and employment, and therefore enjoy different degrees of social mobility. Civil service jobs, which in Greece constitute a very important avenue of upward social mobility for villagers, are primarily occupied by Greeks from southern Greece, whereas positions in commerce, private business, and the tourist industry are dominated by the refugees from Asia Minor, the Vlachs, and the Arvanites. The local Macedonians are still primarily engaged in small-scale agriculture and therefore occupy the lowest position in the hierarchy of occupational specialization.

This situation has not led to the development of class consciousness among the local Macedonians of Florina. They attribute their position at the bottom of the socioeconomic hierarchy not to an opposition between classes, but to an opposition between ethnic groups, especially between local Macedonians and refugees. As Hall et al. (1978:394) put it, ethnicity has become "the modality in which class is lived."

[11] The most prominent group of "refugees" in the Florina area are Pontians, refugees from the Pontos (an area of northeastern Asia Minor near the Black Sea), who speak a distinctive form of Greek and maintain a regional or ethnic identity as Pontians, while at the same time asserting their identity as both Macedonians and Greeks.

Similarly, many local Macedonians also conceptualize the core-periphery relationship that exists between the district of Florina and other areas along the northern border of Greece, on the one hand, and urban centers like Athens and Thessaloniki, on the other, in ethnic terms as an opposition between local Macedonians and Greeks from southern Greece.[12] It is in this context, in which both regional and class conflicts are translated into ethnic terms, that the emergence of a movement for the human rights of the Macedonian minority in Greece must be understood.

At the most general level Macedonians in northern Greece who are involved in the human rights movement seek recognition from the Greek government, as well as from other states and international organizations, that a Macedonian minority does in fact exist in Greece. They want the right to preserve their language and their culture, which is in danger of disappearing because of the long-standing Greek policy of forced assimilation and Hellenization. Toward that end they demand freedoms of expression, religion, association, and movement, which they do not fully enjoy at the present time. They also seek an end to the discrimination they experience on the basis of their ethnic or national identity, particularly in the areas of education and employment. Finally, they seek an end to the harassment and persecution experienced by Macedonians who are openly involved in the struggle for Macedonian human rights.[13]

It is important to note that Macedonian human rights activists in northern Greece explicitly reject the autonomist or irredentist goals of some of the more extreme Macedonian nationalists in the Republic of Macedonia and in Macedonian diaspora communities in Canada and Australia. These views were clearly expressed by one of the leaders of the Macedonian human rights movement in northern Greece in 1990:

> We want recognition and respect as human beings. We want to be free to express who we are—Macedonians, Slav-Macedonians. We want to be free to enjoy the songs and dances of our grandparents with the names they used [i.e., the Macedonian, not the Greek, names] without

[12] This is particularly true for local Macedonians who have developed a Macedonian, rather than a Greek, national identity, but it is also true in a less explicit sense for local Macedonians who have a Greek national identity.

[13] The following account of the violation of the human rights of the Macedonian minority of northern Greece is based primarily on my own fieldwork. Published sources that confirm the accuracy of this account include the entry on Greece in the United States Department of State's *Country Reports on Human Rights Practices* (1990, 1991, 1992, 1993), the chapter on Greece in the report of the Minority Rights Group of London on minorities in the Balkans (Poulton 1993), and the Human Rights Watch/Helsinki report on the Macedonian minority in Greece (1994b).

being accused of being Bulgarians or Communists or agents of Skopje. We have the same language and traditions as the Macedonians of Yugoslavia, but that doesn't mean we want to create a state with them. We don't want autonomy; we don't want to change borders. We want to eliminate borders, not build new ones. We just want to be free to speak our language and preserve our traditions like the Vlachs, the Arvanites, and the Pontians.

Since national identity and religious identity are frequently equated in the Balkans, national conflicts are often defined in religous terms as conflicts between Christians and Moslems (Greeks and Turks) or Orthodox and Catholics (Serbs and Croats). In the conflict between Macedonians and Greeks (who are both Orthodox Christians), however, language is the most important feature that distinguishes the two groups from one another.[14] As a result, it is not surprising that language rights occupy a central position on the agenda of the Macedonian human rights movement.

According to a study of linguistic minorities in Greece done by the Commission of the European Communities, the situation of the Macedonian language in Greece is "extremely precarious" (Siguan 1990:58). The Macedonian language is not officially recognized by Greek authorities in any context. In all educational institutions, all religious services, and all mass media Greek is used exclusively. Macedonian human rights activists assert their right to establish schools for the teaching of Macedonian as well as churches so that they can worship in Macedonian. In addition, they seek the right to produce radio and television programs and to publish books and newspapers in Macedonian.

There are no official restrictions on the use of Macedonian in private or in informal public situations, and people in the Florina region can often be heard speaking Macedonian in such contexts. Nevertheless, a climate of fear and intimidation still exists, a legacy of past decades of repression, discrimination, and forced assimilation, which inhibits many people from speaking Macedonian openly. Elderly Macedonians remember being arrested, fined, imprisoned, and tortured for speaking Macedonian under the Metaxas dictatorship in the 1930s. They also remember how humiliated they felt when they were forced to attend night school in order to learn Greek. Younger people remember elementary school teachers beating them with a switch on the palms of their hands for speaking Macedonian among themselves.

Peter Savramis, a Macedonian living in Melbourne, went to school in a village outside Florina in the 1950s. At the end of the school year his

---

[14] On the relationship between language and ethnic nationalism, see Fishman (1972) and Fishman, Gertner, Lowy, and Milán (1985).

9. While the Greek community of Toronto celebrates Greek Independence Day in March 1991, the Macedonian community of Toronto
marches to protest the Greek government's treatment of the Macedonian minority in northern Greece

teacher told the class he would send little birds to their houses to spy
on them, to see if they spoke Macedonian at home during the summer.
When Peter noticed some swallows nesting under the eaves of his
house, he was scared. He thought the swallows might be the spies his
teacher had mentioned. After all, the swallows came in the spring and
left in the fall just before school started. Where did they go? Maybe they
went to tell the teacher which children had spoken Macedonian over
the summer. Reluctantly Peter decided to kill the birds. He felt sorry for
them, but what else could he do?

Macedonian human rights activists also seek the right to use their
Macedonian names, both first and last, in official contexts. They want
the right to baptize their children with Macedonian names, something
they cannot do now since most Greek Orthodox priests will not baptize
children with Slavic or other "foreign" names. Baptisms are not the
only life-cycle rituals affected by the unwillingness of Greek Orthodox
priests to sanction the use of Macedonian names. One Macedonian living in Florina said that once his grandmother had given the village
priest a list of the names of her dead relatives to be blessed at a memorial service. When the priest saw the list of Slavic names, he said, "What
kind of names are these? These aren't names. Cross them out." It was

only after the Slavic names had been translated into Greek that the priest would read them. So Zlata became Hrisoula (golden), Slava became Doxa (glory), and Krste became Stavros (cross). "But poor old Zlata won't know she's being remembered," the man continued. "How will she know that the Greeks came and gave her a new name? She won't know that her new Greek name is Hrisoula. She'll think we've forgotten her."[15]

Macedonian human rights activists in Florina also seek the right to preserve and develop their traditional culture in an atmosphere free from discrimination and assimilationist pressure. They want the right to perform Macedonian songs, dances, and other rituals without being harassed by police. Pontians and Vlachs are not harassed when they perform their traditional songs and dances.

In the mid-1980s a local band began playing Macedonian songs at baptisms, weddings, and village festivals. In 1988 this band was invited to perform at a festival in the village of Meliti (Ofčarani in Macedonian), a mixed village of local Macedonians and Pontians about ten miles from Florina. When the police learned of this, they notified the village president that no songs were to be sung in Macedonian and that all the dances were to be called by their Greek, not their Macedonian, names. The festival officially ended at eight o'clock in the evening without incident, but there followed a spontaneous "people's festival" presided over by a leader of the Macedonian human rights movement. As soon as the band began singing Macedonian songs, all the Pontians left. The local police chief ordered the music and the dancing to stop. "Why?" asked the Macedonian activist. "Because they are forbidden," said the police chief. "Do you mean that we, the citizens of Meliti, don't have the right to dance these dances?" the activist replied. "That doesn't even happen in Tanganyika." He urged the crowd to get up and dance a traditional Macedonian dance. Just then the microphone was wrestled from his hand, the lights went off, and the festival abruptly ended.[16]

Another example of the kind of harassment Macedonians in the Florina area experience involved a man who traveled from village to village selling fruit and vegetables from his pickup truck. Whenever he entered a Pontian village or neighborhood, he played Pontian songs

---

[15] Mihalis, a Macedonian human rights activist in Florina, remembered a conversation he had with a terminally ill local Macedonian priest of the Greek Orthodox Church. After commenting bitterly that he had worked all his life for foreigners, the priest asked Mihalis to read some prayers for him in Macedonian.

[16] This event was videotaped by a young Macedonian woman from Australia, who was visiting her relatives in a nearby village, and was reported in detail in the Macedonian press in Australia.

over his loudspeaker, and whenever he entered a Vlach village or neighborhood, he played Vlach songs. On one occasion, when he was playing local Macedonian songs in a local Macedonian neighborhood, a police officer stopped him and confiscated his cassettes. In 1990 a local Florina newspaper (*Kini Ghnomi*, August 18, 1990) concluded an article on the government's attempts to suppress expressions of Macedonian folklore by asking, "Is the existence of the nation threatened by popular tradition?"

One of the most flagrant abuses of the human rights of the Macedonians of northern Greece, and one that figures prominently in any statement of the demands of the Macedonian human rights movement, is the explicit exclusion of Macedonians from the general amnesty announced by the Greek government according to which political refugees who left Greece after the Civil War were allowed to return to Greece even if they had been deprived of their Greek citizenship. In 1982 a ministerial decision was issued by Andreas Papandreou's Socialist government that allowed political refugees to return to Greece only if they were "Greeks by birth" (*Ellines to yenos*). This regulation, which gave legal form to a policy that had been in effect for a long time, prevents Aegean Macedonians who are living in the Republic of Macedonia and other eastern European countries, as well as those who eventually emigrated to Canada and Australia, from returning to Greece. One nationalist politician said it would be "national suicide" to allow these "Slavs" to return, but an official of the Greek Communist Party denounced the policy as "racist."[17]

It was under this provision that the group of Child Refugees from Aegean Macedonia attending their First Annual Reunion in Skopje in 1988 were refused permission to enter Greece. Many stories circulate among Aegean Macedonians in Canada and Australia that attest to the difficulties they experience when trying to enter Greece. Macedonians in Canada and Australia who were born in northern Greece and are Greek citizens but who were married in a Macedonian church, who baptized their children in a Macedonian church, or who have been active in Macedonian organizations, are often unable to enter Greece. If their passports list their name or the name of the village where they were born in its Macedonian form, they will almost certainly be refused permission to enter the country. This has happened most frequently to Macedonians trying to enter Greece by land from the Republic of Macedonia, but it has also happened to those arriving by air in Athens. When two determined Macedonians who lived in

---

[17] See Karakasidou (1993:16), Popov and Radin (1989), and United States Department of State (1990:1137).

Australia, but who had been born in Florina, were not allowed to enter Greece from the Republic of Macedonia, they turned around and drove back through the republic into Bulgaria, and then from Bulgaria into Turkey, before successfully entering Greece across the border between Greece and Turkey.

This provision denying political refugees who are not "Greek by birth" permission to return to Greece has also prevented reunions from taking place of family members who were separated after the Civil War and who live on opposite sides of the border between Greece and the Republic of Macedonia. The last wish of a political refugee who had been born in a village near Florina and died in Skopje was to be buried in the cemetery of the village of his birth. Greek authorities, however, did not allow his relatives to bring his body across the border to be buried in Greece. In another instance a man who had two sons living in the republic died in Florina. His sons applied for visas at the Greek consulate in Skopje in order to attend their father's funeral, but their request was denied; they were not "Greeks by birth." The father's body was brought to the Greek side of the border near the village of Niki (Negočani in Macedonian), while the sons came down to the Yugoslav side of the border. They viewed their father's body for the last time from a distance, from across the international border between Greece and Yugoslavia.

There are several other laws that clearly discriminate against members of the Macedonian minority in northern Greece. In 1982 the Greek government decided that it would no longer recognize degrees granted by the University of Cyril and Methodius in Skopje. The specific reason given for this decision was that the Macedonian language was not "widely recognized internationally." Obtaining a degree in Skopje had been an attractive option to students from northern Greece who spoke Macedonian and who were unable to gain admission to a Greek university. Now this option was no longer available to them. Several students who had completed their degrees in Skopje protested this law by staging a hunger strike in Athens.[18]

In 1985 a law was passed allowing for the return of property that had been confiscated by the Greek government from political refugees who left Greece after the Civil War. The law, however, applied only to political refugees who were "Greeks by birth" and who had returned to Greece and regained their Greek citizenship. Macedonians, therefore,

---

[18] In another example of the unwillingness of Greek officials to recognize the Macedonian language, a Greek court refused to convict a Greek driver who had fatally injured someone in Skopje on the grounds that the police documents from Skopje were inadmissible in court as evidence because they were written in the Macedonian language (Popov and Radin 1989:59).

were not only denied the right to return to the villages of their birth, but they were denied the right to regain ownership of their family homes and fields. In many cases their relatives and children who remained in Greece after the Civil War have had to lease back the property they left behind from the government or from the "nationally minded Greeks" to whom it had been given after the war.[19]

Many men who became involved in the Macedonian human rights movement in northern Greece in the 1980s are children of people who were severely persecuted by the Greek state during the Civil War. In some cases these people were persecuted for their support of the Communist resistance, whose goals were to detach territory in Greek Macedonia from the Greek state and establish a "Free Greece" within the framework of the Balkan Federation envisioned by leaders of the Communist parties of Yugoslavia and Bulgaria. In other cases, however, these people were persecuted for their commitment to speaking the Macedonian language and to maintaining their Macedonian identity and culture. Often these charges were so inextricably linked in the eyes of Greek government officials that they were interchangeable. As children, most of these Macedonian human rights activists spoke Macedonian in their homes and first learned Greek when they went to school. While they were growing up, their parents often discouraged them from asking questions about their identity and their past. From their parents' perspective their old ways and their old language had brought nothing but trouble and were not worth saving. Assimilation and upward social mobility were much more important. Many Macedonian human rights activists living in northern Greece continue to experience persecution and harassment at the hands of the Greek government. They are followed; their phones are tapped; and they receive anonymous threatening phone calls. Their businesses are audited; their customers and clients are frightened away; and they lose their jobs.

Other strategies that have been used by the Greek government to deal with the "Macedonian problem" were outlined in a confidential report prepared by the security branch of the Greek police in Thessaloniki and submitted to the Ministry for Public Order in Athens. Among the steps it suggested for eliminating the use of the Macedonian language in the regions of Florina, Edhessa, and Kilkis are the following: supporting cultural organizations that will combat the anti-Greek propaganda of the Slavs; bribing important people in the area to oppose the use of the "Slavic idiom" in their villages; posting members of the military, the police, and the civil service who are from Florina to

---

[19] The texts of these laws have been published in Popov and Radin (1989).

other parts of the country; encouraging military personnel from other areas to marry women from villages where "the idiom" is spoken; and finally, improving the standard of living in the area in order "to neutralize Skopje propaganda concerning the oppression of 'Aegean Macedonia'" (Popov and Radin 1989).

One of the leading Macedonian human rights activists in the Florina area, Christos Sideropoulos, who has publicly identified himself as a Macedonian and who has traveled abroad to meet with representatives of international human rights organizations and members of Macedonian human rights groups in Canada and Australia, was transferred from his civil service position in Florina specifically because of these political activities. Finally, in November 1992, George Misalis, a Macedonian from northern Greece who has lived for over twenty years in Australia and has been active in Macedonian organizations there, was notified by the Greek Consulate in Melbourne that according to the Ministry of the Interior "he had been declared to have forfeited his Greek citizenship [*ithayenia*]" and to have been "crossed off the citizenship register and the municipal roll" of the village of Meliti near Florina where he was born. When Misalis tried to enter Greece from the Republic of Macedonia in the summer of 1993, he was refused permission to enter the country.

MACEDONIAN HUMAN RIGHTS ON TRIAL

In August 1984 Macedonian human rights activists in northern Greece published a manifesto calling for the recognition of the human rights of the Macedonian minority in Greece. Under the name of the Central Organizing Committee for Macedonian Human Rights, they sent this manifesto, which was written in Greek, Macedonian, and English, to all members of the Greek parliament, to all foreign embassies in Athens, to all European governments, to the United Nations, and to several other international organizations as well. The decision to issue such a manifesto had been taken several months earlier at a meeting of over fifty Macedonians from throughout northern Greece. Among them were teachers, businessmen, and farmers, all of whom realized that they belonged to the last generation of Macedonians in Greece who would be able to preserve their identity and their culture. In this effort they were supported by Aegean Macedonians in diaspora communities in Canada and Australia, who soon organized their own Macedonian Human Rights Committees. Contrary to suggestions frequently made by Greek commentators on the Macedonian Question, this early attempt to organize a movement for Macedonian human rights in Greece did not receive support from officials in the Republic of Macedonia. In fact, it was actively opposed by them since it ran the risk of jeopardizing Yugoslavia's relationship with Greece.

In order to publicize their views and enlist support for their cause, members of the Macedonian human rights movement began publishing a small monthly newspaper in Aridhea, a small town to the east of Florina. It was written in Greek and contained a variety of articles ranging from complaints about the persecution of Macedonians by Greek officials to comparisons between the position of the Macedonian minority in Greece and that of minority groups in other parts of the world like the Kurds and the Palestinians. At one point in the early 1990s the paper was forced to close because no printer could be found who was willing to put up with the possibility of government harassment. When publication was resumed in 1993, the paper had a new name, *Zora*, the Macedonian word for "dawn," and included short poems and folktales written in Macedonian and printed in the Cyrillic alphabet.

During the parliamentary elections of 1989, some Macedonians in Florina and other districts in northern Greece cast invalid ballots on which the following text was written:

> I am a Greek citizen and a Macedonian by birth, and that is what I want to remain.
>
> I fulfill all my obligations to the state without enjoying the same rights as other citizens. My human rights are rudely violated and my nationality [*ethnotita*] and my ethnic origin [*yenos*] are not recognized. That is why I take part in these elections with a protest vote—in order to prove my existence, on the one hand, and to denounce the chauvinistic positions of the political parties, on the other.

In the early 1990s the leaders of the Macedonian human rights movement in northern Greece began to develop a more ambitious political program. They announced plans to establish a new political party in cooperation with Ahmet Sadik, the leader of the Turkish minority in Thrace. The decision on the part of the two minority communities to form a joint political party was prompted by a 1991 election law according to which a party had to receive at least 3 percent of the national vote in order to win a seat in parliament. This is a percentage that neither minority community could hope to reach if it were to field candidates independently.

In 1991 Macedonian human rights activists in northern Greece formed the Macedonian Movement for Balkan Prosperity, whose general goals were to oppose racism, nationalism, and militarism in Greece and to work for peaceful coexistence and cooperation among the peoples of the Balkans. More specifically they are committed to gaining "respect for the fundamental freedoms and human rights of the indigenous Macedonians under Greek rule [*epikratia*] in accordance with the laws and the constitution of the state and the principles and declarations of the European Community, the Conference on Security and Cooperation in Europe, and the United Nations." They are also committed to respecting "the bipolar principle of the inviolability of borders." Finally, as Greek citizens who are Macedonians by birth, they hope to serve as "a bridge of peace and cooperation" between Greece and the Republic of Macedonia. The Macedonian Movement for Balkan Prosperity participated in the 1994 elections for the European Parliament under the name "Rainbow" (a European-wide movement representing the interests of a variety of linguistic and cultural minorities). They received over seven thousand votes, a large number of them from the regions of Florina, Kastoria, and Edhessa.

In the early 1990s several incidents took place in the Florina area in which symbols of the Greek state and its rise to power in Macedonia were attacked. Sometime on the night before the celebration of Greek Independence Day on March 25, 1991, the Greek flags on all the public buildings in the village of Meliti disappeared. In Meliti and several other villages near Florina where Macedonians are becoming increasingly politicized, statues of "Macedonian-fighters" have been defaced, knocked over, or used as urinals. From a Greek nationalist perspective these "Macedonian-fighters" are heroes who fought against the "Bulgarian bandits" in the Macedonian Struggle at the turn of the century. The "Bulgarian bandits" they fought, however, were the grandparents of the present-day villagers who now identify themselves as Macedonians and not as Greeks. As one Macedonian activist put it, "those 'Macedonian-fighters' should be called 'Macedonian-eaters.' They didn't fight to free Macedonia; they fought to conquer it."[20]

The response of the Greek state to some of the early activities of the Macedonian human rights activists in the Florina area is illustrated by the outcomes of several court cases in which these activists have been involved. In 1989 a group of twenty men decided to establish an association which they named the Center for Macedonian Culture (*Steghi Makedhonikou Politismou*). The goals of this association, as stated in its constitution, were the enhancement of the cultural life of the people of Florina, the preservation and development of the popular culture of the members of the association, the protection of human rights, and

---

[20] In a large square near the central bus station in Florina stands a statue of Pavlos Tsamis, a "Macedonian-fighter" who served as a brigadier general in the Greek army, as director of the Center for Macedonians Abroad, and as director of the Society for Macedonian Studies. The statue was donated by the Pan-Macedonian Association of Australia.

the defense of Greek national independence. The founders planned to accomplish these goals by organizing lectures, excursions, art exhibits, and folklore performances, as well as by establishing an office and a library.

When the founders of the Center for Macedonian Culture submitted "a request for the recognition of the association" (*etisi anaghnorisi somatiou*) to the Court of the First Instance in Florina, it was rejected in March 1990, on the grounds that the protection of human rights and the defense of Greek national independence were the responsibilities of the Greek state, not of private associations. Several months later a revised constitution, from which the article referring to human rights and national independence had been deleted, was resubmitted by over fifty men to the same court in Florina. In August 1990, the court again rejected the application for the recognition of the Center for Macedonian Culture. This time the political basis for the decision was explicitly stated. The court ruled that because some of the founding members of the association were known to have alleged that a Macedonian minority existed in Greece and had even made such allegations at a meeting of the Conference on Security and Cooperation in Europe in Copenhagen, the true purpose of the association was not that stated in its constitution, but rather "the cultivation of the idea of the existence of a Macedonian minority in Greece, which is contrary to the national interest [of Greece] and therefore the law."

The founders immediately appealed this decision to the Court of Appeals in Thessaloniki on the grounds that it was an unconstitutional violation of "the sovereign individual and social rights which [they] have as Greek citizens and human beings." They also claimed that the preservation of their popular culture constituted "not only an inalienable right, but an obligation, of every citizen, and that such activities contributed to the unity and the integrity of our fatherland rather than to the undermining of its foundations."

In May 1991, the appeal, which a local paper referred to as a "Trojan Horse of Skopje," was rejected by the Court of Appeals in Thessaloniki. The judges devoted more than half of their twelve-page decision to a detailed summary of the Greek nationalist position on the Macedonian Question, complete with appropriate references to the standard Greek nationalist sources on Macedonia: Andriotis (1957), Kofos (1964), and Sakellariou (1983). The judges stressed the fact that the ancient Macedonian kings were Greek, that when the Slavs invaded the Balkans in the sixth and seventh centuries Macedonia was the "bastion" of Hellenism just as it had been in antiquity, that the peasants who spoke a "Bulgaroslavic idiom" in 1900 had a completely Greek national consciousness, and that ever since its founding in 1944 the Republic of Macedonia has attempted to exploit the existence of "the bilingual Greeks of Greek Macedonia" in order to gain an opening to the Aegean.

The Appeals Court of Thessaloniki went on to argue that the formation of the Center for Macedonian Culture in Florina was part of an attempt by "Skopje" to gain control of Greek territory and that it had been instigated by "Slavic organizations abroad." The court expressed the fear that the center would be a vehicle for spreading Slavic propaganda among the young people of Florina and that the name of the association would create confusion because it would give the impression that it referred to the Greek culture of Macedonia, when in fact it referred to a Slavic culture which, according to the court, did not even exist in northern Greece. Finally, the court concluded that the use of the word "Macedonian" in the name of the association was intended to falsify or misrepresent the Greek identity of Macedonia and that it revealed the intention of the founders to destroy the territorial integrity of Greece. For these reasons the Appeals Court upheld the lower-court decision and refused to recognize the Center for Macedonian Culture.

This decision in turn was appealed to the Supreme Court of Greece in Athens, the Arios Paghos, on the grounds that it restricted the exercise of certain inalienable rights in violation of various provisions of the Greek constitution as well as corresponding provisions of the European Convention on Human Rights. The plaintiffs argued that the Court of Appeals' discussion of ancient and modern Macedonian history was irrelevant and that the court improperly took into consideration the intentions of the founders, instead of focusing on the legality of the constitution of the association. The plaintiffs also pointed out that no other association whose name contained the word "Macedonian" had ever been found to create confusion and that no evidence was cited by the court to prove that the association posed a threat to the territorial integrity of Greece. When this appeal too was rejected, the founders of the Center for Macedonian Culture began making plans to bring their case before the European Commission on Human Rights.

From the perspective of the courts in Florina and in Thessaloniki the only real issue in this case concerned the identity of the founders of the Center for Macedonian Culture and the meaning they assigned to the word "Macedonian." If the founders had been real Macedonians—if, in other words, they had been Greeks—then their association would have been recognized immediately. In that case, as in the case of many organizations such as the Pan-Macedonian Association, the preservation of their culture—the preservation, that is, of Greek culture—would have constituted a service to the nation. Because, however, they were *not* Greeks (as the courts correctly concluded), their efforts to preserve their culture (which the courts incorrectly concluded did not exist in northern Greece) and their reference to this non-Greek culture as Macedonian were contrary to Greek national interest and therefore illegal. The courts' claim that the intention of the founders of the association was not to preserve their culture, as stated in the association's constitution, but to promote the idea of the existence of a Macedonian minority in northern Greece cannot stand, for these two goals are one and the same. The founders' attempt to preserve their culture is an explicit assertion that a Macedonian minority does exist in northern Greece.

The inability of Macedonians in the Florina area to register a cultural association with the word Macedonian in its name, like the inability of Turks in Greek Thrace to use the word "Turkish" in the name of any of their associations, is an excellent example of the way in which the activities, purposes, and bylaws of private associations are subject to detailed regulation and control by the Greek state. It also confirms the fundamental incompatibility of the Greek nationalist conception of the *"ethnos* as an integrated entity embodied in the state" and a philosophy of inalienable human rights (Pollis 1987a:160). The issue at stake in this case is an issue of *recognition*—the refusal of the Greek state to recognize the Center for Macedonian Culture. This case, therefore, replicates the central issue of the entire Macedonian conflict—the refusal of the Greek state to recognize the existence of a Macedonian nation, a Macedonian language, or a Macedonian minority in Greece. It also suggests direct parallels to the struggle that was taking place simultaneously in the European Community and the United Nations over the recognition of the Republic of Macedonia by the international community.

Another trial that offers valuable insights into the situation facing Macedonian human rights activists in Greece involved a lawsuit brought by Kostas Gotsis, one of the founders of the Center for Macedonian Culture, against the editor of *Stohos*, an ultranationalist weekly newspaper published in Athens. This paper, which is distributed throughout Greece as well as in Greek communities abroad, is a testament to the evils of militarism, irridentism, xenophobia, and racism, which are often fostered by extreme nationalism. Calls for the reclamation of Asia Minor, Northern Macedonia (the Republic of Macedonia), and Northern Ipiros (Southern Albania) are standard themes of most issues, as are attacks on ethnic minorities in Greece such as the Jews, the "Mongols of Thrace" (the Turks), and the "Gypsy-Skopians" (the Macedonians). *Stohos* frequently publishes photographs of Macedonian human rights activists in Greece and abroad and exhorts its loyal "Greek-minded" readers to "cut out their tongues" and "crush the worms who are eating our roots." It has even offered large sums of money and free trips to Greece as rewards for the "elimination" of

Macedonian activists who are regarded as particularly dangerous enemies of Hellenism.

Kostas Gotsis owns a construction business in Florina. According to
Gotsis, his grandfather was forced into exile in Yugoslavia because he
was a Macedonian, while his grandmother was sent to jail for giving
birth to five sons who fought with the Communists during the Greek
Civil War. Gotsis' father was killed in the Civil War in 1946. Several
years later his land was confiscated, again because he had supported
the Communists. As a child Gotsis was often called a Bulgarian. He
remembers a Greek soldier in the Civil War pointing to him and saying,
"This is a thorn. We need to clean it out. We don't want thorns in our
fields." In the early 1960s Gotsis was injured while working in a coal
mine in Belgium. During his recovery in the hospital, some Jehovah's
Witnesses gave him copies of the *Watchtower* in Macedonian. That was
how he learned to read his mother tongue. Since he has become active
in the Macedonian human rights movement, Gotsis has been followed,
his mail has been opened, and his phone has been tapped.

In 1989 Gotsis sued Yorghos Kapsalis, the editor of *Stohos*, for slan-
der. An article in the paper had described Gotsis as "an agent of Gypsy-
Skopian propaganda." The first two lawyers Gotsis hired to represent
him withdrew from the case because of threats they had received.
When the trial finally took place, it was dominated by the question of
Gotsis' national identity, not the question of whether he had been slan-
dered by *Stohos*. Kostas Gotsis, the plaintiff, had become Kostas Gotsis,
the defendant.

The climax of the trial occurred when Kapsalis' lawyer asked Gotsis
if he were Greek. Gotsis insisted that the question was not relevant and
refused to answer it. He simply took out his Greek identity card and
asked Kapsalis' lawyer if he dared challenge the validity of an official
document of the Greek government. At several points the trial degen-
erated into a shouting match. When Gotsis admitted that many of his
relatives were political refugees in Yugoslavia who were unable to return to Greece, Kapsalis and his supporters, who filled the courtroom,
shouted, "The Skopians are coming!" "Only Greeks can return!" and
"Out with the Bulgarians!" In the end Kapsalis was found innocent,
and the case was dismissed.

Initially Gotsis had intended to state publicly during the trial that he
was a Macedonian, not a Greek, but his lawyer warned him not to; he
threatened to resign from the case if he did. Since Gotsis could not say
that his nationality was Macedonian and since he would not lie and say
it was Greek, he adopted the strategy of not commenting at all on his
national identity, but of holding up his Greek identity card, which
proved that he was a Greek citizen. Gotsis, in other words, tried to

escape from his dilemma by exploiting the fact that Greek national identity and Greek citizenship are equated in Greek nationalist ideology. If Gotsis had admitted that he was a Macedonian and not a Greek, he would have only confirmed in the eyes of the court the validity of Kapsalis' charge that he was an agent of Skopje.

The next important trial involving members of the Macedonian human rights movement took place in Athens in April 1993. Christos Sideropoulos and Anastasios Boulis, both from the Florina area, were charged with criminal offenses as a result of comments they had made in an interview that appeared in the March 11, 1992, issue of *Ena*, a weekly magazine published in Athens. In this interview Sideropoulos was quoted as saying that he was a Greek citizen, but that he had "a Macedonian national consciousness," while Boulis was quoted as saying simply, "I am not a Greek; I am a Macedonian."

By asserting the existence of a Macedonian minority in Greece, Sideropoulos and Boulis were charged with having spread "intentionally false information which might create unrest and fear among the citizens and which might affect the public security or harm the international relations of the country." During the five-hour trial, which was attended by Ahmet Sadik, a Turkish member of the Greek parliament, two Greek neo-Nazi organizations, Golden Dawn and National Crusade, demonstrated outside the courthouse shouting, "We will conquer Skopje!" and "We will wash our hands with the blood of the Skopians!" Sideropoulos and Boulis were both found guilty and were fined 100,000 drachmas and sentenced to five months in prison.

Amnesty International expressed its concern over this case to the Greek authoritites, stating that the prosecution of Sideropulos and Boulis was in violation of the European Convention on Human Rights. In January 1994, after the Greek parliament passed a law ending prosecutions of "offenses committed by or through the press," an Appeals Court in Athens directed that the criminal prosecution against Sideropoulos and Boulis be dropped. Several months later, however, Sideropoulos was scheduled to be tried in District Court in Florina on charges of having presented information that could damage Greece's international relations at the 1990 meeting of the Conference on Security and Cooperation in Europe, where he stated that a Macedonian minority existed in Greece and was being deprived of its basic human rights.[21]

Another Macedonian human rights activist, Father Nikodimos Tsarknias, a priest who has traveled abroad to publicize the situation of

[21] Human Rights Watch/Helsinki (1993, 1994b) cites several additional cases in which people have been arrested and sentenced to prison for criticizing the Greek government's position on the Macedonian issue. See also the United States Department of State's *Country Reports on Human Rights Practices for 1992* (1993:791).

the Macedonian minority in Greece, has also been the target of legal proceedings in the Greek court system. In early 1993, after twenty years of service as a priest, Father Tsarknias was defrocked and excommunicated by officials of the Greek Orthodox Church. He was convicted in an ecclesiastical court on charges of homosexuality and disobedience to his superiors. Father Tsarknias himself, however, insists that he was punished because he publicly asserts that he is a Macedonian and not a Greek.

On December 2, 1994, in civil proceedings in an Edhessa court Father Tsarknias was sentenced to three months in prison for impersonating a priest because he continued to wear his clerical robes. In his defense Father Tsarknias stated that he still had the right to wear his clerical robes because after he had been excommunicated from the Greek Orthodox Church he had become a monk at a monastery of the Macedonian Orthodox Church near Skopje. According to the court Tsarknias was convicted because, as a Greek citizen, he did not have the right to join a non-Greek church. At the conclusion of his trial, Father Tsarknias refused to promise that he would never wear his robes again. Therefore, he was immediately convicted a second time on the same charges and sentenced to another three months in prison.[22]

MACEDONIAN HUMAN RIGHTS AT THE CONFERENCE ON SECURITY AND COOPERATION IN EUROPE

From its inception the movement for the human rights of the Macedonian minority in Greece has had an important transnational dimension. Since the publication of their initial manifesto in 1984, Macedonian activists in northern Greece have worked closely with leaders of Aegean Macedonian diaspora communities in Canada and Australia. On several occasions activists from Florina have traveled to Toronto, Perth, and Melbourne in order to raise money for their cause by presenting firsthand accounts of the situation in northern Greece and by appealing for an end to the factionalism that frequently mars the activities of Macedonian diaspora communities.

This transnational Macedonian human rights network was well developed by 1988, when a variety of protests and demonstrations on behalf of the human rights of Macedonians in northern Greece took place in cities throughout the world. In February 1988, the Federation of Macedonian Associations of Victoria organized a demonstra-

---

[22] This account of Father Tsarknias' trial is based on a report filed by the Greek Helsinki Monitor.

tion to protest the First International Congress on Macedonian Studies, a conference organized by Greek and Greek-Australian academics whose goal was to demonstrate "the Greekness of Macedonia from antiquity to the present." At the First International Reunion of Child Refugees of Aegean Macedonia, held in Skopje in June and July of the same year, a resolution was adopted urging the Greek government to allow Macedonian political refugees to return to Greece. On August 10, 1988, the seventy-fifth anniversary of the Treaty of Bucharest (the treaty that partitioned Macedonia among Serbia, Bulgaria, and Greece), the Macedonian National Committee of Toronto staged a demonstration at the headquarters of the United Nations in New York calling on Bulgaria and Greece to respect the human rights of their Macedonian minorities.

Then in May 1989, an international Macedonian delelgation, consisting of representatives from northern Greece, Canada, and Australia, visited the Center for Human Rights of the United Nations in Geneva, as well as the Council of Europe and the European Parliament in Strasbourg. Members of this delegation had several objectives. They wanted to draw the attention of European officials to the situation of the Macedonian minority in Greece and to lobby for political action that would lead to a change in current Greek policies. They also wanted to gather information about the various political and legal options available to them for the advancement of the human rights of the Macedonian minorities in both Bulgaria and Greece. As a result of these meetings, members of the delegation realized that the most effective course of action open to them was to file a complaint with the European Commission on Human Rights alleging that, because of its treatment of its Macedonian minority, Greece was in violation of the Human Rights Convention of the Council of Europe.[23]

Shortly thereafter, in November 1989, the Yugoslav representative to the United Nations accused Greece of violating the human rights of the Macedonian minority in Greece. This was the first time the Macedonian Question had been raised by the Yugoslav government since the period following the Greek Civil War. Two other incidents offer further evidence that the Republic of Macedonia was beginning to enjoy increasing freedom from the federal government of Yugoslavia to adopt a more nationalist position. In February 1990, a large demonstration took place in Skopje to protest the violation of the human rights of the Macedonian minorities in Bulgaria and Greece. Then in May 1990, 50,000 Macedonians blocked the border crossings between Yugoslavia and Greece in an effort to pressure both the Greek and the Yugoslav

---

[23] For a full account of the activities of this delegation see Radin and Popov (n.d. b).

governments to work toward improving the situation of the Macedonian minority in Greece.

The most impressive accomplishment of the transnational Macedonian human rights movement, however, has been to organize delegations to attend several meetings of the Conference on the Human Dimension of the Conference on Security and Cooperation in Europe, which took place in the early 1990s. The Conference on Security and Cooperation in Europe (CSCE), also known as the "Helsinki process," is an ongoing international political movement dedicated to promoting the causes of peace, human rights, and social and economic cooperation. The CSCE originally involved all the countries of Europe except Albania, as well as the former Soviet Union, Canada, and the United States. In 1975, the leaders of the thirty-five participating states met in Helsinki and signed what have come to be known as the Helsinki Accords, a document containing a declaration of principles governing relations between states that advocates respect for human rights, the self-determination of peoples, the peaceful settlement of disputes, and the inviolability of international borders.

The signing of the Helsinki Accords initiated a series of follow-up meetings to review implementation of the Helsinki provisions. The concluding document of the Vienna meeting of the CSCE, which was signed in 1989, significantly strengthened the human rights provisions of the Helsinki Accords. It alluded specifically to the rights of minorities and to the right of citizens to monitor the human rights performance of the governments of their own countries. It also established a continuous process of human rights review through an agreement to hold three yearly meetings of the Conference on the Human Dimension of the CSCE.

The second meeting of the Conference on the Human Dimension was held in Copenhagen in June 1990. It was attended by an international Macedonian delegation, which consisted of fifteen members from eight different countries. The "internal" delegates included one from Bulgarian or Pirin Macedonia, two from Greek or Aegean Macedonia, and four from the Republic of Macedonia. The "external" delegates included two from Australia, three from Canada, and one each from Poland, Czechoslovakia, and West Germany.[24] The majority of the delegates represented local Macedonian human rights committees or local branches of the Association of Child Refuges from Aegean Mace-

---

[24] This distinction between "internal" and "external" delegates indicates that Macedonians from Bulgaria and Greece are not considered part of the Macedonian diaspora, but are regarded as inhabiting the Macedonian homeland, that is, the geographical area where the Macedonian language has traditionally been spoken, as opposed to the Republic of Macedonia itself.

donia. The leaders of the delegation were particularly pleased that they had been able to assemble for the first time "a united Macedonian delegation on a world scale."

The Macedonian delegation participated in the Copenhagen conference as an officially recognized nongovernmental organization (NGO), as did such groups as the Albanians of Kosovo, the Hungarians of Romania, the Armenians, and the Kurds.[25] In that capacity it attended both the official meetings and the parallel NGO activities, which included a variety of seminars and workshops on human rights issues. The two major goals of the Macedonian delegation were to persuade as many of the official state delegations as possible to address the situation of the Macedonian minorities in Bulgaria and Greece in the final document of the meeting and to raise the issue of Macedonian human rights directly with the governments of Bulgaria and Greece.

Early in the conference Canada, the Federal Republic of Germany, and the Netherlands introduced a proposal on national minorities, a topic that was clearly going to be one of the central issues of the conference. In his introduction to the proposal a Canadian delegate pointed out that since no one could ever draw "a perfect map of Europe," national minorities would always exist. He called for all governments to demonstrate tolerance, respect, and understanding toward these minorities. After noting that Canada and many other participating states have interpreted the term "national minority" as used in the Helsinki Accords to include "ethnic, cultural, linguistic, and religious minorities," he condemned the practice by which some states attempted to evade their CSCE commitments regarding national minorities by claiming that no national minorities existed within their borders. After outlining Canada's multicultural policies and describing the cultural mosaic that constitutes Canadian society, he concluded by stressing the value of promoting the ethnic, cultural, linguistic, and religious identities of all minority groups.[26]

A very different tone was conveyed by the head of the Greek delegation in his presentation to the conference several days later. After emphasizing that the issue of minorities was not only one of human rights

---

[25] This account of the Copenhagen conference is based on the following material: a report written by the Macedonian delegates from Australia; texts of presentations made at the conference by the Canadian, Yugoslav, and Greek delegations; and documents distributed there by the Pan-Macedonian Association of Ontario and the Association of Macedonian Societies in Bulgaria.

[26] The Canadian delegate's glowing description of multiculturalism in Canada failed, however, to deal with the real threat to Canadian sovereignty posed by the continuing phenomenon of Québécois separatism.

but was, above all, an important social problem with major political consequences, he urged member states *not* to "attempt to further codify the rights of persons belonging to minorities," but instead to convene a "meeting of experts" to further study the concept of minorities in order to arrive at a common understanding of the complexities of the issue.

On June 21, the Yugoslav delegation to the conference introduced a "Memorandum Relating to the Macedonian National Minority," which accused the governments of Bulgaria and Greece of a number of specific violations of the human rights of the members of the Macedonian minorities living in their countries. It also charged the two countries with failing to fulfill their commitments to these minorities under the Universal Declaration of Human Rights, the European Convention for the Protection of Human Rights and Fundamental Freedoms, and the concluding document of the Vienna meeting of the CSCE. The Yugoslav memorandum closed by calling on the governments of Bulgaria and Greece to submit reports on the steps they have taken to protect the rights of the Macedonian minorities in their countries at the next meeting of the Conference on the Human Dimension of the CSCE to be held in Moscow the following year.

A few days later the head of the Greek delegation issued a sharp reply to the Yugoslav memorandum in which he accused the Yugoslav delegation of undermining CSCE efforts to safeguard minority rights by manipulating the issue in the service of extremist, adventurist, and irredentist policies. He drew attention to the "negative record of human and minority rights violations in Yugoslav Macedonia" and referred specifically to the mistreatment of the Albanian and Serbian minorities in the Republic of Macedonia.[27] He then defended the human rights record of Greece and pointed out that as "a member of the democratic family of the European Community" Greece has ratified a variety of international human rights instruments. Finally, he stated that the "Macedonian problem" was a nonissue and simply denied that a Macedonian minority existed in Greece. Any assertion to the contrary, he insisted, was an attempt to usurp the name and identity of two and a half million Greek-Macedonians. Not only did this constitute a gross violation of their human rights, but it was also an expression of the systematic policy of cultural genocide being directed against them by officials in Skopje.

The position of the official Greek delegation was supported by an

---

[27] For a detailed account of the human rights record of the Republic of Macedonia, see Human Rights Watch/Helsinki (1994a).

open letter sent to the conference participants by the Pan-Macedonian Association of Ontario, several of whose members were present at the Copenhagen meeting. They accused "Slav-Macedonian émigrés" under the direction of the authorities in Skopje of trying to detach Greek Macedonia from the Greek state under the pretext of human rights—of using, in other words, a "human rights approach" in order to advance territorial claims against Greek Macedonia. In their meetings with other delegations the representatives of the Pan-Macedonian Association of Ontario insisted that the only "real" Macedonians were Greeks.[28]

To complicate the situation further, representatives of the Association of Macedonian Societies in Bulgaria, who were attending the Copenhagen meeting, filed a memorandum in which they argued that the Macedonian nation was an artificial creation of Serbia and that all the Slavs of Macedonia were really Bulgarians. After documenting the persecution of inhabitants of Yugoslav or Vardar Macedonia who had a Bulgarian national identity, this memorandum criticized statements asserting the existence of a "Macedonian Nation" as part of a campaign to conquer all of Macedonia being carried out by "Great Serbian Jingoists." The memorandum concluded with an urgent call for the recognition of the human rights of the Bulgarian minorities of Yugoslavia and Greece. Needless to say, some of the representatives of the thirty-five participating CSCE states were confused by their encounters with these three different delegations, each of which identified itself as a Macedonian delegation, and each of which offered a different definition of who the Macedonians really were.

At one point during the conference a member of the official Greek delegation attempted to prevent the Macedonian delegation from distributing its literature at an information stand which had been set up at the entrance to the main conference center in order to publicize the activities of the various nongovernmental organizations. An attendant at the information stand saw the deputy head of the Greek delegation remove large quantities of the Macedonian delegation's literature. When she notified her supervisor, he asked the Greek delegate to stop. The next day the head of the Greek delegation officially requested that the conference secretariat remove the information stand of the non-

---

[28] At the Moscow meeting of the Conference on the Human Dimension of the CSCE the following year, members of the delegation from the Pan-Macedonian Association of Ontario told a member of the official Canadian delegation that they had come to the conference in order to counter Skopian propaganda. The Canadian representative replied that attending the conference for the purpose of attacking the Macedonian delegation was not consistent with the principles of the conference.

governmental organizations. When this request was denied, the Greek delegation called for the suspension of the Macedonian delegation's right to use the stand. This request, however, was also denied.

Several days later the Macedonian delegation held a press conference, which was sponsored by the Yugoslav delegation.[29] In addition to presenting their case more generally, the Macedonian delegates attempted to publicize this incident as widely as possible. Danish newspapers published articles under headlines that read, "Attempt to Censure the Macedonians" and "Literature of a Minority Removed." As members of the Macedonian delegation later reported, many conference participants were left wondering, "If attempts to deny Macedonians basic rights are made at an international conference on human rights, then what must the situation be like for them in Greece itself?"

The final document of the Copenhagen meeting of the Conference on the Human Dimension of the CSCE, which was adopted by consensus, is a general reaffirmation of the commitment of the participating states to democracy, the rule of law, and human rights, which was expressed in both the Helsinki Accords and the concluding document of the Vienna meeting of the CSCE. The section of the document dealing with the issue of national minorities affirms that "persons belonging to national minorities have the right to exercise fully and effectively their human rights and fundamental freedoms without any discrimination and in full equality before the law." In an attempt to define the term "national minority," the document states that belonging to a national minority "is a matter of a person's individual choice and no disadvantage may arise from the exercise of such choice." More specifically it declares that

> Persons belonging to national minorities have the right freely to express, preserve, and develop their ethnic, cultural, linguistic or religious identity and to maintain and develop their culture in all its aspects, free of any attempts at assimilation against their will.

This explicitly includes the right of national minorities to establish their own cultural associations and to conduct religious and educational activities in their mother tongue.[30]

---

[29] According to conference rules, in order to hold a press conference nongovernmental organizations were required to obtain the sponsorship of an official governmental organization.

[30] The full text of the final document of the Copenhagen meeting of the Conference on the Human Dimension of the CSCE was published by the United States Commission on Security and Cooperation in Europe (June 1990, Washington, D.C.).

MACEDONIAN HUMAN RIGHTS AND
MACEDONIAN NATIONALISM

Macedonian human rights activists—farmers and civil servants from northern Greece, as well as lawyers, businessmen, and manual laborers from Canada and Australia—state unequivocally that they reject the irredentist concept of a "Greater Macedonia" and that they do not want to change present international borders in the Balkans. "The Europeans are tearing down walls and opening borders," they say. "Why would we want to create new ones? That would mean war, and no one wants war." As a model for the future, a model for change, they look not to the violent process of disintegration taking place in Yugoslavia, but to its antithesis, the peaceful process of integration taking place simultaneously in western Europe. In describing their political goals they appeal to the concept of "a United Europe," "a Europe without borders," where international boundaries would be meaningless, travel and communication would be unrestricted, and Macedonians wherever they lived would be united and free.

These Macedonian human rights activists, in other words, look forward idealistically to the end of the nation-state and to the rise of pluralistic transnational communities such as "the new Europe." Until that rather distant goal is realized, however, they are attempting to gain human rights for the Macedonian minorities in Bulgaria and Greece by constructing their own transnational community, a community epitomized by the international Macedonian delegation to the Copenhagen meeting of the Conference on the Human Dimension of the CSCE. Drawing on the personal experiences of discrimination of the "internal" delegates from Bulgaria and Greece as well as the professional expertise of the "external" delegates—judges and lawyers raised in the multicultural societies of Canada and Australia—this delegation effectively exposed the failure of the Greek state with its commitment to a nationalist ideology of ethnic homogeneity and purity to safeguard the human rights of its Macedonian minority. In doing so the transnational Macedonian delegation took full advantage of the forum provided by the CSCE, itself a transnational organization committed to pluralism and the protection of the rights of national minorities defined on the basis of the principle of self-identification. In this way, then, national minorities like the Macedonians are gradually beginning to shift the balance of power in their favor and away from the nation-states like Bulgaria and Greece, against which they are struggling.

It is one of the fundamental ironies of the Macedonian human rights movement, and other comparable movements as well, that coexisting in uneasy tension with an explicit commitment to pluralism and respect for the principle of self-identification lies an implicit commitment to a diametrically opposed ideology—the ideology of Macedonian nationalism. Macedonian human rights activists, who have suffered the negative consequences of the nationalist ideologies of Bulgaria and Greece, are also, to a degree at least, Macedonian nationalists. The *international* Macedonian delegation to Copenhagen was still in the final analysis a *national* delegation, just as the Macedonian *transnational* community is still in the final analysis a *national* community.

Macedonian human rights activists are movitated by a desire to protect the human rights of the Macedonian national minorities in Bulgaria and Greece. They want to preserve or, more accurately perhaps, to create a Macedonian national identity among people who have been for almost a century the targets of Bulgarian or Greek assimilationist policies. The nationalism of Macedonian human rights activists, however, is muted, for strictly speaking it is inconsistent with the human rights discourse to which they are committed. But it is nationalism nonetheless, a counternationalism, which developed at least partially in reaction to the nationalist policies of Bulgaria and Greece. In its more extreme forms Macedonian nationalism is characterized by the same narrowness and intolerance as the Bulgarian and Greek nationalisms, which Macedonians have struggled against for so long. In its more extreme forms Macedonian nationalism, with its irredentist calls for a "United Macedonia," also poses a threat—a rhetorical threat, if not a military one—to the territorial integrity of Bulgaria and Greece.

Macedonian nationalism, which lies in the background of the Macedonian human rights movement, is a major force behind another closely related movement that has developed simultaneously and has involved many of the same individuals and organizations—the movement to win international recognition for the newly independent Republic of Macedonia. And Macedonian nationalism, with the potential threat it poses in this context to the Albanian and Serbian minorities living in the republic, has much less to do with the attempt to create a "United States of Europe" than it does with the rise of Serbian and Croatian nationalism, which have brought about the disintegration of the multinational state of Yugoslavia.

CHAPTER VI

National Symbols and the International Recognition of the Republic of Macedonia

UNLIKE Slovenia, Croatia, and, most tragically of all, Bosnia-Herzegovina, the Republic of Macedonia emerged peacefully in 1991 from the collapse of the former Yugoslavia. Since then it has struggled to gain international recognition as a sovereign state under its constitutional name—the Republic of Macedonia—and to survive as a democratic and pluralist state in the Balkans, a region where nationalism, not pluralism, has long been the dominant political ideology.

This struggle has met with serious obstacles both on the domestic and the international fronts. Over one-fifth of the citizens of the Republic of Macedonia are members of a large and potentially destabilizing Albanian minority, while Macedonia's neighbors either refuse to recognize a Macedonian state or deny the existence of a Macedonian nation or both. To make matters worse, the economy of Macedonia, which was the weakest of the former Yugoslav republics to begin with, has suffered enormously because of the United Nations sanctioned embargo on Serbia to the north, which cut off Macedonia's major rail and highway links to the rest of Europe. The ensuing shortages, unemployment, and inflation have made an already hazardous transition to a democratic political system and a market economy even more difficult.

The disintegration of the former Yugoslavia followed closely the breakup of the Soviet Union and the end of Soviet hegemony in eastern Europe. By 1990 the Communist Party of Yugoslavia had ceased to play a dominant role in the political life of the country, and multiparty political systems were beginning to develop in each of the constituent republics. When Slovenia, Croatia, and then Bosnia-Herzegovina declared their independence in 1991 as part of the rising tide of nationalist sentiment sweeping eastern Europe, Serbia attempted to preserve the unity of the Yugoslav state by military means. The tragic outbreak of nationalist violence and ethnic cleansing that followed drew worldwide attention.

Less well known, however, is the fact that on September 8, 1991, a referendum was held in which Macedonians voted overwhelmingly in favor of establishing a sovereign and independent Macedonian state. A revealing feature of this referendum was the fact that voting was not limited to citizens of the Republic of Macedonia alone. Also participating (in an unofficial capacity) were people who identified themselves as Macedonians regardless of where they were born, where they lived, or what states they were citizens of.[1] The extension of the right to vote—even unofficially—to Macedonians who were not citizens of the republic reveals a blurring of the distinction between two crucial categories, citizens of the Macedonian state, on the one hand, and members of the Macedonian nation, on the other. This distinction plays a crucial role in political life in the Balkans, for it is precisely the conflict between people's obligations as citizens to the states in which they live, on the one hand, and their loyalties to the nations to which they belong, on the other, that lies at the heart of both the domestic and the international problems that face the newly independent Republic of Macedonia. Whether it is the Albanians who are citizens of Macedonia or the Macedonians who are citizens of Greece, members of one nation who inhabit states dominated by another nation pose the ultimate challenge to the emergent democracies of the Balkans and eastern Europe more generally.

According to the 1991 census, the Republic of Macedonia had a population of slightly over two million people. It included 65 percent Macedonians (who are Orthodox Christians), 21 percent Albanians (who are Moslems), 4 percent Turks, 3 percent Roma (Gypsies), 2 percent Serbs, 2 percent Macedonian Moslems, and a small number of Vlachs. The Albanians, many of whom boycotted the 1991 census and therefore insist that they constitute significantly more than one-quarter of the population, are concentrated in the western part of the country near the Albanian border, while the Serbs are concentrated in the northeast near the border with Serbia.

Like the constitutions of the other former Yugoslav republics, the Macedonian constitution, which was adopted in November 1991, reveals a tension between two opposing principles: the principle of constitutional nationalism, according to which the dominant nation in the state is sovereign and members of that nation are privileged over others, on the one hand, and the principle of democracy, according to which all citizens of the state, regardless of their nationality, are sovereign, on the other.[2] In the parliamentary debates that took place while the Macedonian constitution was being drawn up, this very issue—the precise nature of the relationship between the Macedonian state and its diverse citizenry—was a major point of contention. Would the Repub-

---

[1] For a more detailed account of this election see chapter 4, pp. 98–100.

[2] On constitutional nationalism in the former Yugoslav republics, see Hayden (1992). On the role of nationalist ideologies in the dismembering of Yugoslavia, see Denich (1994).

lic of Macedonia be a "national state," a "state of the Macedonian nation"? Would it be a "civil state," a "state of equal citizens"? Or would some compromise be found?

In attempting to resolve this dilemma the coalition government of President Kiro Gligorov, a former Communist and leader of the Social Democratic Union of Macedonia, needed to satisfy both international and domestic critics. In order to gain legitimacy and recognition from the United Nations, the European Community, and other international organizations, Gligorov's government had to demonstrate its commitment to democracy, pluralism, and the protection of minority rights. Domestically Gligorov faced the challenge of striking a balance between the demands of two opposing political forces. On the one hand, he was confronted by the major opposition party, the Internal Macedonian Revolutionary Organization—Democratic Party for Macedonian National Unity (VMRO-DPMNE), an ultranationalist party whose irredentist platform called for the creation of a "United Macedonia." On the other, he was confronted by the demands of the Party for Democratic Prosperity (PDP), the larger of the two Albanian parties in the republic, which was an important member of Gligorov's coalition government. The extreme nationalist position of VMRO-DPMNE was in direct conflict with the minority rights position of the PDP and with the democratic expectations of international organizations.

Although the preamble of the Macedonian constitution offers a nationalist definition of the Macedonian state, the main body of the constitution itself is a much more democratic document clearly influenced by western European models and containing explicit reference to the equality of all citizens before the law.[3] More specifically, the preamble of the Macedonian constitution defines the republic as "the national state of the Macedonian people [*narod*], in which full equality as citizens and permanent coexistence with the Macedonian people is provided for Albanians, Turks, Vlachs, Romanies [Gypsies], and other nationalities living in the Republic of Macedonia." This compromise failed to please either the leaders of VMRO-DPMNE (who had argued that the Republic of Macedonia should be defined as "the national state of the Macedonian people and all citizens living in it") or the leaders of the PDP (who argued that the Albanians should be referred to as one of the two constitutive nations of the Macedonian state). Equally contentious was Article 7 of the constitution, which specifies that "the Macedonian language, written in the Cyrillic alphabet," is the official language of the republic, but which also grants official status to the

---

[3] As Hayden (1992:658) points out, according to the traditional rules of constitutional interpretation the provisions of such preambles, unlike those in the main body of the text, are not legally binding.

languages and alphabets of the "nationalities" in areas inhabited by a "significant number" of people who belong to these "nationalities."

The basic provisions of the Macedonian constitution itself declare that in the republic sovereignty is derived from the citizens of the state. The constitution guarantees that "members of nationalities" have the right freely to express and develop their national identity and culture and more specifically to found cultural associations and to obtain primary and secondary education in their own language. Article 78 of the constitution also establishes a Council for Interethnic Relations consisting of two members from each "nationality" in order to deal with issues concerning the rights of national minorities.

In actual practice the Republic of Macedonia has managed fairly well to live up to these constitutional ideals. As a result it has retained a great deal of the cultural pluralism that characterized life in the former Yugoslavia. President Gligorov, who has expressed his desire to create "a multicultural republic," leads a multiethnic, coalition government whose twenty-four ministers include five Albanians and one Turk. Newspapers are published in Albanian and Turkish; the government broadcasts radio and television programs in Albanian, Turkish, Romany, and Vlach; and a "theater of the nationalities" in Skopje offers performances in Albanian and Turkish. Finally, the government has even set goals for increasing the representation of the national minorities in both the universities and the police force.

The Albanians in Macedonia, however, have expressed dissatisfaction with their minority status in a variety of ways. They boycotted the September 8, 1991, referendum which established the Republic of Macedonia as a sovereign and independent state. Then, in January 1992, they held their own referendum and voted overwhelmingly in favor of "the political and territorial autonomy of Albanians in Macedonia" and the establishment of their own state, to be named the Republic of Ilirida.[4]

With regard to the issue of minority rights more generally, Albanians, like members of the other national minorities in Macedonia, complain of discrimination in the fields of education and employment. They object, for example, to the fact that all citizens of the republic must

---

[4] The destabilizing potential of the Albanian minority in Macedonia is exacerbated by the explosive situation that exists in neighboring Kosovo, the formerly autonomous region of Serbia, whose Albanian majority is growing restive under increasingly repressive Serbian rule. The outbreak of conflict in Kosovo would inevitably spill over into Macedonia and involve the Albanian minority there as well. Extreme Albanian nationalists advocate the creation of a "Greater Albania" that would include the part of Macedonia inhabited by Albanians, the province of Kosovo, and the state of Albania itself. See Xhudo (1993).

carry identity cards written in Macedonian. The government has prepared legislation according to which these identity cards would be
written in two languages, but the leaders of VMRO-DPMNE have successfully blocked its passage. Albanians also object to the citizenship
law of the republic because it allows Macedonians who live in other
former Yugoslav republics (but not members of national minorities
living there) to be granted Macedonian citizenship automatically. Serbs
in Macedonia have similar complaints. They object to the fact that the
Macedonian constitution does not refer to Serbs as one of the nationalities living in the republic, to the fact that there are no programs in
Serbian on state radio and television, and to the fact that priests of the
Serbian Orthodox Church (which does not recognize the Macedonian
Orthodox Church) have been prevented from holding services in the
republic.[5]

The conflict between pluralism and nationalism in Macedonia was
highlighted in the difficult negotiations that took place in parliament
over the long-delayed census, which was finally held in the summer of
1994 under the supervision of the Council of Europe and with the financial support of the European Union. Once again President Gligorov
had to contend with the diametrically opposed demands of the Macedonian nationalists in VMRO-DPMNE and those of the Albanian nationalists in the PDP. In the end the parliament passed legislation di-
recting that some census forms should be printed only in Macedonian
and that others should be printed in Macedonian *and* in the five languages of the national minorities (Albanian, Turkish, Romany, Serbo-
Croatian, and Vlach).

The leaders of VMRO-DPMNE, who had insisted that the census
forms be printed only in Macedonian, announced plans to challenge
the constitutionality of the new census law on the grounds that it was
inconsistent with the designation of Macedonian as the official language of the republic. The leaders of VMRO-DPMNE felt that this law
was an attempt to introduce a policy of "multilingualism" into the republic and was the first step on the road toward federalization. This

---

[5] In a recent report Human Rights Watch/Helsinki concluded that "human rights
problems do exist in the Former Yugoslav Republic of Macedonia, chiefly involving discrimination against various ethnic minorities. . . . This discrimination, however, appears
to be a legacy from earlier times. The government acknowledges the discrimination and
appears to be attempting to work out solutions" (Human Rights Watch/Helsinki 1994a).
The challenges facing the Republic of Macedonia in the area of human rights are illustrated by the controversy that arose when members of the Albanian minority attempted
to establish an Albanian language university in Tetovo in December 1994. According to
the Macedonian government these attempts were illegal and unconstitutional. Police prevented ceremonies marking the inauguration of the university from taking place and
arrested members of the university's founding committee.

dispute over the first census to be held in the newly independent Republic of Macedonia confirms Benedict Anderson's (1991:164–70) observation that a census is a powerful tool that enables states to classify their citizens into national categories and then express this classification quantitatively in order to determine the relative size and political strength of these national minorities.[6]

On the international front the most serious obstacle facing the Republic of Macedonia has been Greece's opposition to the international recognition of the republic under its constitutional name. This conflict between Greece and Macedonia over the name of the republic is part of a larger "global cultural war" (Featherstone 1990b:10) in which these two nations and the states that represent them are fighting for control of powerful national symbols, such as names, flags, and famous ancestors. Both Greek and Macedonian nationalists regard these symbols as essential components of their national culture, as cultural property that by definition belongs to their nation and their nation alone.[7] International recognition of the Republic of Macedonia is a particularly important aspect of the more general conflict between Greece and Macedonia because it raises the issue of the politics of identity to the highest level, the level of international diplomacy.

As Fredrik Barth (1969:13) has pointed out, identity involves both self-ascription and ascription by others. This is just as true for states as it is for individuals. In order to establish its identity as the *Republic of Macedonia*, it is not enough for this former Yugoslav republic to declare its independence under that name; it must also be recognized under that name by other states and by major international organizations as well. Only in that way will its identity be legitimated in the world of international affairs. The Republic of Macedonia, therefore, is engaged in a campaign to become a full member of the family of nations. It is attempting, in other words, to obtain a legitimate place in the international order, to find "a seat at the table as a nation among others" (Malkki 1994:49), and to do so under its constitutional name, the Republic of Macedonia.

Greece's opposition to international recognition of the Republic of Macedonia is based primarily on the claim that the name "Macedonia" is, was, and always will be Greek. After the name "Macedonia," the next most controversial symbol in this conflict has been the sixteen-ray

---

[6] According to the results of the 1994 census, which were generally accepted as accurate by European observers, but which were still contested by leaders of the Albanian minority, Macedonians constituted 67 percent of the population of the republic, Albanians 23 percent.

[7] On the exclusivity of nationalist claims to cultural property, see Handler (1988:157). On "the disputed ownership of history," see Herzfeld (1991).

sun or star of Vergina, which is widely recognized as the emblem of the ancient Macedonian royal family and which was chosen as the flag for the newly independent Republic of Macedonia. From a Greek national-ist perspective, since the ancient Macedonians were Greeks, both the name "Macedonia" and the sun or star of Vergina are Greek, and any use of them by "Slavs" constitutes not only the theft of Greek national property, but also proof that "Skopje" harbors irredentist claims on Greek territory. In addition to posing a threat to Greek national inter-ests, the Greek government argues that international recognition of the Republic of Macedonia would lead to a further destabilization of the southern Balkans.

As evidence for the existence of Macedonian territorial claims against Greece, the Greek government regularly cites several passages in the Macedonian constitution. The preamble to the Macedonian con-stitution links the recent establishment of a sovereign Macedonian state with the creation of the People's Republic of Macedonia (as one of the republics of the former Yugoslavia) at the first session of the Anti-Fas-cist Assembly for the National Liberation of Macedonia (ASNOM), which was held on August 2, 1944. The preamble specifically states that the resolutions of ASNOM provide part of the historical legacy on which the present Macedonian state is founded. Greek objections to this passage are based on the fact that one of the goals articulated by ASNOM in 1944 was "the unification of the entire Macedonian nation," to be achieved by "the liberation of the other two segments" of Mace-donia (Andonov-Poljanski 1985, 2:607).

The Greek government also objects to Article 3 of the Macedonian constitution, which states that "the borders of the Republic of Macedo-nia may be changed only in accordance with the Constitution," as well as Article 49, which states that the republic "cares for the status and the rights" of Macedonians living in neighboring countries and "assists them in their cultural development and promotes ties to them." Some Greek sources interpret this article as legitimating efforts to "liberate enslaved Macedonians" living in Greece. More generally, however, Greece objects to all references to a Macedonian minority in Greece since the Greek government denies the existence of any such minority.

Ironically the Greek constitution contains an article which directly parallels Article 49 of the Macedonian constitution. Article 108 of the Greek constitution states that the Greek government "shall care for Greeks residing abroad and for the maintenance of their ties with the Mother Fatherland," and the Greek government has actively sup-ported the rights of the Greek minority in Albania. What is more, reports occasionally appear in the Greek press claiming that there is a Greek minority in the Republic of Macedonia.[8]

The first major focus of the conflict between Greece and Macedonia over the international recognition of the republic was the attempt by Macedonia to gain recognition from the European Community (EC). On December 16, 1991, the Council of Ministers of the EC announced the conditions under which the EC would recognize the former Yugoslav republics which had declared their independence. In addition to requiring that these republics commit themselves to protecting the human rights of the ethnic minorities living within their borders, the EC also required them to guarantee that they had no territorial claims against any neighboring EC state and that they would not engage in hostile acts against any such state, *including the use of a name which implied territorial claims.*[9]

On January 6, 1992, the Macedonian parliament, which in the words of the Macedonian foreign minister was "pinning its hopes on Europe," adopted two amendments to the Macedonian constitution in an attempt to convince the EC of its peaceful intentions. Amendment 1 stated that the republic had no territorial claims against any neighboring state and that the borders of the republic could be changed only in accordance with "generally accepted international norms," while Amendment 2 stated that the republic would not interfere in the internal affairs of other states. In addition, President Gligorov repeatedly offered to sign a bilateral agreement with Greece affirming the permanence of the international border between the two countries.

Shortly thereafter an EC arbitration commission found that of all the former Yugoslav republics only Slovenia and Macedonia fulfilled the conditions for recognition. In addition, it specifically ruled that the use of the name "Macedonia" did *not* imply territorial claims toward any neighboring state. In spite of the findings of its own arbitration commission, however, the EC announced on January 15, 1992, that it would recognize Slovenia and Croatia, but not Macedonia. This step, although it did nothing to resolve the conflict between Greece and Macedonia, officially marked the demise of the Federal Republic of Yugoslavia.

---

[8] No such minority, however, was identified in the 1994 Human Rights Watch/ Helsinki report on human rights in the Republic of Macedonia (1994a). These Greek claims probably refer to the small Vlach minority in the republic, many of whom were Hellenized in the late nineteenth and early twentieth centuries.

[9] This requirement was included at the insistence of Greece and clearly applied only to Macedonia, since Macedonia was the only former Yugoslav republic that shared a border with an EC state.

When the Council of Ministers of the EC met in May, 1992, they agreed to recognize the Republic of Macedonia, but only under a name that was acceptable to all parties concerned. A month later the EC adopted a position that was even closer to the Greek position on the issue when it announced that it would only recognize the republic "under a name which does not include the term Macedonia." Most observers agreed that the EC states supported Greece on the Macedonian issue, not because of the merits of the Greek case, but because the EC Council of Ministers recognize the right of member states to exercise an unofficial veto on issues that affect their national interests.[10] Furthermore, in exchange for EC support on the Macedonian issue Greece promised to ratify the Maastricht Treaty, which would strengthen the EC by creating a common European currency and a common European foreign policy. In addition, Greece also promised to support EC sanctions against Serbia, a traditional ally of Greece, and to ratify an EC financial protocol with Turkey, a traditional enemy of Greece.

In response to these EC decisions Macedonian officials repeatedly declared that bargaining over the name of a state as a condition for its recognition was contrary to the principles of international law, and they insisted that no other country had the right to change the name under which Macedonia was recognized. Greek Prime Minister Constantine Mitsotakis, on the other hand, celebrated the final EC decision as "an important national victory" (*The Age* [Melbourne], June 30, 1992, p. 8), while a Greek diplomat was quoted as saying "This pseudo little republic must stop bothering us" (*New York Times*, April 5, 1992, sec. 4, p. 2). During this period the international press was full of references to the nationalist hysteria and paranoia sweeping Greece. The entire affair was described as a "shameful diplomatic farce" (*New York Times*, April 5, 1992); the consensus seemed to be that Greece was running the risk of losing its "democratic image" and placing itself "on the margins of Europe." Some European diplomats were unusually blunt. The Danish foreign minister said that the Macedonian issue had made the EC states "hostages of Greece" (*Neos Kosmos*, January 23, 1993, p. 1), while the Italian foreign minister accused Greece of "blackmailing" the EC over the recognition of Macedonia (*Neos Kosmos*, December 19, 1992).

Then, in December 1992, the focus of the dispute between Greece and Macedonia shifted from the capitals of the member states of the EC to New York City, when the Republic of Macedonia applied for admission to the United Nations. The governments of both Greece and Mace-

---

[10] See Nugent (1989:88, 103) for a discussion of the principle of unanimity in the decision-making process of the EC Council of Ministers.

donia were willing to compromise when France proposed a plan according to which the republic would be admitted to the United Nations under the temporary or provisional name "the Former Yugoslav Republic of Macedonia" (usually abbreviated as FYROM), with a permanent name to be chosen later through a process of mediation. Thus "the Former Yugoslav Republic of Macedonia" became a member of the United Nations and took its seat in the General Assembly alphabetically under the letter "T." At Greece's insistence Macedonia was not allowed to fly its flag at the United Nations headquarters.[11]

Throughout this entire recognition process Greeks and Macedonians mounted large demonstrations in Athens, Thessaloniki, and Skopje, as well as in New York, Toronto, Brussels, and Melbourne, to express their respective positions with regard to the international recognition of the Republic of Macedonia. Both the Greek and the Macedonian governments were prevented from taking any steps toward reaching a compromise solution by the extreme nationalist positions adopted by opposition parties in each country. In fact, in the autumn of 1993 the conservative government of Greek Prime Minister Mitsotakis fell in large part because he was portrayed by the opposition as being too willing to make concessions on the Macedonian issue.

In December 1993, the focus of the Macedonian conflict shifted from New York back to western Europe. Just days before Greece was to assume the rotating presidency of the EC, which had now become the European Union (EU), six member states—Great Britain, France, Germany, Italy, Denmark, and the Netherlands—decided to recognize Macedonia under the name "the Former Yugoslav Republic of Macedonia" and to establish full diplomatic relations with it. Two months later the United States and Australia announced that they too would recognize "the Former Yugoslav Republic of Macedonia." Both countries, however, refrained from establishing diplomatic ties with the republic, primarily in order to avoid further antagonizing their large and well-organized Greek diaspora communities. In response to pressure from the Greek community in Australia, the Australian government announced that all government agencies would from that point on refer to Macedonians in Australia as "Slav-Macedonians." Needless to say, the Macedonian community in Australia protested vigorously, ac-

---

[11] During final negotiations over its admission to the United Nations, the Macedonian government attempted unsuccessfully to have "the Former Yugoslav Republic of Macedonia" referred to as a "temporary description" rather than a "temporary name." The Macedonian government was informed at this time by United Nations legal advisors that the name "FYROM" was only for internal United Nations use and did not prevent individual member states from recognizing Macedonia under its constitutional name.

cusing the government of having betrayed the principles of multiculturalism that lay at the heart of Australian society.

Any hopes that these acts of recognition would bring an end to the
two years of economic chaos and political instability that had characterized Macedonia's struggle for international recognition were dashed
when Greece responded by immediately imposing an economic blockade against the republic. This move evoked widespread international
condemnation and prompted the other members of the EU to bring
Greece before the European Court of Justice on charges of having violated the Maastricht Treaty and other EU trade rules. According to the
government of Greek Prime Minister Andreas Papandreou, whose
Panhellenic Socialist Movement (PASOK) had come to power in October 1993, Greece would lift its blockade against "Skopje" and resume
United Nations sponsored negotiations on a permanent name (which
Greece had earlier broken off) only if "Skopje" agreed to adopt a new
flag, guarantee its border with Greece, and eliminate articles of its constitution that Greece found unacceptable.

The Greek blockade against the republic had a devastating effect on
the Macedonian economy, already weakened by the effects of the
United Nations embargo on Serbia. By denying the republic access to
the Greek port of Thessaloniki, the Greek blockade drastically reduced
Macedonia's export earnings and seriously interfered with its import
of food, oil, and other vital supplies. Greek Prime Minister Papandreou
was at least partly right when he said "Skopje's survival depends on
the port of Thessaloniki, not on the number of its ambassadors" (Macedonian Information and Liaison Service, December 14, 1993).

Membership in the United Nations and recognition by the United
States and the EU states have undoubtedly been the major prizes in
the struggle over the international recognition of the Republic of Macedonia. At times, however, it has seemed that no international organization was too small or insignificant to provide a setting for this contest.
For several years after its declaration of independence, every attempt
by the republic to become a member of an international organization
met with opposition from Greece. Every rejection was a victory for
Greece; every acceptance a victory for Macedonia. The veto of Greece
has kept Macedonia from becoming a member of the CSCE, while
Cypriot opposition has prevented it from joining the Nonaligned
Movement.

The Republic of Macedonia has, however, succeeded in becoming a
member of the International Olympic Committee, and its team participated in the 1992 Barcelona Games, although it did so under the Olympic, not the Macedonian, flag. Macedonia has also joined a variety of
other international organizations ranging from the World Bank, the
International Monetary Fund, and the International Atomic Energy

Agency to Interpol, the World Automobile Association, and the International Red Cross. The benefits a landlocked country like Macedonia will derive from its membership in the International Naval Organization are surely more symbolic than practical.

Interesting issues have also arisen as the Republic of Macedonia has attempted to secure the recognition of individual states. Although Bulgaria was the first country to recognize Macedonia as an independent state, Bulgaria does not recognize the existence of a Macedonian nation, a Macedonian language, or a Macedonian minority in Bulgaria. The Bulgarian government insists that Macedonians are Bulgarians and that the Macedonian language is a dialect of Bulgarian. This conflict over the status of the Macedonian language was highlighted during a 1994 meeting between Macedonian President Gligorov and Bulgarian President Zhelev in Sofia during which Gligorov insisted on using an interpreter despite the repeated demands of Zhelev that interpreters not be used.

When Russia recognized the Republic of Macedonia in August 1992, under its constitutional name, it attempted to avoid antagonizing the Greek government through what one Greek account referred to as "incredible orthographic acrobatics" (*Neos Kosmos*, August 6, 1992, p. 1). The Russian minister of foreign affairs insisted that the name of the new state, "Macedónia" (pronounced with a soft "c," a hard "d," and the accent on the third syllable), and the name of the region in Greece, "Makedhonía" (pronounced with a hard "c," a soft "d," and the accent on the fourth syllable) were in fact two different names. And when China recognized the republic under its constitutional name, it expressed its appreciation for Macedonia's "consistent and principled support for the stance of the Chinese government on the Taiwan issue" (Macedonian Information and Liaison Service, October 14, 1992).

Throughout this period Macedonian news media regularly published reports listing each of the countries that had recognized Macedonia and specifying the precise name under which recognition had been accorded. These acts of recognition were significant because they were further proof that the Republic of Macedonia was finally taking its proper "seat at the table" as a full member of the family of nations.

THE POWER OF NAMES

The most hotly contested symbol in the global cultural war taking place between Greeks and Macedonians has been without a doubt the name "Macedonia." Despite the condescending tone of the titles of some articles on the Macedonian Question that have appeared recently in the American press—"What's in a Name?" or "The Name Game," for example—it is clear that names are extremely powerful symbols of identity and that the process of naming is inextricably linked with the process of identity formation. This insight did not escape the notice of a Greek journalist who wrote an article on Macedonia that appeared in a Greek newspaper in Melbourne. "The major problem," he wrote, "is the name. . . . With the name the theft took place, the falsification, and the distortion of history. With the name 'Macedonia' the state of Skopje was created" (*Neos Kosmos*, November 9, 1992, p. 2).

As Pierre Bourdieu points out in his discussion of the "magical power of naming" (1991:236), the power to name is one of the elementary forms of political power precisely because it involves the power to bring into existence that which is being named. Furthermore, possession of a name—the right to identify oneself by a certain name—is equivalent to possession of that which is named. Thus the conflict between Greeks and Macedonians over the name "Macedonia" is ultimately a dispute over which group has the right to everything associated with "Macedonia"—its culture, its history, and even, in the final analysis, its territory.

An amazing variety of names were proposed for the Republic of Macedonia during its campaign to gain international recognition. During the entire negotiation process (which was still continuing in early 1995) the Greek government consistently refused to accept any name for the republic that included the word "Macedonia" in any form whatsoever, whether as a noun or even as an adjectival modifier. By proposing names for the republic that did not include the word "Macedonia," the Greek government was attempting to sever completely the symbolic ties linking the republic and its people with anything Macedonian. More specifically, it was trying to undermine the arguments put forward by contemporary Macedonian nationalists that they, not the Greeks, were the true heirs to the glory of Alexander the Great and the ancient Macedonians. Finally, the Greek government wanted to prevent recognition of the republic under the name "Macedonia" from serving as a basis for the irredentist claims made by extreme Macedonian nationalists to Greek territory in Macedonia.

Needless to say, Greek proposals to change the name of the republic were rejected out of hand by the Macedonian government, which consistently refused even to discuss the possibility of a compromise on the name issue. In their responses to these proposals, Macedonian officials, while asserting historical claims to the name "Macedonia," also specifically sought to allay Greek fears that use of the name Macedonia implied a desire to appropriate the cultural heritage of ancient Macedonia or to seize territory in Greek Macedonia. President Gligorov, for example, made the following statement in a 1992 interview:

We are Slavs who came to this area in the sixth century . . . we are not descendants of the ancient Macedonians. We have borne this name [Macedonians] for centuries; it originates from the name of this geographic region, and we are inhabitants of part of this region. This is the way people can differentiate us from the neighboring Slav peoples, the Serbs and the Bulgarians. Our country is called the Republic of Macedonia, and this is only a part of the territory that is now part of Greece and Bulgaria.[12]

Among the names for the new republic suggested by Greece were "Dardania," "Paeonia," and "Illyria," names used in antiquity to designate regions to the north of ancient Macedonia. Use of these names serves to displace the Republic of Macedonia both spatially and temporally. These names dissociate the republic spatially from the geographical region of Macedonia by identifying it with areas to the north. They also deny its existence in the present by projecting it into the past.[13]

Other names for the republic suggested by the Greek government, such as "the Central Balkan Republic," "South Slavia," and "South Serbia" are metonyms that negate the existence of the Republic of Macedonia by dissociating it from "Macedonia" and identifying it with larger geographical areas and cultural groups, such as the Balkans, the Slavs, and the Serbs.[14] The Greek practice of referring to the republic by the name of its capital city, "Skopje," and names such as "the Macedonian Republic of Skopje" or "Skopian Macedonia" are also metonyms. They operate, however, in the opposite direction by identifying the republic with a smaller geographical unit, a city, rather than with a larger one.

Many names for the republic were proposed by third parties to the dispute that were not acceptable to either the Greek or the Macedonian government. These names represent attempts to qualify the name of the republic in order to undercut its claim to embody Macedonia in either its temporal or its spatial entirety. Names like "Central Macedonia," "Vardar Macedonia," "Upper Macedonia," and "Northern Macedonia" clearly indicate that the republic occupies only a portion of the geographical area known as Macedonia. The name "New Macedonia" similarly serves to dissociate the modern Macedonian state and by extension the modern Macedonian nation from Alexander the Great and the ancient Macedonians.

[12] From the *Foreign Broadcast Information Service Daily Report, Eastern Europe*, February 26, 1992, p. 35.

[13] This process is similar to the "denial of coevalness" as it occurs in anthropological discourse dealing with "the other" (Fabian 1983:31). See also Danforth (1984) and Brown (1992).

[14] The Albanians of Macedonia (who are not a Slavic people) objected strongly to any name that identified the republic as Slavic.

Finally, "the Former Yugoslav Republic of Macedonia," which has been generally adopted as the temporary or provisional name of the republic and which is acceptable to neither government as a permanent solution to the problem, negates the existence of the republic both temporally and spatially. This name implies that the republic enjoys no independent existence in the present; that it is only a "former" republic. In addition, it links the republic metonymically to the "former Yugoslavia," a multinational state that included the Republic of Macedonia in the past, but which no longer exists. As President Gligorov put it, "We are not 'former,' and we are not 'Yugoslav' any more" (*Nea Elladha*, October 30, 1993, p. 2). The widespread use of "FYROM" as an acronym for "the Former Yugoslav Republic of Macedonia" also serves to dissociate the Republic of Macedonia from the name Macedonia and everything it represents. An even more extreme example of this process of dissociation is the occasional use in Greek sources of the term "Fyromians" to refer to the Macedonians themselves.

Perhaps the most interesting proposal to surface during the negotiations between Greece and Macedonia over the permanent name of the republic was the Greek suggestion made in June 1992 that the republic adopt a "double name." One name would be the formal or official name of the republic and would be used "externally" in all of its dealings with other states and with international organizations. This name could not include the term "Macedonia" in any form. The other name would be an informal name for "internal" or "domestic" use only and could include the term "Macedonian." According to this plan, which the Greek press referred to as a compromise, Greece would allow the citizens of the Former Yugoslav Republic of Macedonia to refer to themselves as "Macedonians" at the domestic level as long as they adopted another name for use at the international level.

A year later a different plan was put forth which also called for a "double name," but which was much less attractive to the Greek government. According to this plan Greece would be able to use any name it liked to refer to the republic, but the international community could refer to it by its constitutional name. Both these proposals emphasize that the process of naming, like the process of constructing an identity more generally, involves both self-ascription and ascription by others. The real power in this phase of the contest over Macedonian identity lies in the hands of powerful states and international organizations that are in a position to determine the official name the republic will eventually be able to use in the world of international affairs.

From the Greek perspective the name "Macedonia" is the exclusive property of Greece, and if "Skopje" is recognized as the Republic of Macedonia, Greece will somehow lose its claim to all that the name stands for. As a result, the name "Macedonia" has become the focus of legal battles on several continents in which Greek organizations have attempted to prevent Macedonian organizations from using the name by establishing their own exclusive rights to it first. In November 1992, the Greek government hired a patent agent in Belgium to threaten the Macedonian Information and Liaison Service, a Macedonian news agency based at the time in Brussels, with court action if it continued to use the word "Macedonian" in its name. The Greek government claimed that this organization had infringed on the trade name of the Macedonian News Agency, a Greek news agency based in Thessaloniki. The name "Makedonija," however, had already been registered in Belgium by cultural, sporting, and religious associations founded by Macedonians from the republic in the mid-1980s. In May 1994, a federal court in Washington, D.C., granted the Pan-Macedonian Association of America and Canada (a Greek-Macedonian organization) exclusive rights to the name "Macedonia," a decision that the World Congress of Macedonia for North America (a Macedonian organization) planned to appeal.[15]

An important component of the response of the Greek government to the Republic of Macedonia's efforts to win international recognition was a campaign to bolster *Greek* claims to the name Macedonia. During this campaign the Greek government began to use the term "Macedonia" in prominent and official contexts where the name had not been widely used before. It was as if the Greek government were trying to rehabilitate the name "Macedonia," which for a long time had had negative connotations associated with poverty, backwardness, Turks, and Slavs; as if Greece were trying to reclaim something it had taken for granted, something it only realized was valuable now that it was being claimed by someone else.

One of the earliest and most significant steps in the Greek government's campaign to reclaim the name "Macedonia" was the decision taken in August 1988, to change the name of the Ministry of Northern Greece in Thessaloniki, to "the Ministry of Macedonia-Thrace." As Macedonians were quick to point out, while "Macedonia" was adopted as the official name of the republic in 1944, this decision in 1988 marked the first time that the name "Macedonia" had ever been

---

[15] The confusion caused by two hostile groups both claiming the same name can have embarrassing, sometimes even amusing consequences. An Australian politician gave a pro-Macedonian speech to what he thought was a Macedonian organization, only to find out later that he had in fact been addressing a group of Greek-Macedonians. When asked to provide financing for a new hospital in Thessaloniki by the minister of Northern Greece, a vice-president of an international bank replied that he had already authorized a large loan for Macedonia in Skopje (Martis 1983:101).

officially used by the Greek government to designate a formal administrative unit of the country. It must be noted, however, that the name "Macedonia" (like the names "Thrace," "Epirus," and "Peloponnesos") has long been used unofficially in Greece to designate a particular geographic region that had no administrative bodies or functions associated with it, but which nevertheless had a great deal of cultural and historical significance.[16]

In the early 1990s, when the Macedonian Question had become an important "national issue," the Greek government engaged in a kind of naming frenzy in which an incredible variety of highly visible places, organizations, and objects were given the name "Macedonia" or "Macedonian." The international airport in Thessaloniki was renamed "the Macedonia Airport," and a new press agency that opened there was named "the Macedonian News Agency." When Olympic Airways, the Greek national airline, purchased a new airbus, it was named "Macedonia," as was the Greek entry in a transatlantic sailboat race. At this time the Greek National Tourist Organization also opened a high-profile advertising campaign featuring Macedonia, an area whose potential for tourism had long been ignored. The main slogan of the campaign was "Come to Greece and Visit Macedonia."

Participants in this dispute over the name "Macedonia" often cited what they claimed were analogous situations in other parts of the world in order to support their own particular point of view. People who favored the international recognition of the Republic of Macedonia pointed out that the names of peoples change over time. "Bulgar" originally designated a Turkic-speaking people; now it designates the Slavic-speaking people who assimilated them. Similarly, the Franks were a Germanic-speaking people, while the people who use this name today (the French) speak a Romance language. These examples clearly undermine the Greek claim that because the ancient Macedonians were not Slavs a contemporary Slavic people cannot call themselves Macedonians. Supporters of the Republic of Macedonia also pointed out that Luxembourg is both the name of an independent country and the name of a province of Belgium, and that France has not asked Great Britain to change its name because Brittany is the name of a French province.[17]

Opponents of the international recognition of Macedonia, on the other hand, argued that these examples were not relevant because they did not take into consideration the hostile climate of competing nation-

---

[16] For administrative purposes Greece is divided into fifty-one provinces or nomes, thirteen of which make up the region of Macedonia. See Keefe et al. (1977:ix, 42).

[17] I would like to thank Victor Friedman for pointing these examples out to me.

alist ideologies that dominated Balkan politics in the 1990s. Advocates of the Greek position on Macedonia cited the fact that after World War I the Allies prevented the newly independent state of Austria from adopting the name "German-Austria." As a more recent example, supporters of Greece cited the determined opposition of the People's Republic of China to the attempt of the government of Taiwan to lay claim to the name "China."

In addition to the conflict over the name of the newly independent Republic of Macedonia, which took place at the level of international diplomacy, conflict raged at less visible levels over other kinds of names as well. Particular anger and bitterness were evoked by the controversies surrounding the geographical names of cities and towns in northern Greece, as well as the personal names of the people who inhabit them. In both these cases, however, it was the Greek state, not some international organization, which had the ultimate authority to determine what names would be used in all official contexts. It is not surprising that the Greek state decided that all official geographical and personal names in Greek Macedonia would be Greek. Nevertheless, in both cases Slavic names continue to be widely used in unofficial contexts in northern Greece and even in official contexts in diaspora communities in Canada and Australia.[18]

From a Greek perspective the Macedonian practice of using the name "Aegean Macedonia" to refer to "Greek Macedonia" constitutes a threat to Greek sovereignty over the area, as does the use of Macedonian names like Lerin and Solun for the cities of Florina and Thessaloniki. The Greek practice of using Greek names to refer to places in other countries ("Constantinople" for "Istanbul," "Monastiri" for "Bitola," and "Northern Epirus" for "Southern Albania," for example) is somehow not regarded in the same light.

Arguments over the names of villages in Greek Macedonia generally focus on whether the Slavic or the Greek names are the "real" or the "original" names of these villages. Macedonians claim that the "real" village names are the Slavic names that were in use prior to the 1920s, when the Greek government decreed that they should all be replaced by Greek names. These Slavic names were the names the Greeks "found" when they came to Macedonia and incorporated it into the Greek state in 1913; these were the "traditional" names that the villagers' parents and grandparents always used. Greeks, on the other hand, reply that the "real" village names are the Greek names that they

---

[18] Macedonian activists in northern Greece take great pleasure in the fact that Slavic toponyms (the names of springs, fields, ravines, and hills), which exist primarily in oral tradition, have not been replaced with Greek names.

read on maps and on the signs that stand at the entrance to their villages. Each side accuses the other of having changed the "real" village names.

In the late 1980s and early 1990s immigrants from northern Greece living in Toronto and Melbourne faced the divisive issue of whether to use the Greek or the Slavic name for their village in the name of their village social organization. In some cases this led to the formation of two separate village associations, one composed of villagers who identified themselves as Greeks and insisted on using the Greek name of the village, the other composed of villagers who identified themselves as Macedonians and insisted on using either the Macedonian name of the village or both names of the village together.

In Melbourne in 1989, for example, the Philanthropic Society of Meliti (the Greek name of a village near Florina) split into two factions as a result of the Macedonian conflict. The Greek faction continued to use the name Meliti, whereas the Macedonian faction preferred Voštarani, the Slavic name of the village, and adopted the name "Voštarani (Meliti) Social Club." A few years later in an identical sequence of events, the Macedonian faction of another village organization split off and formed the "Gorničevo-Kelli Community." In this way immigrants from Florina have attempted to deal with the divisions in their diaspora communities caused by the Macedonian conflict by adopting a "double name" solution of their own.

The Macedonian conflict has left its mark not only on the place names of northern Greece, but on the personal names of the individuals who live there as well. As the rural population of Macedonia was incorporated into the three different nation-states that acquired control of Macedonia after the Second Balkan War in 1913, the names of the people who had just become citizens of these states were "nationalized." They were standardized, in other words, and given a form that marked the individuals who bore them as members of the dominant nations in these states. In Greece names like Petrov or Markov (names whose forms were common in rural Macedonia at the turn of the century) were changed to Petropoulos or Markidis, in Serbia they became Petrovich or Markovich, while in Bulgaria they were written as Petroff or Markoff. After the establishment of the People's Republic of Macedonia in 1944 these names were changed to Petrovski or Markovski. The Hellenization of Slavic personal names (both first and last), which took place in northern Greece in the 1920s and 1930s, often involved more drastic changes in the form of the name. In some cases names were translated from Macedonian into Greek; in others cases people received entirely different and unrelated names.

Many people from northern Greece who identify themselves as Macedonians and not as Greeks resent the fact that they were given Greek names even though they were not Greek. This resentment has contributed to their sense of alienation from the Greek state and the Greek Orthodox Church, the two institutions in modern Greek society that have the power to bestow names on people. People from northern Greece with a Macedonian national identity often complain that Greek Orthodox priests, whether in Florina, Toronto, or Melbourne, will not allow them to give Slavic (or even English) names to their children. They complain that they can only give Slavic names to their cows and their dogs.

Baptism, the ritual through which the Greek Orthodox Church assigns names, is a powerful image of what Bourdieu (1991:236) has called the "magical power of naming." Greeks and Macedonians often use the metaphor of baptism when discussing the subject of naming in the context of the Macedonian conflict. That they do so both at the state level and at the individual or personal level is an indication of their awareness of the parallels that exist between the two. Macedonians sometimes refer jokingly to Greece as a powerful but somewhat backward godfather, who still claims the right to choose the name of the newly independent Republic of Macedonia. Greece, they say, wants to baptize Macedonia and name it Skopje.

Although people from northern Greece with a Macedonian national identity have Greek names, which were given to them at baptism and which appear on their identity cards, passports, and other official documents, they also have Slavic names that are used informally in the company of family and friends. One Macedonian human rights activist, a farmer from a village near Florina, said that using his Greek name felt as uncomfortable and foreign to him as wearing a coat and tie. Another Macedonian human rights activist living in Toronto simply said: "We all have two names." Once again the Macedonian conflict has led people to adopt a system of "double names" in which both Greek and Slavic names coexist in uneasy tension.[19]

For people from northern Greece living now in Canada or Australia, the situation is particulary complex. Members of the same family who emigrated at different times (one in the 1920s, the other in the 1970s) or by different routes (one directly from Greece, the other via Yugoslavia or the Soviet Union) may now have different last names. The fact that members of the same family have been assigned different names is perceived as an arbitrary abuse of state power and provokes a great deal of anger and resentment, threatening as it does a sense of individual

---

[19] See Herzfeld's (1987:95–122) perceptive discussion of double images, diglossia, and disemia.

identity, as well as a sense of family unity and generational continuity. In Canada and Australia immigrants from northern Greece also have the option of changing their names, an option not available to them in Greece. A man may chose to use as his legal name the Greek name that his father used or the Slavic name that his grandfather used. Alternatively he may adopt an English name like Peters to avoid having to chose between Petropoulos and Petrov.

For many people from northern Greece with a Macedonian national identity who have settled in Toronto or Melbourne, the opportunity to change their name officially from their Greek name to their "real" Slavic name is a very meaningful one. In the early 1990s an eighty-six-year-old man from a village near Florina asked a social worker at the office of the Australian Macedonian Welfare Council in Melbourne if she would help him fill out the legal forms necessary for him to change his name. When she asked him why at his age he wanted to change his name, he said that when he died he did not want a Greek name on his gravestone.

Macedonian human rights activists in Florina proudly show visitors a grave in a nearby village which has a Slavic name inscribed on it. The man buried there had emigrated to Australia in 1929, before his name had been Hellenized. He returned to Greece in 1982 on an Australian passport, which identified him by his Slavic name. When he died, his family insisted his Slavic name be placed on his grave. Local church and government officials could not object because that was his legal name. In the early 1990s the ultranationalist right-wing newspaper *Stohos* attacked the residents of this village for allowing a "Slav" to be buried in their cemetery and called on them to fulfill their patriotic duty by destroying the grave.

There are many other factors involved when immigrants from northern Greece to Canada or Australia who have a Macedonian national identity confront the issue of whether to change their names. One man, who had come to Melbourne in 1955, decided to change his name after he became an Australian citizen in 1960. His old family name was Stefanov, but it had been changed to Stefanidis by the Greek government. Because he was young and, as he put it, "full of patriotic feelings for Macedonia," he changed his name to Stefanovski, the form of his name that was in general use in the Republic of Macedonia. If he were to change his name now, he said in 1992, he would change it back to Stefanov.

Another immigrant from northern Greece living in Melbourne had kept his Greek name even though he had a Macedonian national identity. He was waiting to change his name until after his father died. His father still lived in Greece, and he didn't want to cause him any trouble.

A Macedonian human rights activist from Florina who was living in Toronto had also decided to keep his Greek name, but for a very different reason. He felt that the existence of Macedonians like himself— Macedonians who were not Greek but who had Greek names—proved that not all Macedonians lived in Yugoslavia. It proved that a Macedonian minority did exist in northern Greece.

THE SUN OR STAR OF VERGINA, ALEXANDER THE GREAT, AND THE ANCIENT MACEDONIANS

After the name "Macedonia" the second most contentious symbol in the conflict between Greeks and Macedonians has been the sixteen-ray sun or star of Vergina. This emblem was virtually unknown to the public and had no political or national significance whatsoever until it was discovered in 1977 adorning a gold chest found in an ancient Macedonian royal tomb at Vergina, a small village forty miles southwest of Thessaloniki. According to Manolis Andronikos, the Greek archaeologist who discovered the royal cemetery of Vergina, this gold chest, or larnax, contained the bones of Philip of Macedon, the father of Alexander the Great. In his publications describing the royal tombs of Vergina, Andronikos has referred to this emblem in a variety of ways: as a "star," as a "starburst," and even as a "sunburst" (Andronikos 1977:41; 1978:55, 67, 75–76; 1980a:pl. 30).

Despite these apparent inconsistencies in his description of this emblem, Andronikos has been completely consistent in his interpretation of its meaning. Andronikos has repeatedly and without qualification interpreted it as a symbol of the Macedonian royal family, or in his words as the "emblem of the Macedonian dynasty" (Ninou and Kypraiou 1979:50, 53; Andronikos 1980b:212). Several well-respected ancient historians, however, have questioned Andronikos' interpretation of this symbol. Borza (1981:82) suggests that given its wide use in Macedonian art it might better be thought of as "a national or ethnic sign" rather than a "royal" one, whereas Adams (1983:4) citing its use as a decorative motif in Greek art more generally concludes that the case has not been made for the sun or star of Vergina as either a "royal" or "national" Macedonian symbol.

A similar difference of opinion exists with regard to Andronikos' claim that the bones contained in the famous gold larnax of Vergina were those of Philip of Macedon, the father of Alexander the Great. Although most Greek archaeologists and a few foreign scholars hold that the tomb in which the larnax was found is that of Philip of Macedon, many foreign archaeologists and ancient historians are more skeptical, suggesting that this tomb might instead be that of Philip III Arrhidaeus, the son of Philip of Macedon (Borza 1990:260).[20]

In the popular press, which has paid little attention to the scholarly debates over these issues, the initial claims of Andronikos have been accepted unquestioningly. To the general public, therefore, the sun or star of Vergina has become an important symbol of the glorious civilization of the ancient Macedonians and the heroic accomplishments of Alexander the Great. By the late 1980s, when the dispute over Macedonian identity was growing increasingly fierce, both Greek and Macedonian nationalists, particularly those in the diaspora, eagerly seized on the sun or star of Vergina as a powerful national symbol that expressed their competing claims to continuity with the ancient Macedonians.

The Australian Institute of Macedonian Studies, for example, an organization of Greek-Macedonian academics in Melbourne, adopted the sun or star of Vergina as its logo, and in 1988 when it sponsored the First International Congress on Macedonian Studies, a photograph of the gold larnax of Philip II was placed on the cover of the congress program, while the sun or star of Vergina itself adorned a variety of plaques, medals, and pins that the institute had produced to commemorate the event. Melbourne's Macedonian community mounted a demonstration against the congress on the grounds that one of its goals was to deny the existence of the Macedonians as a specific ethnic group in Australia. Many demonstrators waved flags with the gold sun or star of Vergina in the center.

In the early 1990s both Macedonian and Greek diaspora organizations carried flags depicting the sun or star of Vergina (against red and blue backgrounds respectively) during their demonstrations for or against the international recognition of the Republic of Macedonia. These same flags could be seen at soccer games when Preston Makedonia (the Macedonian team) played either Heidelberg Alexander (the Greek-Macedonian team) or South Melbourne Hellas (the Greek team). The sun or star of Vergina could also be found on T-shirts and jewelry that these organizations sold, on the letterheads of their stationary, and on the mastheads of their newspapers. At this time the Greek government also began to employ this symbol of ancient Macedonia in more official contexts by issuing a postage stamp of the sun or star of Vergina against a blue background, as well as a new 100-drachma coin depicting the head of Alexander the Great on one side and the sun or star of Vergina on the other.

[20] The bibliography on this hotly debated question is very large. In addition to the references already cited, important sources include Andronikos (1984), Borza (1982b, 1987, 1990:256–66), R. L. Fox (1980), Fredricksmeyer (1981), Green (1989), Hammond (1982), and Lehman (1980).

МАКЕДОНИЈА

ИЛУСТРИРАНО СПИСАНИЕ НА МАТИЦАТА НА ИСЕЛЕНИЦИТЕ ОД МАКЕДОНИЈА Број 472 VIII 1992

10. The flag of the newly independent Republic of Macedonia depicting the "sun of Macedonia" against a bright red background, as shown on the cover of the August 1992 issue of *Makedonija*

The controversy over this symbol, which is always referred to by Macedonians as "the sun," reached its climax in August 1992, when the Macedonian parliament selected it as the "state [*državno*] symbol" of the newly independent Republic of Macedonia and voted to place it against a bright red background in the center of the republic's new "state flag." The sun also figures prominently in the "state anthem" of the republic, which begins "Today over Macedonia is born / The new sun of liberty."

The decision of the Macedonian parliament to place the "sun of Macedonia," a symbol of "Macedonian continuity," on the new flag of the Republic of Macedonia encountered bitter opposition both inside and outside the country. The Albanian minority in the republic objected to this choice on the grounds that it was a Macedonian *national* symbol and therefore not an appropriate choice for the flag of a multinational *state*. In addition, the Greek government, with the support of Greeks throughout the world, expressed outrage at what it considered to be the misappropriation or theft of a symbol of Macedonian Hellenism by a group of Slavs whose ancestors arrived in Macedonia a thousand years after the death of Alexander the Great. As a spokesman for the Greek foreign ministry put it in January 1995, "the symbol is Greek and has been stolen."

In Greek sources this symbol is usually referred to as a star, although it is also referred to occasionally as a sun, sometimes even in the same article. By associating the star of Vergina with the star of Bethlehem and other stars that appear in Orthodox Christian iconography some Greek nationalists have argued that Greek Macedonians have revered the "Macedonian star" as a sacred symbol continuously for thousands of years (*Makedhoniki Zoi*, December, 1991, p. 3 and September, 1992, p. 9). Not surprisingly Macedonian nationalists make similar claims.

From the perspective of many Greeks the republic's use of the star of Vergina is an act of "provocation" that constitutes an insult to their "Hellenic heritage." Because the star of Vergina was found on Greek soil, Greeks claim that its use by the republic constitutes proof of the republic's irredentist designs on Greek territory. The Greek government, therefore, has consistently demanded that the republic adopt a new flag and has prevented the republic from using its flag in a variety of places, including the United Nations, the Olympic Games, and offices of the republic in the United States and Australia. In a final attempt to assert its claim to this symbol of the glories of ancient Macedonian civilization, the Greek parliament in February 1993 passed a bill designating the star of Vergina as an official national symbol of Greece.

Ultimately the conflict between Greeks and Macedonians over who has the right to use the sun or star of Vergina as a national symbol is a conflict over which group has the right to claim continuity with Alexander the Great and the ancient Macedonians. According to Greek nationalist historiography the ancient Macedonians were Greeks: they spoke Greek, had Greek names, and worshiped Greek gods. More specifically, Alexander the Great was a Greek king who united all the city-states of Greece and spread Greek civilization throughout the known world. Since ancient and modern Greeks are linked in an unbroken line of racial and cultural continuity, today only Greeks can be Macedonians.[21]

Serious Macedonian nationalist historiography rejects the idea of any direct continuity between ancient and modern Macedonians by acknowledging that the ancient Macedonians were not Slavs and that the modern Macedonians are the descendants of a Slavic people whose ancestors settled in the Balkans in the sixth century A.D. Nevertheless, these sources do devote significant attention to ancient Macedonia. Most accept the fact that the elite of ancient Macedonia were Hellenized. Some sources state that it has not been proved that the ancient Macedonians were Greek, while others conclude that the ancient Macedonians were a distinct non-Greek people. Many of these sources, however, with their references to "the ancient Macedonian state" as "the first Macedonian state" and their references to "Alexander the Macedonian" spreading the glory of the Macedonian name throughout the world clearly promote the idea of continuity between ancient and modern Macedonia.[22]

Many well-respected ancient historians have attempted to determine whether the ancient Macedonians "were Greeks" in an atmosphere more removed from the competing claims of contemporary Greek and Macedonian nationalists. Much of their work has been based on an essentialist approach to the subject of ethnic or national identity. According to this approach the ancient Macedonians "were Greeks" if their culture was sufficiently similar to ancient Greek culture. Detailed studies of various aspects of ancient Macedonian culture have revealed, as one might expect, that it exhibits both similarities and differences when compared to ancient Greek culture. This has led some ancient historians to describe the ancient Macedonians somewhat ambiguously as "half-Greek" or as living at the periphery of the Greek world (Borza 1982a:17).

Although it is clear that standard Attic Greek was the language of the Macedonian elite, the ancient Macedonian language and its relation-

---

[21] Scholarly works that argue for the "Greekness" of the ancient Macedonians include Daskalakis (1965), Kalléris (1954–76), and Sakellariou (1983).

[22] See Andonovski (1978, 1979), Kofos (1994), Pribichevich (1982:37–64), Stalev and Kabrovski (1991), and Tashkovski (1976:55).

ship with ancient Greek have been the subject of much scholarly de-
bate. Despite some claims that ancient Macedonian was a form of
Greek (Hammond and Griffith 1979:47–49), many ancient historians
and linguists maintain that there is simply not enough evidence to determine exactly what the Macedonian language was.[23] The evidence
from other aspects of ancient Macedonian culture—art, religion, and
political organization—is much more abundant, but no more helpful in
determining whether the ancient Macedonians "were Greek." As Borza
observes (1990:95),

> there is much in Macedonian society that was assimilated from Greece;
> but there is also a great deal that seems to be indigenous and non-Hel-
> lenic. . . . In brief, one must conclude that the similarity between some
> Macedonian and Greek customs and objects are not of themselves proof
> that the Macedonians were a Greek tribe, even though it is undeniable
> that on certain levels Greek cultural influences eventually became per-
> vasive.

Adopting an approach that is much more consistent with the contemporary anthropological perspective on ethnicity as a social category
determined by self-ascription and ascription by others independently
of any "objective" cultural criteria, ancient historians have also investi-
gated Greek and Macedonian perceptions of each other. They have
asked how the ancient Macedonians were perceived in relation to the
ancient Greeks both by the Greeks and by themselves. When the question is posed in this way, the answer seems much more clear-cut: in
their own time the ancient Macedonians were generally perceived by
the Greeks and by themselves not to be Greek (Borza 1990:96).[24]

Ancient Greek literature offers many examples attesting to the fact
that the Macedonians were not considered to be Greeks by the Greeks
themselves. The fifth-century historians Herodotus and Thucydides
described the Macedonians "as foreigners, a distinct people living outside the frontiers of the Greek city-states" (Borza 1990:96), while the
fourth-century orators Demosthenes and Isocrates referred contemptu-
ously to the Macedonians as "barbarians" and as "people of a non-
kindred race" (Badian 1982:42). In addition, although individual Macedonian kings were allowed to take part in Panhellenic festivals like the
Olympic Games (in which only Greeks could participate), Macedonians as a people were excluded from them until quite late on the
grounds that they were not Greek. It was only after the death of Alexander the Great with the increasing Hellenization of Macedonian cul-

---

[23] For this view, see Borza (1990:93), Crossland (1982), and Katačić (1976).

[24] Hammond (1986:535) also concludes that "the Macedonians in general did not consider themselves Greeks, nor were they considered Greeks by their neighbors."

ture and the emergence of Rome as a common enemy in the west that the Macedonians came to be regarded as "northern Greeks" (Borza 1990:96; Badian 1982:33–35). This is precisely the period during which ancient authors, such as Polybius and Strabo, did refer to the ancient Macedonians as Greeks. The most important point to remember in this entire discussion, however, is that the identity of the ancient Macedonians (like that of the modern people who identify themselves as Macedonians) was a social construct constantly subject to negotiation and renegotiation in an ongoing political process.

The discipline of archaeology has played a major role in the conflict between Greeks and Macedonians over the glorious heritage of Alexander the Great and the ancient Macedonians at both the scholarly and the popular levels. In Macedonia, as in many other parts of the world including countries as diverse as Denmark, Israel, Mexico, and China, the discipline of archaeology has often been placed in the service of the state and used to legitimate nationalist claims to history, culture, and territory.[25] Archaeologists can be particularly successful in obtaining government patronage and sponsorship for their research when their work is viewed as bolstering nationalist claims for the antiquity and the historic continuity of the nation. In nationalist conflicts the past frequently serves as a valuable resource which can provide the raw materials from which national symbols can almost literally be mined. Archaeologists not only discover a nation's past through their excavations; they mount and display it before an admiring public in "national" archaeological museums as well.

In Greece archaeologists whose research can be used to demonstrate the Greekness of Macedonia are often described as performing work of great "national significance." This was especially true in the case of Manolis Andronikos. Shortly before his death in 1992, Andronikos was awarded the Great Cross of the Order of the Phoenix, the highest honor given by the Greek state. In presenting him this medal on behalf of the president of Greece, the Minister of Macedonia-Thrace referred to Andronikos as Greece's "national archaeologist" and praised him for "arming the quiver of Hellenism, the quiver of the Greek nation, the quiver of Greece, with arguments that refute the false claims [of those who] misrepresent, falsify, and distort [Greek] civilization and history" (*Makedhoniki Zoi*, April 1992, p. 10).

The role of archaeology in legitimating the Greek nationalist position on the Macedonian issue was also apparent during a public lecture given by Dimitrios Pandermalis of the University of Thessaloniki at a

---

[25] For valuable discussions of the political role played by the discipline of archaeology in a variety of contexts, see Fowler (1987), Silberman (1989), and Trigger (1984). See also Smith (1986:180).

conference entitled "Macedonia: History, Culture, and Art." This conference, which was held at Columbia University in New York in June 1989, was funded by the Pan-Macedonian Association of America and Canada. Pandermalis, one of the most prominent Greek archaeologists working in Macedonia, spoke about his recent excavations at Dion, an important Macedonian cult center located twenty miles south of Vergina at the foot of Mount Olympus. Pandermalis' lecture was accompanied by dramatic slides of skulls gazing up out of ancient shaft graves and white marble heads buried in mud beneath the debris of fallen walls. There followed more slides in which these same marble heads, immaculately cleaned, restored, and mounted, were displayed against beautiful backgrounds of red and blue velvet. This remarkable transformation evoked gasps of awe and wonder from an audience composed largely of members of the Greek-American community of New York. They were witnessing the miraculous resurrection of their glorious ancestors; they were seeing their national heritage come to life before their very eyes.

The tension between archaeology as a scholarly discipline, on the one hand, and archaeology as an instrument for the legitimation of nationalist ideologies, on the other, was uncomfortably evident in another public lecture, this one given by Eugene Borza, a well-respected ancient historian from Pennsylvania State University. Borza's lecture was presented during the Second International Congress on Macedonian Studies, which was held at the University of Melbourne in July 1991. This conference was sponsored by the Australian Institute for Macedonian Studies, which claims to be a nonpolitical organization concerned exclusively with scholarly and academic issues, but which has been described by its own officers as committed to "promoting" the Greek position on the Macedonian Question and "countering the organized propaganda of the Slavs" (*Makedhoniki Zoi*, January 1987, p. 53).

In his lecture, entitled "Images of Alexander the Great," Borza examined the long history of the use of Alexander's image in the West. His paper concluded with a perceptive analysis of the way the modern Greek government has attempted to carefully manage the manner in which Alexander the Great is presented to the world, particularly in international archaeological exhibits such as "The Search for Alexander," which toured major art museums in the United States in late 1980. Some of the Greek archaeologists participating in the conference were so offended by the fact that Borza had in their opinion blatantly politicized what would otherwise have been a purely scholarly event that they walked out of his lecture and threatened to boycott all future papers presented by non-Greek scholars. These Greek archaeologists were only persuaded to rejoin the proceedings when the chair of the conference attempted to placate them with some conciliatory remarks.[26]

At the level of popular discourse both Greeks and Macedonians make extensive use of Alexander the Great as a powerful symbol of the historical and cultural continuity, which, from their perspectives, links them with their glorious ancestors, the ancient Macedonians. Demonstrations held throughout the world in the early 1990s by Greeks and Macedonians in opposition to or in support of international recognition of the Republic of Macedonia were led by men dressed as Alexander the Great, wearing a crested helmet, breast plate, and greaves and holding a shield and a spear.[27] Each group was outraged that the other group had attempted to appropriate its own famous ancestor for such obviously political purposes.

Alexander the Great is also a common figure in the floats and parades that Greek and Macedonian organizations in Canada and Australia contribute to festivals celebrating multiculturalism and ethnic diversity. When Heidelberg Alexander, the Greek-Macedonian soccer team in Melbourne, plays its arch rival Preston Makedonia, the Macedonian team, the Macedonian fans taunt their Greek-Macedonian counterparts by shouting "Alexander's Maso! Alexander's Maso!" And in an obvious attempt to create a bond of historical continuity linking the two most famous Macedonian national heroes—one from antiquity, the other from the early twentieth century—a group of Macedonian nationalists recently established "the Alexander and Delchev Library" on a main street in Preston, a northern suburb of Melbourne inhabited by many Macedonian immigrants.[28]

The Greek and the Macedonian popular presses often contain articles celebrating Alexander the Great and his brilliant military career. Reports appear on both sides discussing expeditions to Afghanistan and Pakistan that claim to have discovered the last descendants of Alexander and his soldiers, who still survive in small villages high in the Himalayas and who still speak either Greek or Macedonian (depending on the perspective of the author). Political journalists on both sides of the controversy also make effective rhetorical use of Alexander the

[26] For a discussion of the political issues raised by "The Search for Alexander," which fully supports Borza's analysis, see Green (1989).

[27] See, for example, the illustration on p. 48.

[28] This unlikely pair of "Macedonian" heroes, Alexander the Great and Gotse Delchev, also appears on the masthead of *Republika*, a small nationalist newspaper which appeared in Skopje in the early 1990s.

Great. The author of an article in a newspaper published by the Pan-Macedonian Association of Melbourne and Victoria invoked the memory of Alexander the Great in support of the Greek position on the Macedonian Question when he suggested that Alexander would surely turn over in his grave "if he knew that the descendants of those Slavs who invaded his land in the 6th century A.D. [were] now attempting to take as their own the very name of his people, their symbols, and their heritage!" (*Makedhoniki Foni* 1992, 2 [18]:10). Conversely the author of an article in a newspaper published by Macedonian human rights activists in northern Greece observed bitterly that if Alexander the Great "were alive today, he would surely not have the right of repatriation or even the right to return for a simple visit to his homeland of Pella [in Greek Macedonia]" (*Moglena*, June 1992, p. 11).

The Greek government has been very active in using the figure of Alexander the Great to promote its position in the Macedonian conflict. After the discovery of the royal tombs of Vergina in 1977, Constantine Karamanlis, then prime minister of Greece and himself a Macedonian, referred to Alexander the Great as "the representative of all the Greeks" and "a symbol of the indissoluble unity and continuity between ancient and modern Hellenism" (Green 1989:155). In the early 1990s Vergina, Dion, and Pella became obligatory stops for foreign politicians visiting Greece. During one such visit the premier of Victoria, Jeff Kennett, whose outspoken support for the Greek position on Macedonia has earned him a loyal following among members of Melbourne's Greek community (and the derisive nickname "Kennetto-poulos" among members of Melbourne's Macedonian community), was presented with a book entitled *Macedonia: The Face of Northern Hellenism*. At this time the Greek government also issued a new 100-drachma coin depicting the head of "Alexander the Great, King of the Macedonians" on the obverse and the sun or star of Vergina on the reverse.

In 1992 Greek-Macedonians throughout the world established an Alexander the Great Foundation, whose purpose was to fight the anti-Greek propaganda of the "Skopians" and disseminate the truth about the Greekness of Macedonia. Constantine Karamanlis, now president of Greece, served as honorary president of the foundation; Dimitrios Pandermalis became president of the foundation's northern Greek branch; and the Pan-Macedonian Association of America and Canada began raising money through the sale of commemorative gold coins issued by the National Bank of Greece. The foundation developed plans to build an International Cultural Center of Alexander the Great at Dion, which would include a monument to Alexander the Great, a museum, a library, and a conference center. In this way the foundation would "baptize present and future generations in the miraculous spirit of Macedonia."[29]

A particularly revealing example of the conflict between Greeks and Macedonians for control of all that Alexander the Great has come to symbolize involves a bust of Alexander that stands in the center of a small square at the corner of Logan and Danforth Avenues in the center of Toronto's Greek community. The square is surrounded by Greek shops and businesses with signs that read, "Nick the Greek Cafe," "Lord Byron's Men's Hair Styling," and "Alexandros' Take Out: Chicken, Souvlaki, Subs, and Burgers."

Although immigrants from southern Greece living in Toronto wanted to present the city with a bust of Theodore Kolokotronis, a hero of the Greek War of Independence of 1821, Greek-Macedonians with the support of the Greek consulate in Toronto insisted that Alexander the Great was a much more appropriate choice. In May 1990, therefore, a bust of Alexander was commissioned at a cost of $80,000, erected, and then donated to the city of Toronto by the Pan-Macedonian Association of Ontario and the Greek Community of Metro Toronto.

Controversy immediately arose over the wording of the plaque that was placed on the base of the statue. The Macedonian community of Toronto objected to the description of Alexander as "King of the Greeks"; they argued that the plaque should read "Alexander, King of the Macedonians." Then the United Macedonians received permission from the mayor's office to lay a wreath at the statue on July 29, 1990, the 2,346th anniversary of the birth of Alexander the Great. The Macedonian-Canadian Human Rights Committee, however, disapproved of this wreath-laying ceremony on the grounds that it was unnecessarily provocative.

When the United Macedonians arrived at the corner of Logan and Danforth Avenues to lay their wreath at the foot of the statue, they were confronted by a group of Greek-Macedonians from the Pan-Macedonian Association of Ontario, who had learned in advance of the Macedonians' plans and had come to prevent them from performing their ceremony. With their bodies wrapped in blue and white Greek flags the Greek-Macedonians formed a human wall around the statue. As the Macedonians approached, a fight broke out that required the intervention of the Toronto police. When they were assured by the police that the Macedonians would not be allowed to lay their wreath at the statue, the Greek-Macedonians left.

According to reports in the Greek press the Greek community of

---

[29] See *Makedhoniki Zoi*, July 1993, English Supplement, p. 1, and the *Macedonian Newsletter* (Pan-Macedonian Association of America and Canada), vol. 3, March 1994, p. 4.

11. A bust of Alexander the Great, donated to the city of Toronto by the Pan-Macedonian Association of Ontario and the Greek Community of Metro Toronto

Toronto had successfully prevented "any dirty hand" from "defiling" this statue of Alexander the Great, a "symbol of the unity and the fighting spirit of Hellenism." The entire event had been "another golden page in the glorious history of the defense of all that is sacred and holy to the Fatherland" (*Makedhoniki Zoi*, October 1990, pp. 48–49).

MAPS OF MACEDONIA AND THE NATIONALIZATION OF TERRITORY

Disputes over the name "Macedonia," the sun or star of Vergina, and Alexander the Great are all part of the larger conflict between Greeks and Macedonians in which each nation claims as its own exclusive property all aspects of Macedonian identity, history, and culture, both ancient and modern. Control of territory in Macedonia, however, is also an issue in this larger conflict, for in a world of nation-states the sovereign territory of the state is without a doubt the most valuable form of national property.

Greek fears that international recognition of the Republic of Macedonia or acknowledgment of the existence of a Macedonian minority in Greece will inevitably lead to the loss of Greek territory in Macedonia seem completely unrealistic to many outside observers. Nevertheless, these fears are deeply felt and are based on historical experience as recent as World War II and the Greek Civil War, when the territorial integrity of Greece was threatened by both Bulgarian and Yugoslav claims to parts of Greek Macedonia. The irredentist rhetoric of ultranationalist Macedonian organizations like the United Macedonians and VMRO-DPMNE only serves to heighten these fears.

The competing claims to Macedonian territory put forth by the various Balkan states have always received clear expression in maps. The important role played by maps in earlier phases of the Macedonian Question has been examined in detail by Henry R. Wilkinson in his book *Maps and Politics: A Review of the Ethnographic Cartography of Macedonia* (1951). In the late nineteenth and early twentieth centuries Serbia, Bulgaria, and Greece all attempted to support their territorial claims in Macedonia with ethnographic maps showing that the majority of the population of Macedonia was Serbian, Bulgarian, or Greek respectively.

Unlike the political maps in common use today, which divide the world up into the mutually exclusive territories of modern states, ethnographic maps are specifically designed to represent the many different religious, linguistic, ethnic, or national groups that inhabit one particular area. They generally do so through the use of complex patterns of shading, barring, and cross-hatching. See, for example, map 2, published in 1878 by K. Sax, an official of the Austro-Hungarian Empire serving in Adrianople.[30] Alternatively ethnographic maps use pie diagrams, or circles or squares of different colors and sizes, to indicate the relative strength of the different groups under consideration. In this way ethnographic maps attest to the fact that several different peoples, with different languages, religions, cultures, and identities may all live in the same place. They bear eloquent testimony to the human diversity and complexity that so often belie nationalist myths of ethnic purity and homogeneity.

[30] This map was reprinted in Wilkinson (1951:80). See also the ethnographic maps of Macedonia prepared for the *Report of the International Commission to Inquire into the Causes and Conduct of the Balkan Wars*, published by the Carnegie Endowment for International Peace in 1914.

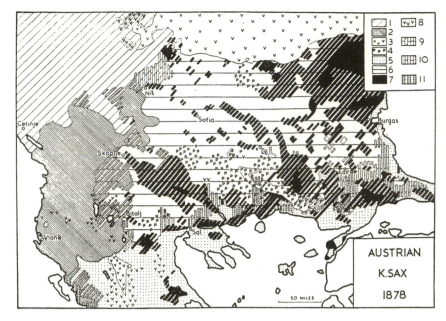

Map 2. An ethnographic map of Macedonia published in 1878 by K. Sax, an official of the Austro-Hungarian Empire serving in Adrianople, as reprinted in *Maps and Politics* (1951)

In sharp contrast to ethnographic maps, modern political maps operate on the basis of what Anderson (1991:173) has called a system of "totalizing classification." Just as a census classifies individuals into mutually exclusive and quantifiable ethnic or national categories, so a political map classifies space into the mutually exclusive and quantifiable territories of particular states. By representing the territory of each state as a uniform, bounded field of one single color, different from that of all its neighbors, a political map expresses visually the nationalist myth of the nation-state as a territorially bounded unit inhabited by a single homogeneous group of people. In fact, the production of such maps played an important role in the creation of nation-states, for these maps were not only models *of* the nation-states they depicted, but were models *for* them as well.[31] The shift from the use of ethnographic maps with their intricate patterns of shading and barring to the use of political maps with their uniform fields of single colors is the cartographic equivalent of the tragic exchanges of populations and the terrible acts

[31] See Thongchai (1988:310, cited in Anderson 1991:173) and Baudrillard (1983:2, cited in Coronil 1992:20) for this application of Geertz's (1973a:93) distinction between "models of" and "models for" to modern political maps.

of ethnic cleansing that have all too often accompanied the creation of modern nation-states.

As Anderson also points out, maps of individual states, resemble detachable pieces of a jigsaw puzzle that can be completely removed from their geographical context. Such maps have become logos that can be infinitely reproduced, easily marketed, and immediately recognized (Anderson 1991:175). Surely no better example of the map-as-logo could be found than the map of Macedonia. The map of "United Macedonia," that is, the map of the entire geographical region of Macedonia including Yugoslav (Vardar), Bulgarian (Pirin), and Greek (Aegean) Macedonia, can be seen everywhere in Macedonian diaspora communities in Canada and Australia. Emblazoned with other popular Macedonian sumbols, such as the head of Gotse Delchev, the sun of Vergina, or the White Tower of Thessaloniki, it can be found on an incredible variety of objects, from posters, napkins, and T-shirts, to key chains, lapel pins, and wall clocks. The map of "United Macedonia" also serves as a logo of many Macedonian organizations, including the Association of Child Refugees from Aegean Macedonia, the Australian-Macedonian Human Rights Committee and the United Macedonians.[32]

Maps play many other important roles in the conflict between Greeks and Macedonians as well. Immigrants from Florina living in Melbourne often tried to settle arguments about whether Macedonia had ever existed as an independent political entity separate from Greece by appealing to historical maps. Macedonians eagerly pointed to the bounded areas labeled "Macedonia," "Epirus," and "Achaia" on maps of the Roman Empire or maps of the travels of Saint Paul in order to support their claim that even at the time of Christ "Macedonia" existed, while "Greece" did not. And if the words "Macedonia" and "Greece" both appeared on a historical map as labels for bounded areas depicted in different colors, Macedonians claimed this proved that "Macedonia" and "Greece" have existed as separate countries or states since antiquity. This clearly illustrates the ease with which mapping conventions can be misinterpreted and used to support anachronistic nationalist claims for the existence of nation-states at earlier

---

[32] In October 1993, the Macedonian Movement for Balkan Prosperity, an organization of Macedonian human rights activists in northern Greece, adopted a new logo for its newspaper, *Zora*. This new logo was a map, but it was not the map of "United Macedonia." In an obvious effort to dissociate itself from the irredentist tendencies of Macedonian nationalists, the Macedonian Movement for Balkan Prosperity had instead adopted as its logo a new map, a map that had never before been a part of Macedonian iconography: the map of the entire Balkan peninsula from Crete and Rhodes in the south to the borders of Slovenia, Croatia, and Romania in the north.

historical periods. Thus maps not only nationalize territory, they also project this nationalization of territory back into the past. In this way they nationalize and territorialize history as well.[33]

In the early 1990s intense controversy surrounded the publication of every new map of the Balkans, as Greeks and Macedonians either praised or attacked publishers for their editorial decisions regarding the newly independent Republic of Macedonia. When the prestigious National Geographic Society published a new map of Europe in December 1992, the Republic of Macedonia was presented as a sovereign state under the name "Macedonia," and its flag was displayed on the back of the map with the flags of all the other countries of Europe. This, plus the fact that the map did not include the word "Macedonia" as the name of a geographical region in northern Greece, provoked angry protests in the Greek press. It seemed to confirm the worst of Greek fears: that recognition of the republic under the name "Macedonia" would deprive Greece of all its claims to the name Macedonia. Similarly, news that the 1994 American Express travel map of Europe depicted "Macedonia" as an independent country prompted a member of the electronic mailing list, Hellas, to urge subscribers to call the American Express public relations office to complain about the serious error that had been made.

Several specific maps have featured prominently in the most recent phase of the Macedonian conflict. For example, map 3, which was circulated by extreme Macedonian nationalists in the late 1980s and early 1990s, depicts a "United Macedonia" as an independent country marked off from its neighbors Albania, Yugoslavia, Bulgaria, and Greece by the broken lines generally used to indicate international borders. The existing international borders of Yugoslavia, Bulgaria, and Greece, which intersect at the center of the geographical area of Macedonia are depicted as strands of barbed wire dividing "United Macedonia" into three "occupied" parts. This map constitutes clear evidence of the irredentist claims of extreme Macedonian nationalists against both Greek and Bulgarian territory.

Other maps, which present the entire geographical region of Macedonia and which are used by virtually all Macedonian organizations, including Macedonian human rights groups, are extremely controversial and subject to widely different interpretations (see map 4). From a Greek perspective these maps are interpreted as "political" maps depicting the future "United Macedonia" of extreme Macedonian nationalists. The presence of such maps in publications of Macedonian human rights organizations is cited by Greek sources as proof that even

---

[33] On the territorialization of history, see Coronil (1992) and Poulantzas (1978).

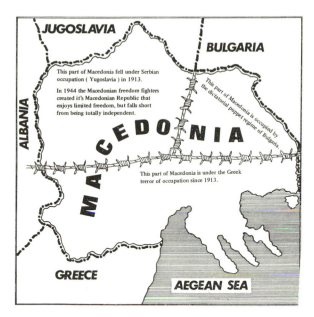

Map 3. A map of a "United Macedonia" circulated in the late 1980s and early 1990s by extreme Macedonian nationalists in Melbourne, Australia

Map 4. An example of the kind of map of Macedonia used by virtually all Macedonian diaspora organizations

Macedonians who explicitly disavow territorial claims against Greece cannot be trusted.

Macedonians, on the other hand, maintain that these are not "political" maps, but rather "ethnographic" maps, which simply indicate the geographical region where Macedonians live and where the Macedonian language is, or more accurately was traditionally, spoken. This claim is undercut to a considerable degree, however, by the fact that this geographical region is surrounded by clearly demarcated borders that define it just as if it were a state. Even though these borders are sometimes labeled "natural," "geographic," or "ethnic" borders, and even though they can be clearly distinguished from the "international" or "state" borders of Albania, Yugoslavia, Bulgaria, and Greece, the simple presence of a line or boundary of any kind cutting through Greek territory and separating Greek Macedonia from the rest of Greece is enough to evoke for Greeks the specter of the creation of a "United Macedonia" as an independent state that would include all of Greek Macedonia.

Many Greeks are offended by the fact that these maps use the Slavic names for cities in Greek Macedonia. They are also troubled by the fact that the peninsula of Halkidiki and the island of Thasos are generally included on these maps as lying within the "ethnic" borders of Macedonia, in spite of the fact that neither of these areas were ever inhabited by significant numbers of Slavic-speaking people. Representatives of the Greek community of Melbourne have complained to the Ministry of Education of the State of Victoria that maps of "United Macedonia" were being used in Macedonian language classes in the Melbourne public schools. In their defense Macedonian teachers argued that if they did not use maps of the entire geographical region of Macedonia, but instead used maps of the republic only, then they would not be able to show Aegean Macedonian students in their classes (whose parents came from Greece) where their families' villages were located. (For an analysis of the maps of Macedonia that appear in new textbooks in the Republic of Macedonia, see Kofos [1994].)

A much more convincing case can be made that the map used on the cover of a booklet of abstracts prepared for the First North American Macedonian Conference on Macedonian Studies (held at the University of Michigan in July 1991) is an "ethnographic" map (see map 5). Unlike the maps used by most Macedonian cultural and political organizations, this map, which was designed by a scholar for use in a scholarly context, does not depict any borders whatsoever around the geographical region of Macedonia, nor does it depict the peninsula of Halkidhiki or the island of Thasos. Without borders this map cannot be

Sponsored by
University of Michigan Center for Russian and East European Studies
University of Michigan Committee on International Academic Affairs
University of Michigan Department of Slavic Languages
University of North Carolina - Chapel Hill Department of Slavic Languages

This Conference was supported in part by a grant from the International Research
& Exchanges Board (IREX), with funds provided by the Andrew W. Mellon Foundation,
the National Endowment for the Humanities, and the U.S. Department of State.
None of these organizations is responsible for the views expressed.

Map 5. A map of Macedonia *without borders* that appeared on the cover
of a booklet of abstracts prepared for the First North American
Macedonian Conference on Macedonian Studies held at the University
of Michigan in June 1991

interpreted as a political map; without borders it cannot be used as a logo. It is not a map of a united Macedonian state.

One of the most interesting examples of the role maps have played in the recent phase of the Macedonian conflict involves a map of Macedonia produced in the 1930s by the Institut Scientifique Macédonien in Sofia. Entitled "A Map of Macedonia within its Geographical Limits," it depicts both "the geographical borders of Macedonia" (which incorporate all three parts of Macedonia) and "the political borders of the Balkan states." This map has been widely used by Macedonians in Canada and Australia because all the cities, towns, and villages depicted on it, including those in Greece, are designated by their Slavic names.

In 1990 the Macedon Publishing Company in Melbourne, publisher of the *Australian Macedonian Weekly*, produced a new edition of this map in order to take advantage of the market generated by the nationalist fervor sweeping the Macedonian community in Australia. This new map contained several very revealing revisions. In an attempt to create a "United Macedonia," cartographically at least, what had been referred to on the original map as "the geographical borders of Macedonia" were now labeled "the true borders" of Macedonia, and what had been referred to on the original map as "the political borders of the Balkan states" were now labeled "the artificial borders" of Macedonia. In another symbolic assertion of territorial claims against Greece, another act of cartographic irredentism, the "true" southern border of Macedonia was relocated so that instead of passing over the summit of Mount Olympus it passed further to the south. In this way all of Mount Olympus was incorporated into the territory of "United Macedonia."

Other changes were made in the original map as well. In order to purify the map of all Bulgarian elements and create a completely Macedonian map, the spelling of several place names (such as Meglen and Debar) was changed by eliminating the back jer, a letter that exists in the Bulgarian alphabet, but which was excluded from the Macedonian alphabet during the codification of literary Macedonian in 1944.[34] The final step in the process of transforming this map into a Macedonian nationalist document involved placing what was to become the new flag of the Republic of Macedonia, the sun or star of Vergina against a bright red background, prominently in the upper right-hand corner of the map.

Several recent maps of Macedonia suggest a solution to the problem posed by the mutually exclusive claims of Greeks and Macedonians to

---

[34] For more information on the codification of the literary Macedonian language, see Friedman (1985, 1986, 1993) and Lunt (1959, 1984).

Map 6. A map of Macedonia that appeared in the *New York Times* on April 17, 1992, illustrating the portrayal of the existence of two Macedonias

Map 7. A map depicting the two Macedonias published in *Time* magazine on October 12, 1992

all that is Macedonian. Maps 6 and 7, which accompanied articles in the *New York Times* and *Time* magazine on the controversy surrounding the international recognition of the Republic of Macedonia, depict two Macedonias. In some maps these two Macedonias are referred to more specifically as "Macedonia (former Yugoslav Republic)" and "Macedonia (region)," but in others no additional clarification or specification is offered. These maps demonstrate that, even though some confusion and ambiguity may arise, the geographical term "Macedonia" *can* be used with two different meanings to refer to two different entities: the newly independent Republic of Macedonia, on the one hand, and the Greek region of Macedonia, on the other. This cartographic solution to the Macedonian Question suggests that there can also exist two separate groups of people both of whom identify themselves as Macedonians: Macedonians (in a national sense) who are *not* Greek, and Macedonians (in a regional sense) who *are* Greek.

CHAPTER VII

Ted Yannas: A Macedonian in Australia

TED YANNAS is a short, heavy-set man with a shaggy black beard that almost hides the rugged features of his square face.[1] Whether he is speaking Macedonian, Greek, or English, his words emerge slowly and precisely with an intensity that suggests a troubled, at times bitter man. He drives heavy equipment for a living and owns his own construction company: Ted Yannas Excavations Pty. Ltd. of Melbourne, Australia.

In his wallet Ted carries a small black-and-white photograph taken one night in 1959 in Thessaloniki. In the photograph Ted, a ten-year-old boy at the time, stands with his parents and his younger brother and sister on a dark street in front of a huge neon sign advertising a local newspaper. The name of the newspaper, and the word spelled out in large capital letters across the top of the photograph, was MAKEDONIA.

Ted's family was from Kladorabi—Kladhorrahi in Greek—a small village in the district of Florina just a few miles from the border between Greece and Yugoslavia. This was the third time they had made the long trip to Thessaloniki to take the medical examinations that were required for emigration to Australia. Ted's father had made the decision to emigrate in 1954 for several reasons. A few years earlier the Greek government had confiscated his family's land because a relative of his had fled to Yugoslavia at the end of the Civil War in 1949. More recently someone had told him not to waste his money sending Ted to high school. Ted would never get a job even if he did graduate. That's when Ted's father knew it was time to leave Greece.

When he applied for a passport, Ted's father was told that he would have to go to the local police station and sign a statement renouncing the Communist Party. He didn't know what they were talking about; he'd never been a member of the Communist Party. He'd only been in trouble once in his life. During the Metaxas dictatorship, when he was eighteen years old, he'd been jailed for acting in a Macedonian performance of *The Bloody Wedding*, a popular play, which was also per-

---

[1] In this chapter, and in the chapter that follows, I have changed the names of all the people mentioned. I have also changed the names of the villages where they were born and some other minor details of their lives as well.

formed in Greek, about a Turkish pasha who kills a beautiful Christian woman because she refused to join his harem. By 1967, when Ted's family was finally given permission to leave Greece, it was too late for Ted to get a good education in Australia. Thinking back on all this, Ted says, "I left Greece with a knife in my back."

When Ted's family came to Australia, they came as Greeks, as Greek-Macedonians. They went to the Greek church, not the Macedonian church, and they tried to avoid what they called "the partisan, the Yugoslav, side of the Macedonians." Ted's mother always used to say, "There's no Macedonia; only Yugoslavia and Greece." One day in school Ted's teacher introduced him to another new boy from Greece. Ted started speaking Greek to him, but the boy didn't speak Greek, so they tried to communicate in broken English. When the boy learned that Ted was from Florina, he asked if Ted knew Macedonian. From then on they spoke Macedonian, and they became good friends.

During their first few years in Melbourne Ted and his family lived with an uncle, Nikos Karelis, who had come to Australia in 1954. Nikos' father had been arrested before World War II on the grounds that he was a Communist and that he was pro-Bulgarian. But he was a royalist; he supported King George. What kind of Communist could he have been? He fled to Yugoslavia in 1945. Nikos himself was put in jail and tortured in Florina during the Civil War. Then he spent six months in a prison camp on Makronisos, an island in the Aegean. Nikos says he suffered a lot at the hands of the Greeks. After he was released, his mother and his brothers went to Bitola to be with his father. As the oldest son, Nikos stayed in the village, but when the Greek government confiscated his family's property, he left for Australia. Nikos' wife remembers the day when her grandfather was driven away in a jeep by the Greek military police. "We never saw him again," she says. "No one knows where he was buried; there were bodies everywhere. They did a lot of bad things. They think we'll forget."

Nikos was the first Macedonian in Melbourne to own a bulldozer. He hired Ted as a driver and got him started in the construction business. Once, several years later, Nikos recommended Ted for the job of digging the foundation for the new Macedonian Community Center in Epping, but the people in charge there refused to hire him when they found out he was a member of Heidelberg Alexander, the soccer team founded by people from Florina who were "pro-Greek." At work Ted would tell Nikos what he'd learned about Greek history in school in Greece. Nikos would say, "No. It wasn't like that. I lived it."

When their financial situation improved, Ted's family moved into their own home, first in Northcote and then in Lalor, two working-class suburbs that spread across the flat plains to the north of Melbourne.

One weekend Ted's father heard that *The Bloody Wedding* was being shown in Macedonian at a movie theater in Preston, a nearby suburb with a large Macedonian community. Ted's father hired a taxi—something he never did—to take the family to the theater. "As much as he was trying to be Greek here in Australia," Ted says now, "he just couldn't wait to see that movie." When they returned home afterward, Ted's father just sat with his head in his hands for hours. He didn't say a word; he just cried.

In the early 1970s Ted was engaged to a woman whose family was originally from a village near Kladorabi. Vera's father had fought with the Communists during the Civil War. When the war was over, he settled in Yugoslavia, where Vera grew up. Vera was a Macedonian. Ted spoke English with Vera and Macedonian with her parents. Ted's parents wanted a Greek wedding—in the Greek church, with Greek music at the reception; they wanted their grandchildren baptized in the Greek church as well. Vera's father agreed.

At first Vera thought that Ted's parents were the same kind of people as her parents, but then she realized they were different. Ted's parents idealized everything that was Greek. Vera thought that attitude was disgusting. Ted had been brought up to believe that the Macedonian language was something inferior and useless, but Vera knew that wasn't true. She'd been to school in the Republic of Macedonia, where Macedonian was the official language. Sometimes they had dinner at a Greek restaurant run by one of Ted's aunts. Vera thought people there danced like Zorba the Greek. When Vera's father wanted to tease Ted, he called him "Gršto"—the Greek boy.

After his father died in 1976, Ted decided to visit one of his father's closest friends in Adelaide. Ted had many things he needed to talk to him about, many questions he needed to ask. "I always thought I was Greek," Ted says now, "but there were things I couldn't explain. My brother and sister just accepted things; they believed what they learned in school. But not me. I always had questions. Why do we have two last names, Yannas in Greek and Yovanov in Macedonian? Why do we speak Macedonian? Why do they call us Bulgarians? My parents would say, 'Don't ask questions. Forget about it. Just leave it alone.'" It was from his father's old friend in Adelaide that Ted finally got some answers. It was then that he learned for the first time about his relatives who had fled to Yugoslavia, about *The Bloody Wedding*, and about his father's renunciation of the Communist Party. Ted's parents had raised him as a Greek, but he was beginning to have doubts. Now he didn't know what he really was.

A year later Ted and Vera took a trip around the world. First they stopped in Toronto to visit some relatives there. Then they went to

Athens, where Ted had some cousins. Vera remembers being shocked by how completely Greek they were. When Ted and Vera finally arrived in Kladorabi after a long trip from Athens, a policeman told them they needed a military permit to visit the village because it was located in a sensitive border area. Ted simply replied, "I didn't need a permit to be born here, so I don't need a permit to visit here," and he walked away. During their stay in Kladorabi, Ted went to a bank in Florina to make the final payment on his family's land, which had been confiscated after the Civil War. All the years Ted's father had been in Australia, he had been gradually buying back his own land from the Greek government. The last stop on their trip was Bitola, across the border in Yugoslavia, where Vera's relatives lived. At a dance held to welcome their overseas guests Vera's relatives announced that they had a visitor from Greece and asked the band to play a Greek song in Ted's honor.

ALEXANDER VERSUS MAKEDONIA

Ever since he came to Melbourne, Ted had been a loyal fan of the Heidelberg Alexander Soccer Club. Ted and his friends called it "our club," because it had been founded by "our people," local Macedonians from Florina. One of Alexander's biggest rivals was Preston Makedonia, a team which had also been founded by people from Florina, but people who identified themselves as Macedonians, not as Greeks. Alexander's other big rival was South Melbourne Hellas, the Greek team, or as some people put it, "the real Greek team." When these teams played each other, Hellas fans called Alexander fans "Bulgarians," Alexander fans called Makedonia fans "Yugoslavs," and Makedonia fans called Alexander fans "Greek-lovers" or "traitors." Some people went to these games for the politics, but back then, Ted said, he and his friends just went for the soccer.

In 1979 Ted was invited to become an official member of the Heidelberg Alexander Soccer Club. Three months later he was elected to the executive committee. Alexander had just bought a new ground and needed to build a clubhouse and some stands. The club was short of money and couldn't afford to hire anyone to do the job, so Ted did all the earth moving for free.

Two years later something happened that changed Ted's life forever. Alexander was scheduled to play a preseason game against Makedonia. This would be the first meeting of the two teams since Makedonia had joined the National Soccer League. Two days before the game a meeting of the executive committee of Heidelberg Alexander

12. "Alexander the Great" circling the field during half-time at the National Soccer League game between Heidelberg Alexander and Preston Makedonia played in Melbourne on February 23, 1992

was called. Tommy Strikos, a member of the committee who worked in the Greek consulate, opened the meeting.

"Gentlemen," he said, "I bring you a message from the consul. We can't play this game. This game has to stop." The consul was afraid that playing the game against Preston would give the Macedonians recognition. The stronger Preston grew, the more people would realize that it was a Macedonian club and the more people would realize who the Macedonians were. Strikos said that the consul was even willing to pay Alexander the ten thousand dollars it would lose by canceling the game. They would just tell Preston that some of their players were injured.

At this point Ted stood up and said, "I don't like this. We're a sporting club, and you want us to get involved in politics."

Strikos jumped out of his chair; he was furious.

"Do you know why you're sitting in that chair?" he shouted at Ted.

"I'm here to help the club," said Ted.

"No you're not!" screamed Strikos. "You're here to help me destroy that race! As good Greeks we have to drown those people in the Yarra River!"

Looking back on that incident years later, Ted says, "At that moment I realized he was talking about *my* people. He was asking me to destroy *myself*. That's when I understood that I was truly a Macedonian. Whatever part of me felt Greek died; it disappeared. My whole life passed in front of me, and I realized I was false. I felt like an adopted child who had just discovered his real parents. All my life had been a lie. I'd been a janissary; I'd betrayed my own people."[2]

After every National Soccer League game the home team buys the visiting team two slabs of beer and one of soft drinks. When Heidelberg Alexander played Preston Makedonia during the 1981 season, no one on the Alexander committee would go into the Makedonia dressing room. Finally someone said to Ted: "You're one of them. You go." A few years later Ted quit Heidelberg Alexander and joined Preston Makedonia. But that's not the end of the story.

After he left the club, Ted learned that John Topalis, Alexander's president, had removed Ted's name from the big mahogany board on the clubhouse wall that listed the names of all the committee members who had served the club since its founding in 1958. "They can't do that," Ted protests. "They can't write me out of the club's history. They can't change my history either. I was part of that club. I built the field myself, and now Topalis erases my name because I'm a Macedonian. What does he think he is? He's a Macedonian too; he just pretends to be Greek. His father was shot by the police in the Civil War because he played in a band that sang Macedonian songs. When I joined Alexander, we spoke Macedonian all the time. No problem. Now they say, 'What's that Bulgarian you're speaking?' So our people leave. Now you have to be 100 percent Greek to be in the club."

Needless to say, officials of Heidelberg Alexander see things differently. One well-educated committee member talks about Ted in very sarcastic terms. "That ethnogenetic process is like Pentecost. The Holy Spirit descends on you and enlightens you, and you become a Macedonian. It's all Slav propaganda."

---

[2] A janissary was a Christian child taken at birth from his family of origin and forced to convert to Islam and serve in the guard of the Turkish sultan during the Ottoman period.

Another club member, who had been a good friend of Ted's, speaks about him more sympathetically.

"I lost my best friend. How can he say he's a Macedonian now? Until a few years ago he said he was Greek. We were the same; we were Greeks from Macedonia. Ted used to have a pile of records a foot high, and a stack of cassettes twice that high—all Greek music. When he stopped listening to them, he gave them all to me. I saw him changing . . . wavering, and I said to him, 'Ted, I don't care. We're friends; let's stay friends. My house is always open to you, but don't talk politics with me. Don't insult me; don't call me stupid and backward.'

"But it didn't work. Whether he got smarter, whether he got stupider, or whether he got paid, I don't know. But it didn't work."

A REAL MACEDONIAN PATRIOT

Now Ted is what many Macedonians call "a real Macedonian patriot." He contributes hundreds of dollars every year to organizations like the Ilinden Foundation, the Macedonian Action Group, and the Australian Macedonian Human Rights Committee. He attends all the demonstrations, rallies, and protests held by the Macedonian community of Melbourne for the international recognition of Macedonia and for the protection of the human rights of Macedonians in northern Greece. He often wears a "Macedonia '91 Folk Festival" hat and a T-shirt with a portrait of Gotse Delchev, or on more formal occasions a red lapel pin in the shape of a map of "United Macedonia."

Ted recently held a surprise birthday party for a friend of his from Florina. Some men came dressed up as nineteenth-century Macedonian bandits, with wooden rifles and cartridge belts crossed over their chests. Their wives wore traditional Macedonian folk costumes. The birthday cake was decorated with a big red map of Macedonia, all of Macedonia. When it came time to cut the cake, the band sang the following verses from "Pearl of the Balkans," a popular new patriotic song:

> There is only one truth.
> There is only one Macedonia.
> Divide her! Tear her to pieces!
> She will still be our most dearly beloved land.

But no one could bear to cut through the center of the cake and divide up Macedonia, so they just took small pieces from around the edge leaving Macedonia united and whole. A Macedonian driving by the hall where the party was taking place stopped his car in the middle of the road to see what was happening. He thought they were celebrating the recognition of the independence of Macedonia and that he had somehow missed the news.

Wherever Ted goes, the conversation inevitably turns to the subject of Macedonia. One Friday night at the bar of the Epping Hotel on High Street in the northern suburbs of Melbourne, Ted was talking with Thanos, a Greek from Katerini. Thanos, unlike most Greeks, was willing to accept the fact that Macedonians existed who were not Greeks, but he was strongly opposed to the creation of a Macedonian state that would include any Greek territory. This wasn't good enough for Ted, though. Ted argued that Korea, Cyprus, and Macedonia were the only three countries in the world that were still divided.

"If I've rented my house to someone for a year," he asked Thanos, "and I want to move back in when the year is over, what do I do? Don't I have the right to take it back?"

Once Ted was talking with a man who had been born in Florina, but whose father had come to Greece in 1922 as a refugee from Pontos in Asia Minor near the Black Sea.

"What am I?" the man asked Ted.

"You tell me what you are," said Ted. "I can't tell you. What are you?"

"I'm Pontian because my father was Pontian. But I'm also Macedonian because I was born in Macedonia. And I'm Greek too because Macedonia is part of Greece."

"You want three identities, and you won't even let me have one!" said Ted. "You're not a Greek. You're a refugee, an Asian. You were *made* a Greek. You're not a Macedonian either. You were *brought* to Macedonia. You don't even speak Macedonian. Our people are the *real* Macedonians. Just because you were born in Macedonia, that doesn't mean you're a Macedonian. You can't *choose* what you are. Blood is passed down from father to son. You can choose what you want to be, but you can't choose what you are.

"I'm a Macedonian, but I'm an Australian citizen too," Ted continued. "That's my choice. I didn't *choose* to be a Macedonian. I *am* a Macedonian. If I was born with black skin, I can't change that. I can choose my nationality, my citizenship, but that doesn't mean I can change the color of my skin. Your national consciousness can change. Fine. But the real essence of who you are can't change. Can the consciousness of a black make him white just because whites raised him and he lives like a white? No. His skin will still be black. You can choose to be a Greek the way I can choose to be an Australian, but you're not. I'm a Macedonian, and if you tell me I'm not, you can get stuffed."

On another occasion Ted said, "We become what people tell us, but that's brainwashing. We don't change in natural fact. When we left Greece, we believed we were Greek. But we were made Greeks. When people ask me now, 'How did you change?' I tell them, 'My grandmother didn't speak Greek. Do real Greeks have grandparents who didn't speak Greek?' All the years I spent in Greek schools were useless. I got older and thought about who I was. Now I'm proud of who I am. I'm a Macedonian. Lots of people say that they're Greek-Macedonians. But you can't be Greek and Macedonian at the same time. You can only brainwash a Macedonian and make him a Greek."

Ted says that ever since he realized he was a Macedonian, his relationships with his fellow villagers have been strained. Most of the other members of the Kladorabi Family Association in Melbourne are Greek. Ted doesn't go to the association meetings anymore. People don't even tell him when they're scheduled to take place; they say he's a troublemaker. Once someone asked Ted to sponsor the calendar put out by the association every year, but there's a Greek flag on it, so he refused. Ted still goes to the village dances, though, in spite of the fact that the master of ceremonies speaks Greek at the microphone and that people there dance mostly Greek dances. Ted is quick to point out that the Greek they speak is very broken and that "they'd break their legs if they ever tried to do the *tsamiko*." "Anyway," he adds, "the *tsamiko* isn't really a Greek dance. It's Turkish; it's from Asia Minor." But what bothers Ted most about these dances is the fact that the president of the Greek Community of Thomastown and Lalor is often invited as guest of honor.

Vera does not enjoy going to the Kladorabi dances because she's afraid there will be trouble, the way there was a few years ago when Ted asked the leader of the band to play a Macedonian song. The leader of the band said that the organizers of the dance had instructed him to play only Greek songs. So Ted went up to a member of the village committee and asked, "Is this function to keep our culture alive in this country or what?" The committee member couldn't say anything, because he knew that back in their village they used to sing songs in that language. After a great deal of discussion the band was finally allowed to play a Macedonian song. But the song Ted requested was a really patriotic song they never sang back in the village. Ted's favorite verses were:

> Come, let us gather
> From all our villages and towns
> To shout together loudly:
> "Get out Greeks! We don't want you."

People were furious with Ted for requesting a song that was insulting to Greeks. Ted's response was, "Why are you so upset? I don't see any Greeks here anyway. Besides, I didn't write the words. It's just a traditional Macedonian song." Ted says that even the Macedonians who are pro-Greek don't like to dance Greek dances all the time.

Much more disturbing to Ted than his alienation from his fellow villagers is his estrangement from his own family. Neither his brother Jim nor his sister Maria speak to him anymore. They are both Greeks.

A few years ago Maria's daughter married a man from a village near Kladorabi who was a Macedonian. She wouldn't get married in a Macedonian church, and he wouldn't get married in a Greek church, so the wedding was held in an Anglican church. At the engagement party they played both Greek and Macedonian music, since the two families shared the expenses, but at the wedding reception the music was all Macedonian, because the wedding was paid for by the groom's family. The groom's father hired a band from Vardar Macedonia that didn't even know any Greek songs. Ted really enjoyed the wedding, but his brother Jim hated it.

On the second floor of the hall where Maria's daughter's wedding reception was being held, a Greek wedding was taking place at the same time. Jim, who had already had a few drinks, said angrily in Macedonian to his uncle Nikos, "Fuck the bloody Yugoslav bastards. I'm going upstairs to dance some Greek dances."

"They're not Yugoslavs!" Nikos shot back. "They're your relatives! That's your sister's daughter who's getting married. You stupid Greek-lover! You have your grandfather's name. Do you know where he is? He's dead and buried in Bitola. Shame on you! You don't know what you are, but other people do. They know what you are. It's in your heart. Your first words were Macedonian. You were born a Macedonian."

JIM YANNAS: A GREEK IN AUSTRALIA

Jim Yannas drives heavy equipment like his brother. He has a full black beard like his brother too, but it's shorter and neater than Ted's. Jim is the secretary of the Greek Community of Thomastown and Lalor and a member of the Heidelberg Alexander Soccer Club. Jim remembers speaking Greek with his parents at home back in Kladhorrahi. It was only his grandmother who spoke "Yugoslav," and she died when he was two. Jim didn't learn "that language" very well until he was about ten, when he spoke it with his friends in the village. Then he forgot most of it because he spoke Greek all the time when he was in high school in Florina. After he came to Australia, he started speaking it again because there were lots of "real partisans" in their neighborhood. When Vera married Ted and moved into their house, "that was the nail in the coffin. That put a full stop to Greek in the family."

"Back then," Jim says, "Ted believed in the Greek-Macedonian part, in what we are—Macedonians with Greek influence, not Macedonians with Yugoslav influence. We're Macedonians . . . Greek-Macedonians . . . the real Macedonians. People from the other side are Slavs. You can change your religion and your political views, but you can't change who you are. You can't change history.

"When does Macedonia appear first in history? With Philip and Alexander the Great. Archaeologists have proved that Macedonian civilization was one and the same with Greek civilization. Macedonian religion was the same as the Greek—the twelve gods of Olympus. The Slavs came later, in the seventh century. Then we were conquered by the Ottomans in 1453. Under the Turks there were Greek and Bulgarian schools in Macedonia. The Bulgarians raided the villages and killed the teachers and priests. Then they built Bulgarian schools and forced people to go there. Some of our people still believe they're Bulgarians. The Macedonian thing was never mentioned in our area. The church in our village was built in 1888 and has Greek writing on the walls. There's nothing Cyrillic anywhere. That makes me believe that our people were Macedonians, Greek-Macedonians, not like *those* people, the other people, the Macedonian Macedonians.

"They say that all the people in Macedonia are Macedonians. They're completely ignorant, especially the recent converts, the newly enlightened ones. I call them Jehovah's Witnesses. They're like people following cults. I'm the way I was born, the way I was taught. Later I looked into it to find out what history has to say. Ted and his friends tried to convert me, but I have a stronger will. I believe in what I know, and I won't change.

"Ted and his friends want to be noticed everywhere they go. They're troublemakers. They get together and drink and carry on like Yugos. They bring the hatred back from the Civil War. What Ted believes in—that's Communist propaganda. The Communists said, 'We'll give you Macedonia.' But my father believed in Greek Macedonia. It was the Communists who chased him out of his house. He hid in the fields so they wouldn't find him. The Communists destroyed our village. The government did too, but . . .

"My father-in-law fought against the Communists. He fought for a liberated Greece. He didn't want Greece to end up like Yugoslavia. Vera calls him a traitor, a Greek spy, but that's not true. He was a loyal Greek, a real Greek patriot. He was a Greek-Macedonian. That's what *we* are. We're not Yugoslav-Macedonians. We're Greek-Macedonians.

"Sometimes people from southern Greece have the impression that Macedonians are all peasants, that they're really second-class Greeks. They think we can't speak Greek; they call us Bulgarians. Somebody here in Melbourne asked me once, 'Why do you speak Greek? You're from Macedonia.' I laughed and said, 'I'm Greek. That's all I know.' It's the people from Yugoslavia who say, 'We're Macedonians, not Greeks.' That's what causes all the trouble.

"How can they say that Macedonians are Slavs, when in the heyday of Macedonia the Slavs didn't even exist? You can't say that you're Macedonian and not Greek. You can't start from the end. If you're going to talk about Macedonia, you have to start at the beginning. In the early days Macedonia was Greek. You can't start a nation from Gotse Delchev in 1903. That's when *their* history begins. They're trying to start a new race that has nothing to do with Greece. They're trying to form a new Slavic-Macedonian race. They say that Macedonia and Greece have nothing to do with each other, that *their* language is the Macedonian language, but it's not. The original Macedonian language was Greek. Their language is just a Slavic dialect. Their alphabet is made up of Russian letters. They don't want to have anything to do with Greece, but you can't rewrite history. In ancient times the Macedonians were one and the same with the Greeks. The *so-called* Macedonians, the *new* Macedonians, are fanatics. They want to take the Greek out of the Macedonian, but they can't. They can't do it in a hundred years. It's been there for four thousand.

"My parents would be ashamed of Ted now. They'd be ashamed of what he says he is. How can he be the only one in the whole family to be a Macedonian? It's an Australian disease. No one back in Kladhorrahi talks like that. No one there wants Macedonia; they all want Greece. People there say, 'What's the matter with Ted?' It's painful for me to see people laugh at him. He changed his nature overnight for no logical reason. One of our cousins saw Ted recently, and Ted started preaching to him about Macedonia. He said, 'Ted, it's not you. It's not the person I knew.' His old friends who were in school with him in Greece are amazed. When they see me, they ask, 'How's Ted?' I tell them, 'He's turned the other way,' and they say, 'No. Not Ted. He wouldn't do that.' But he did."

CHAPTER VIII

The Construction of National Identity among Immigrants to Australia from Northern Greece

As THE STORIES of Ted Yannas and his brother Jim clearly illustrate, the nationalist conflict between Greeks and Macedonians has had powerful, often disruptive, effects on the personal lives of many people from northern Greece, both those who continue to live there and those who live in diaspora communities in Canada and Australia. Most scholarly work on ethnic nationalism, however, has focused on the construction of national identity as a large-scale, collective phenomenon and as a long-term historical process. It has not paid sufficient attention to the construction of national identity as a short-term biographical process that takes place over the course of the lifetime of specific individuals. For this reason, as Eric Hobsbawm has pointed out (1990:78), much too little is known about people's "thoughts and feelings towards the nationalities and nation-states which claim their loyalties."

Many important questions are raised by focusing attention on the construction of national identity at the individual level. How do people develop a sense of national identity? How do they choose a national identity when more than one possibility is available? How and why do people change their national identity? Finally, how is it possible for two brothers to adopt different national identities and to disagree about what nationality they both really are?

In nationalist discourse a person's identity is usually regarded as something permanent, innate, and immutable. It is often thought to consist of some natural or spiritual essence that is identified with a person's blood or soul. While generally avoiding such overtly biological or spiritual metaphors, much anthropological writing has held that people share a particular ethnic or national identity because they possess certain cultural traits in common. People are Greek, in other words, because they speak Greek, have Greek names, and attend the Greek church.[1]

---

[1] Brass (1976:226), for example, states that "objective cultural distinctions" are necessary conditions for the creation of different ethnic or national groups.

It was the work of Fredrik Barth (1969) that was largely responsible for the rejection by many anthropologists of this essentialist notion of ethnic and, by extension, national identity. Instead of defining ethnic groups as "culture-bearing units," groups whose members share a common culture that distinguishes them from members of other groups, Barth defined them as "categories of ascription and identification." According to this approach the crucial feature of ethnic identity is "the characteristic of self-ascription and ascription by others" (1969:10–13). Barth's insights make it possible to understand how the boundaries between ethnic and national groups are able to persist despite the fact that people are constantly flowing across them, as well as how ethnic and national categories are maintained despite the fact that membership in these categories is always changing.

Once the assertion of ethnic or national identity is no longer equated with "belonging to" a particular culture or exhibiting certain cultural traits, once it is understood as a form of political consciousness, as an often explicit and self-conscious political choice, then we are in a position to understand how separate groups with distinctly different identities can exist even when there are no "objective" cultural differences that distinguish them. Because the existence of two groups and the existence of the boundary between them depends exclusively on the "subjective experience of difference" (Sahlins 1989:270), it is possible for people who share a common culture to adopt different ethnic or national identities. Once we abandon the notion that adopting a particular identity is necessarily the result of being a member of a certain culture, we can consider the reverse: that being or becoming a member of a certain culture is rather the result of adopting a particular identity. In other words, people may *not* in fact be Greek because they speak Greek, have Greek names, and attend the Greek church. On the contrary, they may speak Greek (and not one of the other languages they know), use the Greek (and not the Slavic) form of their names, and attend the Greek (and not the Macedonian) church because they are Greek, that is, because they have chosen to identify themselves as Greek.

Barth's work emphasizes the active role individuals play in what are often highly contested struggles involving the creation and distribution of new identities. While states with their powerful military, educational, and ecclesiastical bureaucracies often attempt to impose national identities from above, it is ultimately the individual who chooses what national identity to adopt, or in some cases whether to adopt any national identity at all. Such a situational approach to identity not only avoids the problems associated with an essentialist approach; it also draws attention to the fact that identity is a social construction whose existence and meaning "are continuously negotiated, revised and revitalized, both by ethnic group members themselves as well as by outside observers" (Nagel 1994:153).[2]

A situational or constructionist approach to identity, while taking into consideration the role of personal choice in the process of identity formation, must also remain sensitive to the role played by external factors that limit or constrain the choices individuals face as they construct the identities that shape their lives. For identity formation is not entirely a matter of self-ascription; it is a matter of ascription by others as well. Identities are shaped or structured by powerful political, economic, social, and cultural forces, the most important of which inevitably involve the hegemonic power of the state. State policies, the ideologies that legitimate them, and the institutions and organizations that realize them, all influence the process of identity formation as individuals are socialized and become citizens of particular states. To a great extent states have the power and the resources to determine what choices are available to people and what the rewards or the sanctions will be when they exercise these choices and adopt specific identities.

The degree to which state hegemony constrains individual choice in the construction of national identities varies tremendously. At one end of the spectrum stand nation-states whose ideologies of national homogeneity and ethnic purity lead them to limit quite narrowly the choices available to their citizens. Despite the best efforts of a nation-state to ensure that all its citizens develop one and the same national identity, however, the hegemonic power of the state is never absolute. Some individuals are always willing to endure severe persecution by asserting an identity that defines them as members of an ethnic or national minority.

At the other end of the spectrum stand countries like the United States, Canada, and Australia, whose democratic and pluralist ideologies place significantly fewer constraints on the identities their citizens may adopt. In the case of third- or fourth-generation immigrants from Europe the choice of identity may become sufficiently fluid and free from stigma that one can begin to speak of ethnicity as a "life-style choice," or a "matter of taste," something to be adopted one day and discarded the next (Jusdanis n.d.:27).[3] For first-generation immigrants like Ted and Jim Yannas, however, it is clear that ethnicity is not simply

---

[2] On a situationalist approach to ethnicity, see Okamura (1981) and Morin (1982). For an excellent study of the way local interests influence the process of nation formation, see Sahlins (1989).

[3] Gans (1991) has referred to this development as the "emergence of symbolic ethnicity." See also Waters (1990).

a "life-style choice," although perhaps for their children or grandchildren it may become one.

The construction of identity among immigrants from nation-states in the Balkans who have settled in large pluralist democracies is a particularly complex process because it is influenced by hegemonic constructions that have their origins in both the countries where they were born and the countries where they have settled. These immigrants bring with them identities constructed in their homelands and face the challenge of reconstructing them in the diaspora. From the perspective of these immigrants themselves, particularly those whose identities were denied in their homelands, the most salient feature of the politics of identity in the diaspora is the fact that they now enjoy the freedom to express an identity which they were unable to express freely before.[4]

For the purpose of understanding the role of diaspora communities in the transnational conflict between Greeks and Macedonians, it is precisely this point that is most relevant. Although many groups experience serious discrimination in the United States, Canada, and Australia, for white immigrants from Europe full enjoyment of the rights of citizenship in these countries is compatible with a fairly wide range of ethnic identities. Immigrants who are members of national minorities in the Balkans, for example, experience considerably more freedom to assert their identities in the United States, Canada, and Australia than they do in their countries of origin. More specifically, it is much easier to be a Macedonian in Australia than it is in northern Greece. Macedonians in Australia acknowledge this with their frequent expressions of gratitude and appreciation for the fact that in Australia they enjoy the right to express freely their identity as Macedonians. They often add with bitter irony that Macedonians in Greece, the "birthplace of democracy," do not enjoy these same rights.

From an anthropological perspective, however, it is clear that, although Macedonians in Australia do enjoy a degree of freedom with respect to the expression of their ethnic identity that is not available to them in Greece, the choices facing them in Australia are certainly not unlimited. They are constrained by a complex set of hegemonic forces that have to do with both multicultural politics in Australia and nationalist politics in the Balkans. From the perspective of the English-speaking majority that dominates Australian society at all levels, it makes very little difference whether immigrants from northern Greece identify themselves as Greeks or Macedonians. Regardless of their choice of

---

[4] For a valuable discussion of the process of identity formation among transnational migrants in the late twentieth century, see Schiller, Basch, and Blanc-Szanton (1992).

identity at this level, they remain "Europeans," "ethnics," or "people of non-English speaking background," as opposed to "real Australians."[5]

Immigrants from northern Greece to Australia, like immigrants to Australia from anywhere else in the world, encounter constraints in the process of constructing new identities for themselves in another sense as well. Their choices are limited by the ethnic categories that exist in the official discourse of Australian multiculturalism and that dominate government bureaucracies, social service agencies, and the educational system. Immigrants choose from among the many "ethnic communities" that together constitute Australian society; they become members of the "Italian community," the "Polish community," or the "Turkish community."

It should be immediately apparent that the ethnic categories of Australian multicultural discourse replicate or reproduce almost precisely the national categories of nationalist discourses throughout the world. Immigrants from the Balkans to Australia have more freedom to chose an identity than their fellow villagers they left behind, but the choices they face are essentially the same. Whether they live in Australia or the Balkans, they must be Serbs or Croats, Greeks or Macedonians.

The truth of Pellizzi's (1988:155) observation that "in exile nations become ethnicities" is confirmed by the parallels that exist between the construction of national identities in the Balkans and the construction of ethnic identities in Australia. The disintegration of Yugoslavia and the emergence of Croatian, Serbian, and Macedonian national identities in the Balkans is part of the same transnational chain of events that has led to the demise of the Yugoslav community in Australia and the development there of Croatian, Serbian, and Macedonian communities. The hegemony of national categories of identity is such that even in multicultural Australia they cannot be escaped. In Australia, as in northern Greece, it is difficult for a person to preserve or construct a regional or ethnic identity that has no counterpart at the national level. It is difficult for a person to resist becoming either a Greek or a Macedonian and to remain simply a "local Macedonian," just "one of our people."

Central to the study of identity formation at the individual level, therefore, is the process by which individuals who have previously defined themselves in terms of regional or ethnic identities often associated with rural villages, local dialects, and oral cultures, come to acquire a sense of national identity associated with the literate culture of an entire state. Cultivating a sense of national identity in people who previously did not have one—turning "peasants into French-

[5] On ethnicity and intolerance in Australian nationalist ideology, see Kapferer (1988).

men" (Weber 1976)—not to mention instilling the "proper" national identity in people who have somehow managed to acquire the "wrong" one, is the ultimate goal of all national movements. Needless to say, it is a long, complex process that may take place peacefully or violently, and that may destroy as many identities as it creates. This is particularly true in the case of an ethnic group that inhabits a frontier zone on the border between two nation-states, each of which attempts to impose a different national identity on members of the contested group. With the nationalization of ethnic identities and the politicization of local cultures, a national identity develops like a thin veneer on top of preexisting regional or ethnic identities. Gradually an ethnic group whose territory is divided by a national boundary grows divided itself as its members develop two different and mutually exclusive national identities.

For the Slavic-speaking people of northern Greece this process, which had its beginnings in the mid-nineteenth century, is still continuing in the last decade of the twentieth century both in northern Greece and in diaspora communities in Canada and Australia. Inhabitants of the same villages, members of the same families, who have adopted different national identities, continue to argue over whether they are Greek or Macedonian. They continue to argue over what they really are.

GREEKS AND MACEDONIANS IN MULTICULTURAL AUSTRALIA

Since the end of World War II immigration has dramatically transformed the nature of Australian society. In 1947 Australia's population stood at just under seven million people, 90 percent of whom were Australian-born and English-speaking. With the arrival of over four million immigrants during the next forty years Australian society became one of the most ethnically diverse in the world. By 1988, the year it celebrated its Bicentenary, Australia had a population of over sixteen million people who came from more than a hundred different ethnic groups. Over 20 percent of its population were immigrants, and 20 percent more were Australian-born children of at least one immigrant parent.

Until the early 1970s Australia's immigration program was dominated by a "White Australia Policy" and a firm commitment to the doctrine of assimilation. The goal of this program was to insure that Australia remained a homogeneous, English-speaking society dominated by an "Anglo-Celtic" majority. However, the need to "populate or perish" (presumably at the hands of the "yellow peril" to the north), and the need to provide a constantly growing supply of labor to keep pace with the rapid expansion of the Australian economy, called for the development of an immigration program on such a large scale that any attempt to maintain a homogeneous "British" society through a policy of assimilation was doomed to failure.

In the early 1970s, therefore, both the "White Australia Policy" and the doctrine of assimilation were abandoned. In its place the Labor government of Prime Minister Gough Whitlam adopted an explicit policy of multiculturalism, a policy of cultural pluralism that was based on two fundmental principles: "the recognition and affirmation of the diverse cultural, linguistic and religious backgrounds of the Australian people, and the promotion of equality of opportunity for all Australians regardless of their backgrounds" (Jupp 1988:926). This shift in policy constituted an implicit recognition of the basic demographic facts of Australia's immigration history. Not only had assimilation not occurred, but members of cultural and linguistic minorities had failed to acheive a significant degree of upward social mobility. The adoption of a multicultural policy also implied an awareness that assimilation was an unrealistic policy and that cultural pluralism did not in fact present a real threat to the cohesion of Australian society. The ultimate goal, then, of Australian multiculturalism was the creation of national unity while at the same maintaining the diversity and complexity of a multiethnic society. This goal of creating a single society, a single political structure, composed of a variety of ethnic groups all retaining important components of their original cultures, stands in marked contrast to the desire of nation-states in the Balkans and elsewhere to create homogeneous and ethnically "pure" societies dominated by one and only one national culture.

The rise of multiculturalism as the dominant ideology governing many aspects of Australian society was motivated in part by the increasing assertiveness of second- and third-generation "ethnic Australians." This new attitude led to the growth of ethnic community organizations and migrant groups, which in turn made significant demands on the Australian government at both the state and federal levels to provide "new Australians" with improved social services, particularly in the areas of education and welfare. As a result, the principle that interest groups based on the ethnic identity of their members were legitimate elements in the formulation and administration of government policies gained widespread acceptance.

By the 1980s the Australian government's commitment to multiculturalism had spawned an elaborate bureaucracy designed to improve the delivery of social services to immigrants and their children, particularly those of non-English-speaking background, who were still dispro-

13. Second-generation Greek-Australian dancers at a folklore festival presented by immigrants from northern Greece living in Melbourne on November 3, 1991

portionately concentrated in low-status and low-paying occupations. At the federal level the Australian Institute of Multicultural Affairs was established in 1979 to promote the awareness and tolerance of diversity at all levels of Australian society. At the state level ethnic affairs commissions were formed to monitor the performance of a wide variety of state government agencies to ensure that they were meeting the needs of the different ethnic communities. In addition, ethnic communities' councils and other immigrant organizations were established to serve as political pressure groups to lobby the government on issues of equal access and equal opportunity.

Particular attention was paid to the field of education. The Child Migrant Education Program of 1970 gave way to the Commonwealth Multicultural Education Program of 1979. Significant government funding supported the teaching of "community languages" or "languages other than English" (LOTE) to children of "non-English-speaking backround" (NESB) through programs in English as a second language, mother-tongue maintenance, and second-language acquisition. These programs were complemented by bilingual day schools and part-time ethnic schools run by the ethnic communities themselves.

Government policies with regard to the mass media were changing in similar directions. By the mid-1970s government-supported "ethnic radio stations" in Melbourne and Sydney were regularly broadcasting in twenty-six languages other than English. In 1978 the Special Broadcasting Service (SBS) was established specifically to provide multilingual radio as well as multicultural television services, which supplemented an already thriving tradition of private ethnic newspapers. Comparable developments were occurring in other areas of Australian society as well. Significant improvements were made in the government's ability to provide healthcare, welfare, and other social services to members of ethnic communities in their own languages and in a culturally sensitive manner. By the 1980s municipal libraries had begun to buy books in community languages, and telephone interpreter services were being provided in a variety of languages as well.[6]

In many ways the multicultural nature of Australian society is epitomized by the city of Melbourne, the capital of the state of Victoria, located in southeastern Australia on the Yarra River at the head of Port Phillip Bay. Melbourne, with a population of 3.2 million, is the second largest city in Australia, as well as the most heavily industrialized. While overall 25 percent of Melbourne's population are "overseas-born," in some working-class areas of the city this percentage rises to 40 percent. When the children of the "overseas-born" are included, these percentages double. Almost 75 percent of the "overseas-born" in Melbourne are from Europe, while approximately 20 percent of the total population of the city speak a language other than English in the home.[7]

According to the 1986 census 337,000 people in Australia stated that they were of Greek ancestry, and 148,000 of them (44 percent) lived in Victoria. Of the 138,000 people in Australia who listed Greece as their birthplace, 66,000 lived in Melbourne. According to the same census, of the 277,000 people in Australia who stated that they spoke Greek at home, 113,000 lived in Melbourne.[8] Greek is spoken by more

---

[6] This brief summary of the development of Australian multiculturalism draws on essays in Jupp (1988). Other useful sources include Ata (1986), Foster and Stockley (1984, 1988), Goodman, O'Hearn, and Wallace-Crabbe (1991), Jupp (1984), and Sesito (1982). See Bottomley (1992), Castles, Kalantzis, Cope, and Morrissey (1990), Jakubowicz (1981), and Kapferer (1988) for important critiques of multiculturalism on the grounds that it involves a trivialization or folklorization of the concept of culture, that its emphasis on cultural differences ignores differences in class, socioeconomic status, and access to power, and finally that it fails to question more fundamentally the need to draw boundaries of exclusion and inclusion. I hope to present a more thorough discussion of Australian multiculturalism and Australian nationalism in a future book that will deal exclusively with the conflict between Greeks and Macedonians as it has developed in the Australian context.

[7] These statistics are from the Australian Bureau of Statistics (1991).

[8] Bureau of Immigration Research (1990a:3, 36; 1991:239) and Clyne (1991:42).

Australians than all other languages except English and Italian. In the 1970s the Greek population of Melbourne was concentrated in inner-city neighborhoods like South Melbourne, Northcote, and Richmond. By the late 1980s, however, many Greeks had moved to the middle-distance and outer metropolitan suburbs of Preston, Thomastown, and Lalor. While Greeks in general remain employed in low-skilled jobs in manufacturing and in the retail trades, many second-generation Greeks have experienced a significant degree of upward social mobility.

The Greek community of Melbourne is one of the largest in the entire Greek diaspora; it is also one of the most visible and active ethnic communities in a city renowned for its cultural diversity and cosmopolitanism. At the heart of the Greek community of Melbourne are thirty-six Greek Orthodox churches and over a hundred clubs, societies, and associations that are based on place of origin in Greece. There are also a multitude of women's groups, youth groups, and pensioners' clubs, as well as many athletic, philanthropic, cultural, political, business, and professional organizations, including soccer teams, Boy Scout troops, folk dancing groups, student unions, and teachers' associations. Modern Greek is taught in twenty-five elementary schools and thirty secondary schools in Melbourne and in all four universities in the city. In addition, the Greek community of Melbourne has a large, well-organized system of private ethnic schools. It is also served by several Greek newspapers and private Greek radio stations. Finally, the Greek Consulate General in Melbourne, with its Office of Press and Information and its Educational Advisor, plays a prominent role in the affairs of the Greek community there.[9]

According to the estimate of the ethnic composition of the Australian population prepared for the Bicentenary in 1988 (Jupp 1988:124), there are 75,000 people of Macedonian ethnic origin in Australia, 46,000 of whom are thought to have come from the Republic of Macedonia in Yugoslavia, 28,000 to have come from Greece, and 1,000 from Bulgaria. In an essay on the Macedonians prepared for the Jupp volume, Peter Hill estimates that there may be a total of 100,000 people of Macedonian ancestry in Australia (1988:691). In all Australia 3 percent of those born in Greece (about 4,000 people) reported Macedonian ancestry, while 4 percent of those born in Greece (about 5,000 people) spoke Macedonian at home. Well over half of both of these groups lived in Victoria. If these numbers are doubled to include the second and third generations, there are at least 6,000 to 7,000 people in Melborne who speak Macedonian at home, who identify themselves as

---

[9] For accounts of the Greek community in Australia, see Chapter IV, note 8.

Macedonian, and whose families are originally from Greece (Bureau of Immigration Research 1990a:30, 34).

Census data on the Macedonian community of Australia are extremely unreliable for several reasons. Until recently Australian census forms asked people simply to list "country of origin" for themselves and their parents. People who identified themselves as Macedonians, therefore, appeared in the Australian census data as "Yugoslav-born," "Bulgarian-born," or "Greek-born." In the 1986 census people were asked for the first time to state their "ancestry," defined in an information booklet accompanying the census forms as "the ethnic or national group from which you are descended." At this time 42,000 people in Australia listed their ancestry as Macedonian. Of these, 21,000 were born in Yugolsavia, 4,000 in Greece, and the rest in Australia. Almost half of the people of Macedonian ancestry in Australia lived in Victoria, the vast majority of them in Melbourne. According to the 1986 census there were 46,000 people in Australia who spoke Macedonian at home, 21,000 of whom lived in Melbourne.[10]

Even since the inclusion of the ancestry question on the census forms, the number of people of Macedonian ancestry and the number who speak Macedonian have undoubtedly been underrepresented. Out of fear of persecution at the hands of Greek authorities or out of confusion about the meaning of the question, many Macedonians listed their ancestry and their language as Greek or Yugoslav. According to Hill (1988:691) Macedonian is the fourth most widely spoken language in Victoria, after English, Italian, and Greek.

The Macedonian community of Melbourne is similar to its Greek counterpart in many ways and has the same range of social, cultural, and political organizations. It is, however, significantly smaller in size. There are only four Macedonian churches in Melbourne; Macedonian is taught at only five primary schools, six high schools, and none of the universities in Melbourne; and there are no private ethnic schools run by the Macedonian community. Furthermore, because it has a much smaller educated and professional elite, and because there is no Macedonian consulate to support its activities, the Macedonian community of Melbourne is much less powerful and influential both economically and politically in the life of the city. This is true at the state and the federal level as well.

While the Greek community is divided in many ways, the Macedonian community is even more divided. One of the major divisions in the Macedonian community is that between immigrants from Yugoslav (or Vardar) Macedonia and immigrants from Greek (or Aegean)

---

[10] Bureau of Immigration Research (1990a:35, 1990b:37, 1991:261) and Clyne (1991:43).

14. A new house in a Macedonian neighborhood in Epping, a northern suburb of Melbourne

Macedonia. Because many Aegean Macedonians arrived in Australia in the 1950s, while the largest number of Vardar Macedonians emigrated to Australia in the late 1960s, the Aegean Macedonian community is better established in Melbourne; its members speak better English and have enjoyed more upward social mobility. In addition, the two communities have different geographical centers. The majority of Aegean Macedonians in Melbourne live in the northern suburbs of Preston, Thomastown, Lalor, and Epping, while the Vardar Macedonians of Melbourne are concentrated in the western suburbs of Footscray, Sunshine, Altona, and Keilor.

Relationships between the Greek and the Macedonian communities in Melbourne and throughout Australia started to deteriorate in the mid-1980s. With the formation of organizations like the Australian Macedonian Human Rights Committee and the Association of Child Refugees, Aegean Macedonians began to assert more forcefully their identity as Macedonians. Many people who had previously identified themselves as Greeks began to identify themselves as Macedonians. In protest marches at the Greek embassy in Canberra in 1986 and 1987, Macedonians demanded that the Greek government recognize the existence of a Macedonian minority in Greece and grant them their basic human rights.

At the same time nationalist feelings were mounting in the Republic of Macedonia, as the hold of the Communist Party of Yugoslavia grew weaker in the years after Tito's death and as the final breakup of Yugoslavia drew near. As a result many immigrants from Vardar Macedonia who had previously identified themselves as Yugoslavs also began to identify themselves as Macedonians. In this way a Macedonian national community came into being in Melbourne and in other large cities in Canada and Australia. In Melbourne, for example, a new Macedonian newspaper, the *Australian Macedonian Weekly*, began publication, and the Federation of Macedonian Associations of Victoria was organized in an attempt to bring some unity and cohesion to the Macedonian commmunity of Melbourne.

In response to the politicization of the Macedonian community, the Greek community of Melbourne became increasingly forceful in its claims that "Macedonia was, is, and always will be Greek." One of the events that contributed most to the polarization of the Greek and the Macedonian communities in Melbourne was the First International Congress on Macedonian Studies, held at La Trobe University in the northern suburbs of Melbourne in February 1988. The conference was sponsored by the Australian Institute of Macedonian Studies, a group of Greek-Macedonian academics and professionals who have frequently claimed that the institute is a nonpolitical organization concerned only with scholarly and academic issues, but who have also stated that the goals of the institute are "to counter the organized propaganda of the Slavs," "to stop the uncontrolled corruption of the terms 'Macedonian language' and 'Macedonian culture' in Australian educational circles," and "to promote Greek positions" (*Makedhoniki Zoi*, January 1987, p. 53). At this time officials of the institute argued that public funds should not be used "to teach the Slavic idiom of Skopje and name it [the] Macedonian language" and that the Australian government should not recognize the existence of Macedonians, but only the existence of Yugoslavs, Bulgarians, and Greeks.

The Macedonian community of Melbourne responded to the congress vigorously. Its leaders denounced the congress as an "affront to the dignity of the Macedonian people" and said that its goals were to deny the existence of "the Macedonians as a specific ethnic group" and "to wipe out the Macedonian culture and language in Australian schools and universities." The Federation of Macedonian Organizations of Victoria organized a demonstration against the congress and urged people to attend in order to "defend [their] rights in multicultural Australia." The demonstrators wore red T-shirts bearing the name and the face of Gotse Delchev; they carried red flags with the gold sun in the center; and they held signs that read, "Macedonians exist and they are not Greek," "Aegean Macedonians migrated to Australia to

15. The delegation of the Australian Institute of Macedonian Studies at the celebration of Greek Independence Day in Melbourne on March 22, 1991

escape Greek terror and racism," and "Movement for a free, united,
and independent Macedonia."[11]

Relationships between the two communities in Melbourne continued to deteriorate as the international conflict between Greeks and
Macedonians intensified. This conflict reached a peak in 1991–92 when
the Republic of Macedonia, having declared its independence, was actively seeking recognition as a sovereign state on the international po-

[11] For a more detailed account of the First International Congress on Macedonian
Studies, see Danforth (1990).

RALLY FOR GREEK MACEDONIA

No Recognition of the Skopjan Republic under the Hellenic name "MACEDONIA"

DATE:

SATURDAY 22nd FEBRUARY

VENUE:

CARLTON GARDENS

TIME:

12 NOON

BE THERE AND SHOW AUSTRALIA WE LOVE MACEDONIA

NO "MACEDONIA" FOR SLAVS

16. A leaflet announcing a demonstration held by the Greek community of Melbourne on February 22, 1992

litical scene. During this time the streets of Melbourne were often filled with angry demonstrations; Greek, Macedonian, and English newspapers covered the Macedonian conflict in great detail; and whenever people from Florina met they argued passionately about Macedonian identity, history, and politics.

GREEK-MACEDONIANS, AEGEAN MACEDONIANS, GRKOMANI, AND SKOPIANI

The preceding description of the Greek and the Macedonian communities of Australia has been presented as an account of two dichotomous and mutually exclusive ethnic or national communities. Such an account, however, replicates and perpetuates the hegemonic constructions of both Australian multicultural discourse and Balkan nationalist discourse. In doing so it obscures the fact that there exists a group of people from the region of Florina and from other areas of northern Greece who speak both Greek and Macedonian, who share one common regional or ethnic identity, that of "local Macedonians," and who have been divided into two hostile factions, each of which has adopted a different national identity.

These are the people whose lives have been most dramatically affected by the recent politicization of the Macedonian Question. Individual villages and families have been split, with one villager, one brother, identifying as a Greek, the other as a Macedonian. As the history of the construction of a Macedonian national identity presented in chapter 3 attests, this is not a new phenomenon. At the turn of the century villages in the Florina area were divided into "Bulgarian" Exarchists and "Greek" Patriarchists. During the Civil War inhabitants of these same villages were divided into "Macedonian" Communists and "Greek" royalists. Now people from these same villages, members of these same families, whether they live in Florina or Melbourne, are being forced to decide whether they are Greeks or Macedonians. Although guerrilla bands and military force are not involved in the present phase of the Macedonian struggle, many of the other agents employed by the competing Balkan nation-states at the turn of the century—teachers, priests, scholars, and consuls—still figure prominently in the conflict between Greeks and Macedonians over which group has the right to call itself Macedonian.

In many cases the choices made and the positions taken in the past have parallels in the present. Migrants to Australia from villages that supported the patriarch in the early 1900s often identify themselves as Greeks, whereas Australian-born children and grandchildren of families that supported the Communists during the Civil War often identify themselves as Macedonians. There are, however, many cases where new choices are made, and new identities constructed. In forming village associations some immigrants decide to adopt the "original" name of the village, the "Macedonian" name, instead of the official Greek name. Other immigrants who identify themselves as Greeks have seen their children grow up and become Macedonians.

Since the majority of local Macedonians in the Florina region were poor farmers from small villages, they emigrated to Australia in large numbers. Like other immigrants from Greece, Yugoslavia, and southern Europe more generally, they often settled in the cities of Perth, Adelaide, Woolongong, Sydney, and Melbourne. The institutions founded by the early local Macedonian immigrants from Florina to Melbourne testify to the divisions in their community that have been created by the different national ideologies that have competed for their loyalty over the past century. This is particularly true in the case of the church, the institution that lies at the center of many southern and eastern European diaspora communities.

In 1950 a group of immigrants from Florina, who identified themselves as Macedonians and who opposed communism, founded a "Macedonian Church of Saints Cyril and Methodius" in affiliation with the Bulgarian Orthodox Church of North and South America and Australia, which at that time was independent of the Holy Synod in Sofia. Years later, however, after the diaspora church and the Holy Synod in Sofia had been reconciled, a priest from Bulgaria was sent to Melbourne who insisted that the Church of Saints Cyril and Methodius was a Bulgarian church and that its members were all Bulgarians. In 1985 the trustees of the church, who identified themselves as Macedonians, renounced the jurisdiction of the Bulgarian Orthodox Church and attempted to gain control of the church. The Supreme Court of Victoria, however, ruled against them, and the Church of Saints Cyril and Methodius remained the property of the Bulgarian Orthodox Church. As a result the Macedonian community of Melbourne abandoned the church, and now, because there are very few Bulgarians in the city, the church has been left with virtually no congregation.

Another group of immigrants from Florina, who identified themselves as Macedonians, but who supported communism, founded the Macedonian Orthodox Church of Saint George in 1959, which eventually became affiliated with the Macedonian Orthodox Church in Yugoslavia. By the 1990s this church had become one of the most powerful insititutions in the Macedonian community of Melbourne and in all of Australia. Finally, in 1967 a third group of immigrants from Florina, who identified themselves as Greeks, established a Greek Orthodox Church of Saints Cyril and Methodius. Thus the tripartite division of Macedonia among Bulgaria, Yugoslavia, and Greece is perfectly replicated in the different affiliations of the churches founded by local Macedonian immigrants from Florina who settled in Melbourne.

While the population of the district of Florina has remained stable at somewhat over 52,000 people since 1971, one estimate suggests that there may be 27,000 people from Florina who now live in Australia.[12] According to a survey conducted by Hill (1989:125) there are over 10,000 people in Melbourne whose families are from a group of fourteen villages in the Florina area that have large and active village associations in Melbourne. In addition, immigrants from the city of Florina itself and from at least ten other villages in the area have also settled in Melbourne. It is quite possible, therefore, that as many as 15,000 people from the Florina area are living in Melbourne, heavily concentrated in the northern suburbs of the city.

Immigrants to Australia from Florina have a complex and multilayered system of categories with which they conceptualize the various collective identities that both unite and divide them. At the level of ethnic identity the categories that were and are important in village social life in northern Greece continue to organize social interaction among immigrants from Florina living in Melbourne. The major ethnic groups, which are generally referred to in Greek as "races" (*ratses*) or "elements" (*stihia*), are the refugees from Asia Minor (the majority of whom are Pontians), the Vlachs, the Arvanites, people from southern Greece, and the "local Macedonians," who are often referred to simply as "locals" (*dopii* in Greek, *tukašni* in Macedonian) or as "our people" (*dhiki mas* in Greek, *naši* in Macedonian). According to widely accepted ethnic stereotypes, the refugees are "hardworking," the Vlachs are "clever," and the local Macedonians are "peaceful," "simple," and "backward." At the most general level, the level of national identity, all the refugees, the Vlachs, the Arvanites, and the people from southern Greece in the Florina area and in Greek Macedonia more generally identify themselves as Greeks. The local Macedonians, however, are divided: some identify themselves as Greeks, others as Macedonians.[13]

The term *dopios* ("local," "native," or "indigenous"), which is derived from the word *topos* ("place," "country," or "land"), links the people

---

[12] Personal communication from the representative of the district of Florina to the Greek parliament, who visited Melbourne in 1992.

[13] It should be noted that while local Macedonians in the Florina area speak both Greek and Macedonian, local Macedonians in southern parts of Greek Macedonia (in Kozani and Halkidhiki, for example) speak only Greek. Members of the latter group all have a Greek national identity.

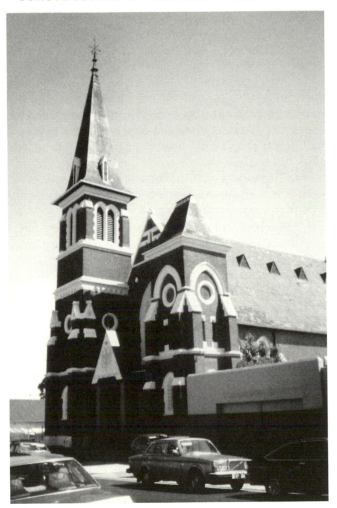

17. The Greek Orthodox Church of Saints Cyril and
Methodius in Preston

referred to by this term with a particular place, a particular geographical area. *Dopios* (or in more formal contexts *topikos*) is used to refer to
the "local language," the local dialect of Macedonian spoken in the
Florina area, and to the "local dances," which are characteristic of the
area. The precise boundaries of this locale, the exact size of the place
referred to, varies greatly depending on the political orientation of the
speaker.

The Greek term *dhiki mas*, like its Macedonian equivalent *naši*, is used
to refer to "our people," as opposed to "foreigners" or "strangers"

(*kseni* in Greek, *tuǵi* or *čuždi* in Macedonian). These terms designate relative social boundaries and are used in a segmentary or hierarchical manner to define categories of inclusion and exclusion at various levels of identity. People who are defined as *dhiki mas* or *naši* can include relatives, fellow villagers, people from the same region, people of the same ethnic group, or people of the same nationality. For example, a local Macedonian from Florina whose son was going to marry a woman from a village near Edhessa or even Bitola, who was also a local Macedonian, could describe his future daughter-in-law as "a foreigner from another village, but one of ours," because she was an outsider with respect to her village identity, but an insider with respect to her ethnic identity. She is from another village, but she is a local Macedonian, not a refugee or a Vlach.[14]

When local Macedonians from Florina use the terms *dhiki mas* and *naši* to designate their own ethnic group, the defining feature of this group is generally said to be language. "Our people" are people who speak "our language," the "local language," the Macedonian language. At this level of the segmentary hierarchy, the terms *dhiki mas* and *naši* clearly contrast with and exclude refugees and Vlachs. More significantly, these terms also contrast with and exclude "Greeks," that is, "Greeks" in an ethnic rather than a national sense. "Greeks" in this ethnic sense are people who speak Greek as their native language, as opposed to people whose native language is Macedonian or Vlach; they are Greeks from southern Greece, from "old Greece," from the Greek state as it existed prior to 1913. Greeks in this sense are also referred to as "real" or "genuine" Greeks, Greeks "from south of Mount Olympus," as opposed to local Macedonians, Pontians, and Vlachs, even though these local Macedonians, Pontians, and Vlachs identify themselves as Greeks at the national level.

Elderly local Macedonians I spoke with in Florina in the early 1990s referred to the Ilinden Uprising of 1903 as "our revolution" in contrast to the Greek Revolution of 1821, and they described the end of the Balkan wars as the time when "the Greeks came." One old man said more pointedly, "The Greeks came and found me here, I didn't go looking for them. They registered me as a Greek by force" (*me eghrapsan me to zori Ellina*). Several people referred to the television channel that broadcast programs in Macedonian from Skopje as "our [*dhiko mas*] channel," as opposed to "the foreign [*kseno*] station," the Greek channel that broadcast in Greek from Athens. Finally, a man who identified himself as a Macedonian and not a Greek and who had recently re-

---

[14] For further discussion of the opposition between *kseni* and *dhiki mas*, see Herzfeld (1987:154ff.) and Danforth (1989:170–71).

turned to Florina after living in Canada for many years, said, "I was a foreigner there, and I'm a foreigner here too."

It is significant that even local Macedonians from Florina who identify themselves as Greeks in a national sense often speak of the opposition between themselves as "our people," on the one hand, and "Greeks" (in an ethnic sense), on the other. This usage is seized on by their fellow villagers who have a Macedonian national identity as evidence that their claim to Greek identity is invalid, that they are not "really" Greek. For example, two local Macedonians from Florina were arguing at a picnic sponsored by their village association in Melbourne. George identified himself as a Greek, Con as a Macedonian. At one point in the conversation George (describing all the different groups of people he came in contact with at the slaughterhouse where he worked) said, "We have Italians, Maltese, Greeks, and our people [dhiki mas]." Con interrupted him immediately, "Wait a minute! A few minutes ago you said we were Greeks, and now you're separating 'our people' from 'Greeks.'" George got angry and accused Con of twisting his words. By blurring the distinction between "Greek" as an ethnic category and "Greek" as a national category and equating the two, Con claimed that it was impossible for "our people" (or Pontians or Vlachs, for that matter) to be "real" Greeks.

The term "Macedonian" can also be used in either an ethnic or a national sense. When it is used in an ethnic sense to contrast with Pontians and Vlachs, it implies nothing with regard to national identity. The term "Macedonian," however, can also be used in a national sense to contrast with Serbs, Bulgarians, and Greeks. People who use the term in this way frequently, but not always, have a Macedonian national identity. Speakers often shift from one level of meaning to another in a single sentence, as when a woman from Florina, who was attending a folk dance festival in Melbourne, said, "Half the Macedonians are Macedonians, and half the Macedonians are Greeks." In other words half the local Macedonians have a Macedonian national identity, while half of them have a Greek national identity. Similarly, a man from Florina living in Melbourne who has a Greek national identity said, "I'm a Macedonian. But if there's a war between Greece and Macedonia, then I'll shoot the Macedonians." He meant that although he was a Macedonian in an ethnic sense (and not a Pontian or a Vlach), he had a Greek national identity and would fight for Greece against people who had a Macedonian national identity.

Because of the segmentary nature of the terms dhiki mas and naši, the category distinction between insiders and outsiders can be used in a variety of ways depending on the political views of the speaker. In relatively apolitical contexts, local Macedonians from Florina refer to people who speak "our language" (Macedonian) as "our people" regardless of whether they live to the north or the south of the border between Greece and the former Yugoslavia. In more politicized contexts, people from Florina with a Macedonian national identity refer to people from as far north as Skopje as "our people" because they speak Macedonian, even though they speak standard literary Macedonian rather than the local dialect of Macedonian spoken in villages in northern Greece. People from Florina with a Greek national identity, however, deny that people from north of the border between Greece and the former Yugoslavia are "our people" on the grounds that they do not speak the local dialect. From this Greek nationalist perspective those people are "Serbs," "Yugoslavs," or "Skopians."

People from Florina who have a Greek national identity insist that all inhabitants of Greek Macedonia regardless of their ethnic identity are Macedonians.[15] They also insist that because Macedonia is a region of Greece, like Crete or the Peloponnesos, all Macedonians are Greeks.[16] One local Macedonian immigrant from Florina to Melbourne who had a Greek national identity described himself this way: "I'm a Greek first. I come from Macedonia. I'm a Greek-Macedonian." Another said: "We're Greeks. We're Macedonians . . . Greeks, not Slavs. We're local Greek-Macedonians." In more formal contexts officials of Greek-Macedonian academic and political organizations speak of "Macedonian Hellenism" and "Macedonian Greeks."

When local Macedonian immigrants from Florina to Australia who have a Greek national identity talk about their relatives and fellow villagers who have a Macedonian national identity, they adopt a variety of strategies, all of which have in common a refusal to acknowledge the legitimacy of their national identity as Macedonians. On the one hand, they say that people who identify as Macedonians are really Slavs or Bulgarians who simply "present themselves" as Macedonians. On the other, they argue that all local Macedonians are really Greeks and that those who deny their Greek identity are people who for political or financial reasons have decided to support the cause of a foreign government, the government in Skopje. They call such people "Skopians" or "Yugoslavs" to stress their political affiliation with a foreign state. For example, a leader of an organization of immigrants from a village

---

[15] I would call this a regional use of the term.

[16] This argument is suspect on two counts. Whereas the term "Greek-Macedonian" is frequently heard, the supposedly analogous terms "*Greek-Cretan" and "*Greek-Peloponnesian" do not exist. The term "Greek-Cypriot," however, does exist (as do "Slav-Macedonian" and "Turkish-Cypriot"). Such usage suggests significant parallels between Macedonia and Cyprus, two geographical regions inhabited by both Greeks and non-Greeks, which have long been important "national issues" in Greek political life.

near Florina who identify as Greeks explained the success of the rival organization of immigrants from the same village who identify as Macedonians by saying, "The Skopians get a lot of Yugoslavs to go to their dances." People from Florina with a Greek national identity also call their fellow villagers who have a Macedonian national identity "autonomists" on the grounds that the assertion of a Macedonian national identity is evidence of a desire to incorporate the territory of Greek Macedonia into an independent and united Macedonian state.

According to people from Florina with a Macedonian national identity, however, all local Macedonians, all "our people," are Macedonians in a national sense, not Greeks. "Macedonian" as an ethnic category, in other words, is equated with "Macedonian" as a national category. From this politicized Macedonian nationalist perspective all Macedonian-speaking inhabitants of Macedonia regardless of whether they live in the Republic of Macedonia, Bulgaria, or Greece are Macedonians in a national sense. Macedonian nationalists downplay the cultural and linguistic differences that separate these three groups of Macedonians in order to stress the single national identity that supposedly unites them. People from Florina who are firmly committed to their Macedonian national identity are referred to as "good Macedonians" or "good patriots." In informal English-speaking contexts, Macedonians also use the term "Maso" to refer to themselves and other people with a Macedonian national identity.

Macedonian nationalists claim that there can be no such thing as a "Greek-Macedonian," the term used by Greeks to refer to people who have a Greek national identity and a Macedonian regional identity. As an article in the *Australian Macedonian Weekly* (November 18, 1987, p. 2) put it, there are only "Macedonians from Greece" and "Greeks from the part of Macedonia that falls within the political boundaries of Greece." According to another article in the same paper, "You can't sit on the fence and call yourself a Yugoslav-Macedonian or a Greek-Macedonian. In Australia you are either a Macedonian pure and simple or not." As Ted Yannas put it, "You can't be Greek and Macedonian at the same time. You can only brainwash a Macedonian and make him a Greek." From a Macedonian nationalist perspective, the only legitimate use of the term "Greek-Macedonian" is to refer to someone who has one Greek and one Macedonian parent.

This claim that Greek and Macedonian are mutually exclusive categories of national identity is supported in several ways. A young Macedonian woman who taught Macedonian in a bilingual education program at an elementary school in Melbourne where Greek was also taught said, "There's no Greek-Macedonian language. There's only the Greek language and the Macedonian language." This perspective is frequently supported by analogies between national identities and biological species. Mile, a Vardar Macedonian who worked as a delivery man in Melbourne, was talking with a Greek who identified himself as a Greek-Macedonian. "How can you be a Greek-Macedonian?" Mile asked. "How can you be a horse and a donkey at the same time? You can't be both." When an immigrant to Melbourne from Florina who identifies himself as a Macedonian was told that he was really a Greek-Macedonian, he replied, "No, that can't be. You're either a cat or a dog." Using a different set of metaphors, metaphors of gender and sexual orientation, both of which are in this context believed to be biologically determined, a Macedonian nationalist told me that when he hears people identify themselves as Greek-Macedonians he asks them, "Oh, so you mean you're Greek and Macedonian? Are you also male and female? If you're Greek and Macedonian, then you must also be male and female, so you're a poofter."[17]

Another strategy Macedonian nationalists use to undermine the claim to Macedonian identity of people whose national identity is Greek, but who also claim to be Macedonians, is to laugh and say, "If you really want to be a Macedonian, then why don't you identify yourself as a Macedonian on the census?" Macedonians, in other words, know full well that in countries like Canada and Australia, where there are large diaspora communities of both Greeks and Macedonians, at the level of ethnic or national identity Macedonian and Greek *are* mutually exclusive categories, and *they*, not the Greeks, are the Macedonians.

The term "Greek-Macedonian" is also used with a very different meaning by immigrants from Florina to Melbourne who do everything they can to remain neutral in the extremely politicized atmosphere that has been created by the recent intensification of the Macedonian conflict. These people try to avoid identifying themselves as either Greeks or Macedonians. They say that they are neither one nor the other; that they are lost, mixed-up, or confused; that they don't really know what they are. People in this situation often identify themselves as "Greek-Macedonians," that is, Slavic-speaking local Macedonians who have been assimilated to Greek culture, people who speak two languages and participate in two cultures. All too often the voices of people who adopt this perspective, who identify in this way, are drowned out by nationalist voices on both sides of the issue proclaiming the irreconcilability and mutual exclusivity of Greek and Macedonian identities.

---

[17] Poofter is a British and an Australian slang term referring to a homosexual or an effeminate man. On the negative implications of category confusion, see Douglas (1966).

People with a Macedonian national identity refer to local Macedonians who have adopted a Greek national identity as "*Grkomani*." They define the term in a variety of uncomplementary ways. A *Grkoman* (*Grekomanos* in Greek) is "a Greek lover," "a fake Greek," "a Johnny-come-lately Greek," or a Greek who has been "made" or "manufactured." A *Grkoman* is someone who is not really Greek, but only "pretends to be Greek." Macedonian nationalists contrast someone who is "a Macedonian, one of our people, but a *Grkoman*" with someone who is not one of "our people," but is a "genuine Greek." A statement published by Macedonians in Canada (cited in *Stohos*, April 15, 1992, p. 6) defined a *Grkoman* in greater detail as follows: "A *Grkoman* is a Macedonian who wants to be called a Greek, who refuses to accept his true Macedonian national origin, who is ashamed of his past and the language he speaks, who is afraid to call himself Macedonian, ... a person who collaborates with the Greeks against all Macedonians." One Macedonian I spoke with in Melbourne compared *Grkomani* to transvestites, people who claim to be something they are not. "They are lost, ignorant souls," he said. "They are fence-sitters, people who sit on two chairs, and they are bound to fall."

It is clear, then, that just as Greek nationalists insist that all local Macedonians are Greeks, so Macedonian nationalists insist that all local Macedonians are Macedonians. Regardless of which national identity local Macedonians adopt, their choice is not accepted by their relatives and fellow villagers who have adopted the opposite identity. What is more, their self-ascribed national identity is often rejected by people who have the same national identity as they have, but whose claim to that identity is more secure. Local Macedonians from Florina who identify as Greeks are dismissed as "Bulgarians" by "real Greeks" from southern Greece. As a local Macedonian with a Greek national identity told me, "No matter how pro-Greek [*Ellinofilos*] I am, they won't ever accept me as a genuine Greek." Conversely, local Macedonians from Florina who identify themselves as Macedonians are often suspected of being *Grkomani* by Vardar Macedonians. When supporters of Heidelberg Alexander (the "Greek-Macedonian team") play South Melbourne Hellas (the "real Greek team"), they are called "Bulgarians." When they play Preston Makedonia (the "Macedonian team"), they are called "*Grkomani*." "Neither side wants us," one Heidelberg Alexander fan said. "The Greeks call us Bulgarians, and the Yugoslavs say, 'You're *Egejci* [Aegean Macedonians]. Get out.' Both sides use us when they need us, and then they betray us when they don't."

This is the real tragedy of people like Ted Yannas. Because they belong to an ethnic group that is marginal to both nations, an ethnic group that inhabits a border region where the territories of two states meet, they are not accepted as full members of either nation, even the one they themselves identify with.

HOW CAN A WOMAN GIVE BIRTH TO ONE GREEK AND ONE MACEDONIAN?

In the early 1990s the attention of the Greek and the Macedonian communities of Australia was focused on the Macedonian conflict. The most burning issues confronting the two communities were the struggle of the Republic of Macedonia to gain international recognition under its constitutional name and the parallel, but somewhat less immediate, struggle of Aegean Macedonians to gain recognition from the Greek government as an ethnic or national minority. During this time conversations among Greeks and Macedonians in Melbourne inevitably turned to questions of identity. At weddings, soccer games, village dances, and picnics they argued endlessly about what made a person Greek or Macedonian, and about how people could ever know what a person's nationality really was.

Peter Savramis is a Macedonian, not a Greek. He left his village near Florina and came to Melbourne in the early 1970s. Peter takes great delight in arguing with people in Greek, Macedonian, and English about the Macedonian Question. He prides himself on being able to present his position articulately, convincingly, and without getting in a fight. Peter often talks about the Macedonian conflict at construction sites around the city where he works installing heating and air-conditioning systems.

One day in the fall of 1991 an Italian contractor introduced Peter to Kostas, a Greek carpenter who would be working with him on a new house.

"This is my friend Peter," the contractor said. "He's a Macedonian, but he speaks Greek."

With a look of suspicion, Kostas asked Peter in heavily accented English, "What kind of Macedonian are you? Are you one of the ones who makes trouble?"

"No," Peter replied. "We're just trying to protect our culture from the Greek government."

"What do you mean?" asked Kostas.

Peter suggested they speak in Greek.

"Where are you from?" asked Kostas in Greek. "Are you one of the ones who wants to take our land?"

"Wait a minute," Peter said. "I'm a Macedonian. What land are you talking about?"

"You speak good Greek!" said Kostas, somewhat surprised.

"Yes," said Peter. "I speak pure Greek. I learned it in school."

"You're a Greek-Macedonian," said Kostas.

"No! I'm a Macedonian." replied Peter.

Kostas was starting to get angry. "But you can't understand those Yugoslavs who want to take our land."

"When it comes to language," Peter explained, "a Macedonian from Greece and a Macedonian from Yugoslavia can understand each other perfectly. They speak the same language."

"Why does it bother you if I'm Macedonian?" asked Peter. "Are you Greek?"

"Yes."

"If I said that you weren't Greek, wouldn't you tell me to get stuffed?"

"Yes."

"It's the same for me. If you say I'm not Macedonian, I'll tell you to get stuffed."

"But you're a Greek-Macedonian," insisted Kostas again.

"I'm a Greek citizen," said Peter, "but I'm a Macedonian by birth. You could have an Australian passport, but by birth what are you?"

"A Greek," replied Kostas.

"It's the same with me," said Peter. "I'm Macedonian by birth. If a hundred years ago they divided Greece up, and Italy and Bulgaria and Turkey each took a part, what would you be?"

"I'd still be Greek," replied Kostas.

"That's right," said Peter, shaking his hand. "And I'm still Macedonian. I am what I am, and you are what you are. If you say I'm not a Macedonian, then I'll say you're not Greek."

An analysis of the indigenous theories of identity that underly arguments like this confirms the value of David Schneider's (1968, 1969, 1984) discussion of blood and law as two of the most powerful symbols expressing the unity of people who share a common identity, whether in the domain of kinship, religion, or nationality. According to Schneider, blood is regarded as a "natural substance," a "shared biogenetic material." It is a biological essence, an objective fact of nature, that is given at birth and that is often thought to constitute a permanent and unalterable aspect of a person's identity.[18] By contrast, another aspect of a person's identity is that determined by law, by what Schneider

---

[18] On blood as a symbol of shared national identity, see Handler (1988:37), Herzfeld (1992:11, 22–47), and Just (1989).

calls "a code for conduct," that is, a particular pattern of behavior, a particular social relationship which is dependent for its continued existence on the performance of a particular social role (1968:21–29). It is understood that this aspect of a person's identity is neither natural nor permanent, but that it can either be changed or terminated. In the conversations of immigrants from Florina to Melbourne either of these two powerful symbols, blood or law, can serve as a criterion for determining a person's identity.

According to both Greek and Macedonian nationalist perspectives national identity is something that is naturally and biologically given. It is determined first and foremost by "blood" or by "birth." This biologized conception of national identity is expressed both explicitly and metaphorically. A person of Greek nationality is "Greek by birth, origin, or descent" (*Ellinas to yenos*). As a man from Florina who identifies himself as a Macedonian and not a Greek said, "No one buys his nationality; no one chooses his mother. I inherited this nationality. It's my inheritance, the milk of my mother."

Metaphors identifying the personified national homeland as parent also support this biologized conception of national identity. As we have seen, Greece is often referred to as the "mother fatherland," while Macedonia is referred to both as "mother Macedonia" and as the "fatherland." Macedonian nationalists frequently use biological metaphors equating the category of national identity with the category of biological species. When people from Florina who identify as Macedonians deny the legitimacy of the identity of their relatives and fellow villagers who identify as Greeks, they use images suggesting the immutability of biological species: "Wheat is wheat, and corn is corn. You can't change one into the other. Even if you call it corn, it's still wheat. Its nature doesn't change." Or as a supporter of the United Macedonians put it, "A maple tree is a maple tree. You can't inject oak tree into it." Macedonian nationalists often explain the incompatibility of Greeks and Macedonians with a proverb that also draws on the analogy between nationality and biological species. In commenting on the long history of conflict and hostility between Greeks and Macedonians, they say, "sheep and goats don't mix."[19]

People from Florina who identify themselves as Macedonians argue that all Slavic speakers in northern Greece are "really" Macedonians and not Greeks because their "mother tongue" is Macedonian and not Greek. They contrast the "natural" environment in which they learned Macedonian—at home, in the family, speaking with their parents and

[19] In this proverb the sheep represent Macedonians (who are stereotypically docile and naive), while the goats represent Greeks (who are stereotypically clever).

grandparents—with the "artificial" environment of the educational system in which they learned Greek. Real Greeks, they say, don't have grandparents who speak Macedonian. They also attempt to undermine the legitimacy of the Greek national identity of people who speak Macedonian by making fun of them when they say *in Macedonian*, "We are Greeks" (*Nie sne Grci*) or "We Greeks are clever" (*Nie Grci sne eksipni*).[20] From a Macedonian and even a Greek nationalist perspective, such people may seem incongruous, their nationality suspect, but from an anthropological perspective the claims to Greek national identity of people who were born in Greece but speak Macedonian and not Greek are just as legitimate as the claims to Macedonian national identity of people who earlier in their lives identified themselves as Greeks.

The contrast between a person's "genuine" national identity, which is biologically given at birth, and a person's "artificial" national identity, which is acquired somehow later in life is conveyed by a humorous if somewhat bitter comment overheard by a Macedonian from Melbourne while visiting the village where he was born in Florina. A Greek woman from southern Greece who had married a local Macedonian from the village told some men who had gathered in the village café "You aren't real Greeks." An old man, a local Macedonian, replied, "You are a Greek with hormones. We are Greeks by injection." This self-deprecating undermining of the legitimacy of the national identity of Slavic-speaking local Macedonians who identify as Greeks is reminiscent of Kofos' (1989:259) reference to Macedonians as people who have been "immunized with 'Macedonian' national ideology." There are also parallels between Macedonian nationalists' references to *Grkomani* as suffering from a "disease of the mind" and as constituting "a cancer inside the Macedonian nation" (*Stohos*, April 15, 1992, pp. 4, 6) and Kofos' use of images of medical pathology, particularly the image of "mutation" to describe the development of Macedonian national identity.[21]

While the idea that national identity is a natural, biological given is a basic tenet of both Greek and Macedonian nationalist ideologies, in arguments among immigrants from Florina to Melbourne over whether they are really Greeks or Macedonians, this position is most often taken by people who identify themselves as Macedonians. People who identify themselves as Greeks, on the other hand, are much more likely to argue that national identity is determined by what Schneider has called "a code for conduct," that is, a particular relationship with the Greek state, which people enter into as they are socialized into

[20] The word *eksipnos* (clever or smart) is a Greek word.

[21] On this imagery see chapter 2. See also Papadopoulos' image of the enemies of Greece as "cancerous growths" in chapter 5, note 4.

Greek society. Through this process of socialization people develop a commitment to the Greek state as well as a sense of being a part of the Greek nation. Given the identity of the Greek state and the Greek nation, the legal relationship between a Greek citizen and the Greek state, which involves the performance of a particular social role, is equated with membership in the Greek nation. People who are Greek citizens, in other words, must have a Greek national identity; people who were raised in Greek society must be Greeks.[22]

Immigrants from Florina to Melbourne who identify themselves as Greeks frequently argue that their relatives and fellow villagers who identify as Macedonians cannot "really" be Macedonians on the grounds that there has never been a Macedonian state. When a Greek tells a Macedonian "You can't be a Macedonian because there's no such country [*kratos*]," he implies that because there is no Macedonian state as a legal entity and no Macedonian citizenship as a legal relationship, there can be no Macedonian nation and no Macedonian national identity.[23] Given the identity of state and nation in Greek nationalist ideology, Greece's refusal to recognize the Republic of Macedonia as an independent state can be seen as the equivalent of refusing to recognize the existence of a Macedonian national identity.

The Greek nationalist argument is more straightforward when it comes to asserting that people from Florina, people who were born and raised in Greece, must have a Greek national identity. On one occasion a man who identified himself as Greek said, "I was born under Greece, I went to school under Greece, I believe in Greece, and I'll never change." In an attempt to put an end to a long and frustrating discussion, another man said, "We're from Greece, so we're Greek. Let's just forget it."

More specifically people with a Greek national identity often argue that because many people from Florina who claim to be Macedonians have Greek, not Macedonian, names; because they attend the Greek, not the Macedonian, church; because they are literate in the Greek, not the Macedonian, language; and finally because they all have Greek, not Macedonian, passports, they must therefore be Greeks. A column that ran in the *Australian Macedonian Weekly* in September 1988 entitled

---

[22] Some people from Florina define national identity as a product of socialization at the family, rather than the state level saying: "You are whatever your parents raise you to be."

[23] This argument, of course, ignores the fact that nations that have no states to serve as national homelands can and do exist (the Palestinians and the Kurds are obvious examples), as well as the fact that the Republic of Macedonia has existed as one of the Federated Republics of Yugoslavia with its own government, educational system, flag, and nationality since 1944. It also ignores the fact that in 1991 the Republic of Macedonia declared its existence as an independent and sovereign state.

"Myths of Macedonian History" refuted these arguments by pointing out that many Aegean Macedonians had Greek names and were literate in Greek because of the assimilationist policies of the Greek government. The author of this column also pointed out that Aegean Macedonians had Greek passports because they were Greek citizens and that citizenship did not determine ethnic or national identity.

When confronted with the Greek argument that because they came to Australia on Greek passports they are therefore Greeks, many immigrants from Florina who identify themselves as Macedonians simply say, "No. We're Macedonians with Greek passports." This response, however, never succeeds in convincing people with a Greek national identity that such a possibility exists. More argumentative Macedonians often reply, "You say that we're Greeks because we were born under Greek rule. Does that mean that your grandfather was Turkish because he was born under Turkish rule?" One Macedonian ridiculed the Greek argument by asking rhetorically, "If you were born on a farm does that make you an animal?" The force of these replies is to demonstrate that just because people were born in a certain place, in the territory of a certain state, and are therefore citizens of that state, they are not necessarily members of the nation that is identified with that state.[24]

The relevance of Schneider's analysis of the symbols of blood and law to the present discussion of the construction of national identity among local Macedonians from Florina is clear from the analogies often drawn between trying to determine what a person's "real" national identity is and who a person's "real" mother is. At a village picnic in Melbourne Sam, a man from a village near Florina who identifies himself as a Greek, said, "My blood is Macedonian. My real mother is Macedonian. But my adoptive mother is Greece. And you can't spit in the face of your adoptive mother." Faced with a clear choice, metaphorically speaking, between a relative to whom he was related by blood and one to whom he was related by law, Sam chose to place greater emphasis on the legal relationship and to remain loyal to his adoptive mother. In this way he explained the fact that he had a Greek national identity.

Ted Yannas used the same metaphor, the metaphor of adoption, to explain how as an adult he realized that he was actually a Macedonian, even though he had lived all his life as a Greek. "I felt like an adopted child who had just discovered his real parents," he said. "All my life had been a lie. I'd been a janissary; I'd betrayed my own people." Ted

---

[24] Place, here identified with "country of origin" and viewed as a determinant of citizenship as a legal relationship, must be distinguished from place in the sense of the earth and soil, which figure in biological metaphors of national identity as a kind of "rootedness" (see Malkki 1992; Bottomley and Lechte 1990).

Yannas, unlike Sam, however, chose metaphorically to privilege his relationship with his biological parents. In this way he justified his newly discovered Macedonian national identity.

As these two examples illustrate, immigrants from Florina to Melbourne can decide whether they are Greeks or Macedonians either by invoking the existence of a "blood" tie or by invoking the existence of a social relationship. National identity in this case, therefore, is a matter of choice, a matter of self-identification or self-ascription. Immigrants from Florina recognize the role of conscious choice and individual decision making in their discussions of national identity, but only to a degree. They talk about people with a Greek national identity as people who "want" or "believe in" Greece. Conversely they refer to people who have a Macedonian national identity as people who "want" or "believe in" Macedonia or Skopje. People who identify as Greeks or Macedonians are also described as being "on the Greek side" or "on the Macedonian side," as belonging to one "political faction" or the other. This terminology suggests that whether immigrants from Florina identify themselves as Greeks or Macedonians is a matter of conscious political choice. They *are* Greeks or Macedonians because they *choose* to be Greeks or Macedonians.

Macedonians who are involved in the Macedonian human rights movement in Australia are the most likely to acknowledge that national identity is a matter of self-ascription. They have been influenced both by the discourse of multiculturalism in Australia, where ethnic identity is specifically stated to be a matter of self-identification, and by the discourse of international human rights organizations such as the United Nations or the Conference on Security and Cooperation in Europe, where membership in a national minority is considered to be a matter of individual choice.[25] Such an approach to the issue of ethnic and national identity (as opposed to the essentialist approach so characteristic of most nationalist ideologies) clearly serves the interests of Macedonians in their struggle to gain recognition as a nation on the international scene and as an ethnic or national minority in Greece as well as in Canada and Australia.

In many cases, however, the acknowlegment of the self-ascriptive nature of national identity is merely a token gesture of respect, one that is all too readily abandoned in favor of a more nationalistic approach. A man involved in the Macedonian human rights movement in Melbourne talked about a fellow villager who identified himself as Greek

[25] See, for example, the final document of the Copenhagen Meeting of the Conference on the Human Dimension of the Conference on Security and Cooperation in Europe, which has been published by the United States Commission on Security and Cooperation in Europe (1990).

this way: "I respect Tom for what he believes he is. He has the right to believe in something, and he believes he's a Greek. But he's really a Macedonian like us." Another immigrant from Florina involved in the Macedonian human rights movement described the underlying biologically given Macedonian national identity of a fellow villager who explicitly identified himself as Greek as existing "inside his blood, without his wanting it."

People from Florina who identify themselves as Greeks exhibit this same tendency to contrast people's beliefs, people's assertions of what they are, on one the hand, with what they "really" are, on the other. A woman who identified herself as Greek and who taught Greek in a public elementary school in Melbourne expressed this contrast implicitly when she said, "I know Greeks from Florina who say they're not Greek." *Her* knowledge that they *are* Greeks somehow transcends in importance and legitimacy *their* assertions that they are *not*. Another immigrant from Florina who identified himself as a Greek expressed the contrast this way: "You can change your consciousness [*sinidhisi*], but you can't change what you really are. My son can have an Australian consciousness, but he can't be Australian. He can feel like an Australian, but he can't be one. . . . A person who went to Skopje after the Civil War can change consciousness. Now he believes there; now he has a Slavic consciousness. But he can't be a Macedonian. He's Greek."

Because all local Macedonians from Florina accept the fact that they belong to the same ethnic group, they believe that they all must also have the same national identity. People who have a Macedonian national identify believe that all local Macedonians are Macedonians, whereas people who have a Greek national identity believe that all local Macedonians are Greeks. Members of both groups dismiss as mistaken and illegitimate the self-ascribed identity of anyone who asserts an identity different from their own.

Macedonians justify dismissing the self-ascribed Greek national identity of their relatives and fellow villagers by arguing that it is motivated by fear and that it is a product of the assimilationist policies practiced by the Greek government since 1913. As one Macedonian put it, "They were forced to become Greeks." A leader of the Macedonian human rights movement in Melbourne said that in an open society like Australia, where people can freely identify as they wish, their self-ascribed national identity will correspond with their biologically given national identity. When deliberate attempts have been made to eradicate an ethnic group, however, then people's self-ascribed national identity will not correspond with their biologically given identity. In such cases people's "real" identity is determined not by self-ascription but by biology.

Greeks justify dismissing the self-ascribed Macedonian national identity of people from Florina in a similar manner. They argue that it is a conscious choice, which in many cases is motivated by the pressure tactics of local "Skopians" or by economic self-interest. Macedonian human rights, they say, has become a big business; human rights activists collect a lot of money from the community and spend it any way they want. But a Macedonian woman from Florina who completed her university studies in Melbourne explicitly rejected the idea that her Macedonian identity was a matter of conscious choice. "The Greeks are denying my people the right to be who they are, not who they want to be. I don't choose to be Macedonian. I *am* Macedonian. I'm Macedonian because I was born to the family I was and in the place I was. I'm not Macedonian beause of any political act of my own." From both the Greek and the Macedonian nationalist perspectives, therefore, a person's self-ascribed national identity as a product of conscious political choice is generally rejected in favor of a reified conception of national identity grounded in biology.

Because a person's national identity can be defined as biologically determined or as acquired through a process of socialization, and because a person's self-ascribed national identity, whether it is based on biology or socialization, can either be accepted at face value or rejected in favor of another identity based on a different principle, the question of whether the Slavic-speaking people of northern Greece are Greeks or Macedonians is ultimately contestable. People from Florina will continue to argue about blood, birth, language, education, consciousness, belief, and passports as criteria of national identity. Parents and children, husbands and wives, brothers and sisters will continue to disagree about what they really are.

At a village dance in Melbourne a man who identified himself as Macedonian and not Greek told me a story about two brothers from a village near Florina. One had settled in Yugoslavia after the Civil War; the other had remained in Greece. Eventually they both came to Australia (one on a Yugoslav passport, the other on a Greek passport) where they lived together with their mother in the same house in Melbourne. They were constantly arguing with each other because one brother identified himself as Greek while the other brother identified himself as Macedonian. Finally they confronted their mother; they asked her how a woman could give birth to one Greek and one Macedonian.

The narrator of the story did not tell me what the mother replied. Instead he offered his own answer to the question. "It's *not* possible," he said emphatically. "By blood, by birth, they're both Macedonians."

I am sure that if the narrator of the story had been a Greek I would also have been told that it was not possible for a woman to give birth to one Greek and one Macedonian, but I would have been told that both brothers were *Greek*. As an anthropologist, however, I offer a different answer to this question. I suggest that it *is* possible for a woman to give birth to one Greek and one Macedonian. It *is* possible precisely because Greeks and Macedonians are not born, they are made. National identities, in other words, are not biologically given, they are socially constructed.

MACEDONIAN LIVES

There are several different positions local Macedonian immigrants from Florina to Australia have taken when it comes to articulating a sense of national identity. Some state straightforwardly and openly that they are Greek, others that they are Macedonian. Still others avoid ascribing to themselves either of these two mutually exclusive national identities and attempt to maintain a neutral stance in what has become a highly politicized environment. This is a particularly difficult challenge given the power and pervasiveness of "Greek" and "Macedonian" as categories of ethnic identity in Australian multicultural discourse and as categories of national identity in Balkan nationalist discourse.

There are many factors that influence the process of identity formation as it takes place among immigrants from Florina to Australia. Balkan history, village politics, family situation, and individual biography all play important parts in this complex process. People may identify themselves as Greeks for a variety of reasons. They may come from a village that supported the patriarch in the early twentieth century or a family that supported the Greek government during the Civil War. They may come from a wealthy family or have grown up in the city of Florina itself, or they may simply have been the youngest child in the family and grown up speaking Greek in the home because their older brothers and sisters had already started school. They may have left Greece as adults, having been fully socialized into Greek national society as a result of completing high school or serving in the military. Alternatively, they may be involved in a profession that can be practiced more readily in the Greek community of Melbourne with its large private educational system and its well-established professional and business elite. They may also have married into a family with a strong sense of Greek national identity. Finally, they may be afraid that if they publicly identify themselves as Macedonians, they may not be able to return to Greece or that their relatives still living in Greece may be harassed by Greek government officials. One person, for example, refused to discuss the Macedonian issue with me, saying, "It's too political, too dangerous. I don't want to talk. The people in the Pan-Macedonian Association might find out what I said, and I'd get in trouble."

Alex Petridis: 100 Percent Greek

Alex Petridis grew up in Lofi, a small village ten miles from Florina whose inhabitants are all local Macedonians. One of his most powerful childhood memories is watching his grandfather dance the "local dances" holding a shepherd's crook, slapping his feet, and shouting, "Opa." Alex's grandfather was a merchant; he knew Greek and Macedonian, but his grandmother only knew Macedonian. Alex always spoke Greek with his parents. They were apolitical; they never talked to him about the Civil War, and he never asked about it.

While he was in high school in Florina, Alex joined a folk dance group. He also studied folk dancing and performed in a folk dance ensemble when he moved to Thessaloniki. After he came to Melbourne in 1971 at the age of eighteen, he was hired to teach folk dancing to the youth group of the Pan-Macedonian Association of Melbourne and Victoria. Several years later he founded his own folk dancing group in order to "promote Macedonian culture, the culture of northern Greece, and all of Greek culture." Alex isn't interested in politics, just in teaching Greek culture and Greek traditions in Australia. He also works in the restaurant business. His wife is from Greece too, from a small village in southern Greece near Sparta.

When asked about his own personal sense of identity, Alex says, "I feel like a local Macedonian, not a Slav, more like a Greek. We locals are 100 percent Greek. We lived there before the Slavs came. If someone calls me a Slav, I'll swear at him. I'm not a Slav; Slavs are Bulgarians, Serbs, Russians. I don't feel Australian either. I express myself best in Greek, I'm involved in Greek culture, I work with Greeks. I feel Greek; I just feel more Greek."

Jeff Papakostandinou: A Greek First

Jeff grew up in the village of Neret—Polipotamo in Greek. His mother didn't know Greek, so Jeff spoke "the local language" with her, but with his father he spoke mostly Greek. Most of the fifteen hundred people from Neret who live in Melbourne are Macedonians; many of them went to Yugoslavia in the 1940s and came to Australia from there. The five hundred people who still live in the village are all Greeks.

Shortly after he arrived in Melbourne in 1973 as a young man of nineteen, Jeff went to work in a factory with his father. At lunch one day they joined a group of men from their village. When Jeff's father asked him for a cigarette, one of the men they were sitting with said angrily, "Aren't you ashamed?" Jeff's father thought he was referring to the fact that he was smoking a cigarette in front of his son, but the man said, "Forget the cigarettes. Aren't you ashamed to speak Greek? Here we're all Macedonians. Greece is gone." Jeff and his father were stunned; they had been reprimanded for speaking *Greek*. In Greece they had always been ashamed to speak *Macedonian*.

Several years later Jeff married a woman who had been born in Australia but whose parents came from Florina. She had grown up speaking Macedonian at home, and she learned English at school.

"I'm Greek," she says, "but I don't speak Greek. When Greeks ask me why, I tell them, 'We're from the part of Greece where they speak Macedonian at home.' I was born in Australia, I speak Macedonian, and I come from Greece. I'm Greek, Greek-Macedonian. I can never be Australian; I don't feel Australian. We're not Yugoslavs either. We're Greeks. But we speak Macedonian."

Since coming to Australia and particularly since getting married, Jeff's Macedonian has improved a great deal. He and his wife speak Macedonian at home. Their children speak Macedonian and English. When they're a little older, Jeff plans to send them to afternoon school to learn Greek.

In Jeff's opinion the Macedonian Question doesn't exist in Greece. Everyone there "wants Greece." When people ask him what he is, he says that he's a Greek first. Then he says that he's a Greek from Macedonia.

"I'm a Macedonian, but not with the meaning that *they* use. I'm a Greek; I'm a northern Greek. No one can say I'm not a Macedonian. But I can't say I'm Macedonian alone. I'm a Macedonian from Greece. My nationality [*ethnikotita*] is Greek, but I'm Macedonian too. I was born in Greece; all my official papers are Greek. I love Greece."

When asked who can identify themselves as Macedonians, Jeff says that the Macedonians can use the name too, but that both Greeks and Macedonians have to respect it. As for Australia, Jeff says, "I would fight for Australia; I care for Australia. Our future is here."

People from Florina may identify as Macedonians for a variety of reasons as well. They may come from a village that supported the exarch in the early twentieth century or a family that supported the Communists during the Civil War. They may have been born in a small, poor village inhabited exclusively by local Macedonians, or they may have been the oldest child in the family and grown up speaking Macedonian with their parents and grandparents. Alternatively, they may have left Greece for Australia at a young age and may not have been fully social-ized into Greek national society, but only into the "local" society of their family and village. People who left Greece after the Civil War, settled in Yugoslavia or some other eastern European country, and then emigrated to Australia from there are almost certain to have adopted a Macedonian national identity. People who remained in Greece, but who experienced harassment and persecution at the hands of the Greek government in the years following the Civil War, may also have developed a Macedonian identity. Finally, people who marry into a family with a strong Macedonian identity, or who have no relatives still living in Greece are likely to develop a Macedonian iden-tity as well.

Angelo Papadopoulos: A Fanatic Macedonian

Angelo Papadopoulos was born in 1935 in Neokazi—Neohoraki in Greek—a village on the main road from Florina to the Yugoslav bor-der. When he was baptized, his godfather, who spoke no Greek, gave him the name Blaže. That's a nickname for Vangel, which in Greek is Evangelos, but his mother still calls him Blaže. That's his *real* name.

Angelo's first memories are of the German occupation. "There was no Greek state then," he says. "We were free; we spoke Macedonian." That was when Angelo joined a Macedonian youth organization called Gotse Delchev. There were a hundred children in it and only six in the Greek youth organization. "I knew I was a Macedonian way back then. I've never said I was Greek. I never said I was Macedonian either—in Greece. I would have been killed."

After the Germans withdrew from Greece, Angelo's father was pre-paring to cross the border into Yugoslavia to join the Macedonian resis-tance fighters. Angelo remembers his grandfather telling his father, "You are my only son, but you must die for your mother tongue, for Macedonia." Later during the Civil War the Greek soldiers stationed in Neokazi made the children march around the village singing a little song in Greek:

> I am a Greek, a Macedonian. That is my pride, my honor.
> And I say it with joy, so that it will reach the heavens.

But as soon as the soldiers turned their backs, the children began singing another song, a song in Macedonian they had learned several years earlier when they belonged to the Gotse Delchev organization.

The flag of Gotse Delchev waves
In the struggle for Macedonia.

When Angelo's father returned to Neokazi in 1948, he was arrested and accused of being a Bulgarian and a Communist. With the village president and several Pontian refugees testifing against him, he was found guilty and sent to a prison camp on the island of Makronisos for several years, as were several of his uncles and cousins. When the military junta came to power in 1967, the authorities closed Angelo's store. He was removed from the village school committee and from the board of directors of the village soccer team, a team he had founded and supported all his life. That was when Angelo knew it was time to go to Australia.

Since then Angelo has identified himself publicly as a Macedonian and supported Macedonian causes. But in 1988 when he heard Nicholas Martis, the former minister of Northern Greece who spoke at the First International Congress on Macedonian Studies, say that there were no Macedonians in northern Greece, Angelo became "a fanatic Macedonian."

Tom Vasili: A Child Refugee

Tom Vasili was born in Greece, but he didn't learn Greek until he went to school in Romania. Tom grew up in the village of Breznica—Vatohori in Greek—near the Prespa Lakes to the west of Florina. Everyone there spoke Macedonian. In 1947 he learned to read Macedonian when he went to the elementary school run by the partisans during the Civil War. Breznica was a training center for partisan recruits; the radio station for Free Greece was based there as well. In 1948, however, Tom and over one hundred other child refugees were taken from the village first to Yugoslavia and then to Romania. There Tom attended schools run by the Communist Party of Greece, which at that time recognized the Slavic-speaking people of northern Greece as "Slavo-Macedonians." While also studying Russian, Romanian, Greek, and Macedonian, Tom was trained as a mechanical engineer.

In 1956 the Communist Party of Greece changed its policy with regard to the Macedonian Question and announced that it would no longer recognize the existence of a separate Macedonian nation. In protest Tom and his fellow students refused to attend Greek classes at the technical college in Romania where they were studying. Officials of the Communist Party of Greece told them, "You are Greeks. Why don't you go to Greek classes?" Tom stood up and replied, "We are Macedonians. We have a Macedonian language and Macedonian schools, and that's enough." Because he spoke out so openly, the Communists had Tom expelled from the college.

Shortly thereafter the Greek government declared an amnesty and began to allow some of the child refugees to return to Greece. Tom went back to Breznica and immediately applied for a visa to emigrate to Australia to join his father who had already settled there several years earlier. But Tom applied for his visa under the name Stefanidis, the name his family had officially used in Greece. Tom's grandfather's name had been Vasil Stefanov, a Macedonian name, but the Greeks had changed it to Stefanidis. In Romania Tom's name had been changed to Stefanovski, because people said that real Macedonian names end in "-ski." Unbenownst to Tom, however, before his father left Greece for Australia he had Tom's last name officially changed to Vasiliou to try to free him from any association with the family's history of leftist activities. Since his arrival in Melbourne Tom has been active in a variety of Macedonian organizations, including the Movement for the Liberation and Unification of Macedonia and the Macedonian human rights movement. Now he uses the name Tom Vasili.

Some local Macedonians from Florina living in Australia have adopted a third position with regard to the question of national identity. They attempt to maintain a neutral stance in the conflict between Greeks and Macedonians by refusing to identify themselves publicly with either one of the two mutually exclusive national groups. In many cases they want to preserve the unity of their village organizations, which provide them with their primary sense of identity; in some cases they may value both national cultures and not want to restrict themselves by identifying themselves exclusively with either one. Finally, they may be genuinely unable to choose either one of the two mutually exclusive national categories to identify themselves with. On several occasions people who had adopted this third position refused to discuss the Macedonian conflict with me. When I asked a man I met at a village picnic if he were a Greek or a Macedonian, he said, "I can't talk. I can't say anything." Then he gestured to the people dancing a "local" dance on the cricket field in front of us and said, "These are my people; this is my village. That's all I can say."

John Dragoulis: "We're All One People"

One man who was extremely hesitant to talk with me finally agreed to do so only on the condition that I not use his name or the name of the village he came from. John Dragoulis, as I will call him here, is an unemployed factory worker who came to Australia over twenty-five years ago. He is very concerned about his father who still lives in Florina. People there have told his father to warn John not to get involved in Macedonian organizations in Australia.

The village association John and his fellow villagers have formed in Melbourne uses the Greek name of the village in all official contexts. The calendar they put out every year and the invitations to all their social functions are in Greek as well. The association is *not*, however, a member of the Pan-Macedonian Association. Instead it is a member of the United Villages Family Association, an organization composed of the associations of eight villages in the Florina area, whose members all want to stay out of politics and keep their villages "united." One village—Ayia Paraskevi in Greek, Sveta Petka in Macedonian—decided to use the name Saint Pat in official contexts in order to avoid having to choose between the Greek and the Macedonian name. At some village dances the master of ceremonies speaks English, at others he speaks Greek, but most of the villagers attending the dances speak Macedonian among themselves. The officers of some village associations instruct the bands they hire to play both Greek and Macedonian songs, but to avoid any really "patriotic" or political songs. The officers of other village associations tell the bands they can *play* Macedonian songs, but they ask them not to *sing* any lyrics in Macedonian.

John and his family go to the Greek Orthodox Church "out of habit." They have been to the Macedonian church a few times, but it seems strange to them to hear the liturgy in Macedonian. John's daughter was recently married in a Greek church. The groom was born in Australia and speaks Macedonian, but he doesn't like politics. At the wedding they played both Greek and Macedonian songs. At the reception John requested one of his favorite Macedonian folk songs, "Young Macedonian Girl" [*Makedonsko Devojče*], especially for his daughter, because that's what she was—a young Macedonian girl.

John has read a great deal about the ancient Macedonians. He owns the volume on Macedonia in the Cambridge Ancient History series, and he knows about the Macedonian kings, Demosthenes, and Alexander's military exploits. He also knows about Gotse Delchev and the Ilinden Uprising. He recently learned the Macedonian alphabet so he could read Macedonian as well as Greek newspapers.

As far as his own identity is concerned, John says he knows that he is a Macedonian, not a Greek, but he emphasizes that he is not "against the Greeks." He would never "come out" and assert his Macedonian identity publicly the way some people do; he would never suggest that his village association adopt the Macedonian name of the village. His main concern is to avoid jeopardizing the neutrality and the unity of his village association.

"My first identity," he says, "is my village identity. Let each individual believe what he wants *as an individual*, but keep the village neutral. I don't want to leave my people [*laos*]; I want to keep them together. We're all from the same village. Not, 'You're Peleponnesian, and you're Russian.' We're all Macedonian. Some people believe they're Macedonians; other people believe that they're Greeks. But we're all one people. We can't have one person saying he's Macedonian and another that he's Greek."

Chris Psalidas: A Cultural Person

Chris Psalidas is a writer and poet. He was born in the 1950s in "Florina cum Lerin," as he put it. When he came to Australia eight years later, he was fluent in Greek and Macedonian, but because his family settled in a Macedonian neighborhood in Melbourne, he stopped speaking Greek and grew up speaking English and Macedonian. In high school he used to say he was Greek, but later he realized that he couldn't call himself Greek the way people from Athens did. He had to qualify it, so he began saying he was Greek-Macedonian. After graduating from university he taught in a high school with lots of Greek students. He went to night school to "resurrect" his Greek. During that time he devoted himself to studying Greek literature and culture.

When the Macedonian Drama Group was formed in 1984, Chris realized that he had an opportunity to explore another part of his identity, a part he had never been able to express before. He wrote a play in English and then translated it back into the rural Macedonian dialect he had learned as a child in Florina. Then in 1987 he went to Skopje on an International Teaching Fellowship. There he learned standard literary Macedonian.

Members of the Macedonian Drama Group called Chris a Macedonian when he worked with them. But in 1990, when a short story of his won first prize in a competition sponsored by the Greek Australian Cultural League, Greek newspapers referred to him as "Chris Psalidas, the Greek poet." That's when Macedonians started saying, "Now Chris has become Greek," and, "Here is Chris going the other way."

When people ask him what he is, Chris says, "I'm a cultural person. I write and dream in English. I played Australian rules football, not soccer. First and foremost I'm an Australian, but I also feel Macedonian. I've never felt politically about the issue; I'm not siding with one group or the other. My psyche, my soul, is big enough to accommodate more than one culture. Our people, the people of Florina, embody the spirit of multiculturalism. I write about ideas, not ethnicity. I get criticized for not supporting one side or the other, but I'm Chris Psalidas, not the Greek or the Macedonian. There is material in both cultures to be explored. I'd be a fool to deny either one."

Ann Koziri: "We Just Don't Know Who We Are"

Ann Koziri spoke poignantly about being trapped between two national identities, two national cultures; about being forced to make a choice she did not want to make. Ann and her husband left Florina in the 1940s and worked on a farm in Gippsland until 1965 when they came to Melbourne to provide a better education for their children and to be with more "Europeans."

"We go to both sides," said Ann, "and we don't talk against either one. That's our policy."

"We can't be Yugoslav," she continued, "and we can't be Greek. At Epping [the Macedonian Community Center] you're not allowed to speak Greek; you can't do Greek-Macedonian dances. But we're Greek-Macedonians. At Aristotelis [the association of immigrants from Florina who identify as Greeks] we speak Macedonian among ourselves, but not very loudly. They say that it's a neutral club, but it's Greek neutral.

"We have a different culture from the Greeks. We can't be all the way Greek or all the way Macedonian. We belong to two races [*ratses*]. I don't want to give up what I am. I'm Greek in a way. I went to Greek schools; I learned the Greek ways. I don't want to be told, 'You're Macedonian and not Greek.' I don't want to be called names. It hurts. We can't say that Peloponnesians and Cretans don't exist. How can people say that *we* don't exist?

"Sometimes I think we just don't know who we are. Somehow we got lost."

"BORN-AGAIN MACEDONIANS"

One of the most interesting aspects of the study of the construction of national identity among local Macedonians from Florina living in Australia is the fact that a significant number of them change their national identity from Greek to Macedonian some time after their arrival in Australia.[26] These people have crossed the social boundary between the

[26] While this analysis focuses exclusively on the construction of a Macedonian national identity among people who previously had a Greek national identity, a similar (but much less traumatic) transformation has also taken place among people from the Republic of Macedonia who previously had a Yugoslav identity.

two ethnic or national groups and redefined themselves by shedding their old identity and assuming a new one, a process similar in many ways to that of religious conversion. As Berger and Luckmann point out (1967:157–63), conversion experiences generally involve dramatic transformations of a person's social reality. When people "switch worlds" and adopt a new national identity in this way, they need to find new significant others who are willing to accept their new identity. They also need to reinterpret the meaning of their past in order to bring it into line with their understanding of the present.

In a recent study entitled *Ethnic Options: Choosing Identities in America*, Mary Waters (1990) documents the fact that identities often change through time, both over the life cycle and across generations. Parents may try to hide or deny a particular identity that their children "rediscover" as they approach adulthood themselves. An identity may be adopted if world political events give it enhanced prestige, or conversely it may be shed if it becomes stigmatized. In most cases these changes in identity are not perceived by the actors themselves as changes but are seen as the correction of an error or the achievement of a new insight that is accurate in contrast to the earlier understanding that was mistaken.[27]

Given the common nationalist view of the immutability of identity, conversion from one identity to another is bound to raise serious questions of authenticity and legitimacy, for if national identity is a fact of nature, something determined by blood or by birth, then it is "unnatural," if not impossible, to change it. As Handler (1988:51) puts it, from a nationalist perspective people "cannot choose what they naturally are." The new identities people ascribe to themselves may be challenged or even rejected by others. This is particularly true when national identity is manipulated in an obvious way to serve personal self-interest (Sahlins 1989:223). When the construction of identity is contested in this way, the criteria people use to define their identity and assess its legitimacy are often explicitly cited. Such arguments over the relevance of various criteria for the determination of group membership make the process of identity formation unusually accessible to anthropological analysis.

People who are the most likely to experience this conversion from a Greek to a Macedonian national identity are men and women who grew up in Greece after the Civil War and then migrated to Australia as young adults in the late 1960s and the 1970s. These are the people for whom the conflict between an ethnic identity as local Macedonians, on

---

[27] According to Berger and Luckmann (1967:160) this realization often takes the form: "Then I *thought* . . . now I *know*."

the one hand, and a national identity as Greeks, on the other, is most acute; these are the people whose villages, whose families, whose very selves, have been divided by the need to choose between the mutually exclusive categories of Greek and Macedonian national identities. There are several factors that influence local Macedonians from Florina to change their national identity from Greek to Macedonian, just as there are several points in their lives when this change is most likely to occur. Of all the factors responsible for this conversion experience the most important clearly have to do with the multicultural nature of Australian society, which stands in sharp contrast to the nationalist emphasis on assimilation and homogeneity that characterizes most aspects of modern Greek society.

When they arrived in Australia, these local Macedonian immigrants from Florina encountered a well-established Macedonian community with its own institutions, organizations, and political leaders, and with a strong sense of Macedonian national identity. Many of the leaders of the Macedonian community in Australia were Aegean Macedonians from the same villages as these more recent immigrants. Other members of the Macedonian community were Vardar Macedonians from Yugoslavia. Many of the more recent immigrants from Florina had never met Vardar Macedonians until they came to Australia. In Greece they had always been taught that the people who lived across the border from them in Yugoslavia were "Serbs." They had no idea that they had relatives and fellow villagers living there. When he first met the Vardar Macedonians living across the street from him in Melbourne, one local Macedonian from Florina thought, "My God! These people are the same as we are!"

Often people from Florina realized only gradually that their decision to come to Australia was a permanent one. In many cases this realization played an important part in their development of a Macedonian national identity. In addition, the stigma and the fear that in Greece had always been associated with everything Macedonian began to disappear after several years in Australia. One immigrant from Florina remembered driving through the streets of Melbourne with his windows down playing Macedonian songs on his car stereo. When a police car pulled up next to him, he panicked and immediately turned off the music. Then he realized that "it wasn't a crime to be a Macedonian in a democratic country like Australia."

Another immigrant from Florina associated the emergence of his Macedonian national identity with becoming financially secure in his new home. "At first when we decided to come to Australia," he said, "we just wanted to leave Greece. We had no money, no fields, no work. So we just left. We came to Australia to fill our stomachs, to be well dressed and clean. We didn't come looking for Macedonia; we didn't come looking for identity. Then we got jobs; we got married; we bought cars and big houses. That's when we began to look for our identity. Here in Australia we realized we didn't have to be Greeks."

The death of a parent or other close relative still living in Greece often made it easier for a person to develop, or to express publicly, a Macedonian national identity. One man said, for example, that as soon as his elderly father (who still lived in Florina) died, he would change his name from Angelopoulos, the Greek name he had used officially all his life, to Gelev, his "real" Macedonian name.

Marriage is another important event that can contribute to a transformation in a person's sense of national identity.[28] When local Macedonians from Florina who have a Greek national identity emigrate to Australia and later marry other immigrants from Florina who have a strong sense of Macedonian national identity, they may develop a Macedonian national identity as well. This is often the case when their spouse has grown up in Australia or in the Republic of Macedonia, rather than in Greece.[29]

In many cases the development of a Macedonian national identity occurs when young people who have been raised as Greeks reach adulthood and undergo a kind of identity crisis in which they rebel against their parents' values and construct their own identity as independent adults. This often involves them in an exploration of their family history, a search for their "roots," a process that can be triggered by a visiting "their village" in Florina, by meeting some of their relatives in the Republic of Macedonia for the first time, or by hearing new versions of important events in Macedonian history—versions that are quite different from those they learned in school in Greece. A man who remembered a high school teacher in Florina saying that the Macedonian-fighters of the early twentieth century saved the people of Macedonia from the Bulgarians believes now that he learned the real truth when he came to Australia, that the Macedonian-fighters were sent from Athens to kill local Macedonians because they wanted a free Macedonia.

In still other cases people reject their Greek national identity and adopt a Macedonian one as a result of what they come to perceive as

---

[28] On the construction of a new social identity at marriage, see Berger and Kellner (1964).

[29] During my fieldwork in Melbourne I learned of only one person who had had a Macedonian identity and then developed a Greek identity. This man had married the daughter of a partisan who had been raised in Yugoslavia and who identified herself as a Macedonian. They raised their children as Macedonians. When his wife died, he remarried. His new wife was Greek. "I married a Greek," he says, "so I have to be Greek now." His children say he has become a *Grkoman*.

Greek nationalist propaganda. A woman from Florina remembered hearing on a Greek radio program in Melbourne that the Macedonian language had been created in 1944. She knew that was a lie because her grandmother had spoken that language all her life.

From the perspective of people who undergo this conversion experience, the development of a Macedonian national identity does not involve the construction of a new identity. Instead it is regarded as the discovery or realization of a true identity, which they had previously been unaware of. The most common image used to describe this conversion process is that of "waking up." People say they "awoke to their real Macedonian consciousness." They contrast their experience of "waking up" with that of their relatives and fellow villagers who remain "asleep" and continue to identify themselves as Greeks.[30] People who realize their "true" Macedonian identity in this way are sometimes referred to by other Macedonian's as "Masos who used to be *Grkomani.*"

Because national identity is defined as something permanent and immutable from the essentialist perspective which so often characterizes nationalist ideologies, people who change their national identity often become easy targets of ridicule and scorn. This is certainly true of those immigrants from Florina to Australia who identified themselves as Greeks in the past but now identify themselves as Macedonians. They are often referred to sarcastically by Greeks as "born-again Macedonians," "newly enlightened ones," or as "Jehovah's Witnesses."[31] Their conversion may also be attributed to having become paid agents of "Skopje" or to having been brainwashed by "Skopian" propaganda. From the Greek perspective, Greeks who "turn Macedonian" are simply regarded as traitors.

Maria Kondou: "I Don't Want Anything to Do with Greece Anymore"

Maria Kondou grew up in a village right on the border between Greece and Yugoslavia, about ten miles from Florina and ten miles from Bitola. She spoke Greek with her parents because her village was "pro-Greek." No one there spoke Macedonian in public; she couldn't even

[30] On this image of "awakening from sleep," see chapter 1, note 4.

[31] The use of religious imagery here not only suggests parallels between nationalism and religion in general; it also suggests that religious conversion is a much more widely accepted and understood phenomenon than conversion from one national identity to another. On the position of Jehovah's Witnesses in Greece, see Pollis (1987a, 1987b, 1992). On the relationship between nationalism and religion more widely, see Herzfeld (1992) and Kapferer (1988).

count to ten in Macedonian. But when she came to Australia in the early 1970s at age eighteen, she lived with her uncle's family, and they all spoke Macedonian. She was shocked; she couldn't believe it. It was as if she had been given a cold shower. Within a few years she could speak Macedonian fluently.

When Maria talked about her sense of identity, her face was flushed; her voice full of emotion.

"When I came to Australia, I would have said I was Greek because I grew up with the Greek ideology. I can't say I'm 100 percent Macedonian. I was born a Macedonian; I am a Macedonian. But it will take time for us to come to our senses. One thing is for certain though, we'll never be 100 percent Greeks, even if they cut off our heads.

"There was a wall. We were on the Greek side, but now the wall is falling. We remain up in the air, without a name. My village is still my home, but it's a Greek environment.

"Now I say I'm a Macedonian. I'm not a Greek-Macedonian. I realized I never was Greek; they just made us think we were. I'm fed up with the Greek ideology; I don't want anything to do with Greece anymore."

Two experiences were instrumental in helping Maria realize that she was a Macedonian. The first occurred in the early 1980s when her oldest child Kathy was attending a Greek elementary school in Melbourne. Maria and her husband had decided to send her to a Greek school because they thought they would return to Greece someday. On March 25, they went to school with Kathy to watch the children celebrate Greek Independence Day. When they entered the school and saw all the children in their blue and white uniforms standing beneath the posters of the heroes of the Greek War of Independence, Maria turned to her husband and said, "What are we doing? Are we going to go in there and shout, 'Long Live Greece!'? Let's go!" And they left. Kathy was baptized in the Greek church, but Maria's two younger children were baptized in the Macedonian church, and they are learning Macedonian and English, but not Greek.

"We were only fooling ourselves. I came here as a Greek, and then slowly I began to understand. Our instincts didn't let us shout, 'Long Live Greece!' any more. But why couldn't our parents have given us a hint about who we were? I had to come to Australia to find out that my grandmother was from Bitola."

The other experience that really affected Maria's sense of who she was took place in church one Sunday.

"We went to the Greek church because we were used to the chanting. But we went as Christians, not as Greeks. I went for religion, not politics. But once the Greek archbishop came to church and started saying,

'We Greeks should do this,' and 'We Greeks should do that.' I didn't like it. Now the priest says, 'Whoever speaks Macedonian can't take communion.'

"They know us; they know who we are. They know we speak that language. We speak Macedonian. We know Greek; but we don't speak it. We aren't in a Greek church or a Macedonian church; we're in an Orthodox church. Over the past ten years, 95 percent of the Aegean Macedonian women I know have left the Greek church for the Macedonian church. The Greeks drove us away."

Lou Kostidis: "How Can My Father's Father Be Kostovski and I Be Kostidis?"

Lou Kostidis owns a fish shop in the northern suburbs of Melbourne. The people who introduced me to Lou in the fall of 1991 told me he was a *Grkoman*. His father had been tortured and sent into exile by the Greeks after the Civil War. Lou did not want to talk to me about the Macedonian conflict; he was afraid.

Several months later I was suprised to see Lou again at a formal dinner dance held at the Macedonian Community Center in Epping in honor of the first Australian gathering of the Association of Child Refugees from Aegean Macedonia. It was the first time Lou had ever been to the Macedonian Community Center. He was sitting with Sam Mitrevski, his cousin's husband, who was involved with the United Macedonians of Victoria and with the local chapter of VMRO-DPMNE. Sam had been telling Lou stories about Gotse Delchev and the other heroes of the Ilinden Uprising, whose pictures hung on the Community Center walls. Lou said he wanted to learn to read Macedonian. He liked the patriotic Macedonian songs people were singing, but unlike most people there he did not know the words to them.

Two weeks after the dinner dance Lou agreed to speak with me at his house. Lou told me he had come to Australia in 1968 at age twenty-one. That was when he saw a Macedonian church and the Macedonian alphabet for the first time. Lou's father's father had been in Australia for many years. "We're not Greeks. We're a different nationality," he told Lou, but Lou just said, "Don't make trouble." When his grandfather died three years later, Lou went through his possessions. From his military discharge papers, Lou learned that his grandfather had served in the Greek army in Asia Minor in the 1920s. The name on all his grandfather's papers was Kostovski. Lou burned them. He was embarrassed, but now he regrets it. If he had known then that he was a Macedonian, he would have kept them. They prove he isn't Greek.

"How can my father's father be Kostovski," he asked, "and I be Kostidis?"

As I was leaving his house, Lou showed me a bronze relief of Alexander the Great that was hanging on the wall of his living room. He had bought it when he'd been a member of the Heidelberg Alexander Soccer Club, but now he supported Preston Makedonia. Then Lou showed me a small white doily decorated with the head of Gotse Delchev, which was displayed prominently on his mantle piece. He had taken it from the table at the dinner dance for the Child Refugees.[32]

Sam Mitrevski says that when he married Lou's cousin, he was strict with her relatives; he pushed them. "Lou used to be a *Grkoman*," Sam says, "but he's changing. He thinks for himself now."

Pete Filipov: "His Eyes Light Up When He Speaks Macedonian"

Pete Filipov has been active in the Macedonian community of Melbourne on both the political and the cultural fronts. His parents were from a village near Florina whose inhabitants had always identified themselves as Greeks.

Pete's father Philip Sahinis came to Melbourne in 1949; the rest of his family came in 1956 when Pete was ten years old. Philip Sahinis was one of the founders of the Greek Orthodox Church of Saints Cyril and Methodius in Preston. He was also one of the founders of the old Florina Association, which later became the United Villages Family Association. Pete says that his father spoke Macedonian at home and talked about "our people" and "the Greeks." He even told Pete not to marry a Greek. To other people, though, Pete's father always presented himself as a Greek. Now Pete says his father was a *Grkoman*. But it wasn't his fault; he didn't have any choice. The concept of being a Macedonian didn't exist for him back then. Pete's father hated the Communists, so he was pro-Greek. As he saw it, if he wasn't a Greek, then it meant he was a Communist. He believed that nothing Macedonian could ever be any good, but he resented always being looked down on by the Greeks.

As a boy Pete grew up believing strongly that he was Greek. He was a Greek from Macedonia or a Macedonian from Greece; it didn't matter. At that time there was no dichotomy between being Greek and being Macedonian. Pete was baptized Petros Sahinis, and that's the name he used until high school. Then when he started making more

[32] For other examples of the juxtaposition of Alexander the Great and Gotse Delchev, see p. 171.

Anglo-Australian friends, he was called Pete. He studied Greek at university in the 1970s; he liked to listen to Greek music and read Greek poetry.

In the late 1970s Pete spent six months in Florina visiting relatives. He saw how the local Macedonians were made to hate their own culture by the Greek state. It really disturbed him. That was when he began to read books like *The Autobiography of Malcolm X* and *Pedagogy of the Oppressed*. They helped him understand the oppressed mentality of the Macedonian people.

Pete has always loved the Macedonian language he grew up with. His wife says his eyes light up when he speaks Macedonian. In the mid-1980s Pete was invited to give a presentation on Macedonian at a conference on the role of foreign languages in the Australian schools. That was his first public appearance as a Macedonian. In 1986 Pete attended the Seminar on Macedonian Language, Literature, and Culture, which is held every summer in Ohrid. The following year, just before his first child was born, Pete changed his name from Petros Sahinis to Pete Filipov, so that his child would not be born with a Greek last name.

Pete writes poetry in Macedonian and in English. He wrote one poem about an aunt of his who was like a mother to him. He wrote it in Macedonian, in the village dialect that his aunt spoke. When his aunt's daughter—Pete's cousin—who still lives in Florina, heard the poem, she was furious. "If you want to write a poem in Bulgarian," she told him, "write it about your own mother!"

When Pete became active in the Macedonian community, many of his father's friends and fellow villagers accused him of being an autonomist and of going over to the Macedonian side for the money. In the early 1990s, at the height of the conflict between the Greek and the Macedonian communities in Melbourne, Pete Filipov spoke out publicly on behalf of the Macedonian cause several times. This prompted a few of his father's friends to write letters to the Greek newspaper in Melbourne expressing their outrage at what had happened to the son of Philip Sahinis, "a real Greek patriot" who was "proud of his Greek origin and his Greek name." One man, who had served in the Greek army with Pete's father, was particularly offended at "the anti-Greek propaganda" Pete was promoting. After observing sarcastically that until a few years ago Pete Filipov was named Petros Sahinis, he wrote that Philip Sahinis would roll over in his grave if he could see what his son was doing now. "Perhaps it is easy to use a Slavic name (Filipov) and make it your own," he concluded, "but it is humanly impossible to steal the name of our Macedonia and make it Skopian."

CONCLUSION

From the Greek nationalist perspective of the author of this letter, "Petros Sahinis" is really a Greek who has illegitimately adopted the Slavic name "Pete Filipov." In the same way, he argues, "the Skopians" are really Slavs who are attempting to appropriate illegitimately the Greek name "Macedonians." While Pete Filipov may have succeeded, the Macedonians, he insists, will fail.

Although the author of this letter perceptively recognizes certain parallels between the construction of national identity at the individual and at the national level, his predictions as to the future course of the Macedonian confict appear to have proved wrong. Recent events on the international political scene suggest that just as Pete Filipov succeeded in constructing an individual identity as Pete Filipov, so the Macedonians will succeed in establishing a national identity as Macedonians. At an individual level a man named Petros Sahinis can legally change his name to Pete Filipov without difficulty in Australia (although he could not do so in Greece). At a collective level the governments of Canada and Australia with their explicitly multicultural policies accept the principle of self-ascription and have recognized the existence of Macedonians as an ethnic group. Macedonian diaspora communities in these and other countries, therefore, are generally known as Macedonian communities, with only the Greek community raising its voice in protest.[33] Greece, however, with its nationalist ideology of ethnic homogeneity and purity continues to deny the existence of a Macedonian minority within its borders, a position that will prove increasingly difficult to maintain as Greece seeks to become a more integral part of the European Union.

In the international political arena the issue is somewhat more complex. The recognition of ethnic or national minorities is one thing; the recognition of states another. International organizations like the Conference on Security and Cooperation in Europe, which accept the principle of self-ascription, have generally recognized the existence of a Macedonian minority in Greece. It is at this level of the Macedonian conflict that the Macedonian transnational community has played a particularly important role and has achieved some degree of success.

[33] A significant exception to this generalization has been the March 1993 decision of the Australian government to begin referring to Australia's Macedonian community in all official contexts as "Slav-Macedonians." This decision came in response to the wave of criticism Australia's large Greek community leveled at the Australian government for its recognition of the "Former Yugoslav Republic of Macedonia."

International organizations, however, have been much slower to recognize the existence of the Republic of Macedonia as an independent and sovereign state. This is the level at which Greek opposition has proved most effective. For a long time Greece pressured international organizations like the European Union and the United Nations not to recognize the Republic of Macedonia under its constitutional name. It also delayed significantly the recognition of the republic by individual countries with large Greek diaspora communities like the United States, Canada, and Australia. By the spring of 1994, however, the Republic of Macedonia had succeeded in achieving widespread international recognition, although controversy still surrounds the issue of what its permanent official name will be. And while the conflict between Greeks and Macedonians over which group has the right to identify itself as Macedonian may have different outcomes in the different arenas in which it occurs, the arguments are the same whether they take place on the floor of the United Nations General Assembly in New York, at meetings of the foreign ministers of the European Union in Brussels, in coffeeshops in Florina, or at soccer games and village picnics in Melbourne.

It is my hope that the detailed analysis presented in this chapter has demonstrated the complexity of the process of identity formation as it takes place at the individual level among local Macedonian immigrants from Florina to Melbourne. This same complexity characterizes the lives and identities of Macedonians in other parts of the world, as well as those of many other people who are members of ethnic minorities and diaspora communities in today's transnational world. These people are caught between mutually exclusive national identities. They are marginal participants in several national cultures and full participants in none, people who are struggling to construct a coherent sense of themselves from a complex, multilayered set of identities—class, religious, regional, ethnic, and national. Although these identities may coexist easily on some occasions, they conflict sharply on others, and this conflict often brings with it a great deal of uncertainty, alienation, and pain.

It is also my hope that the analysis presented here has convincingly exposed the dangers of oversimplified nationalist ideologies with their explanations of national identity in terms of some natural or spiritual essence. In addition I hope it has exposed the weaknesses of earlier anthropological approaches to the study of identity with their arguments that people are members of ethnic or national groups because they share some set of common cultural traits. Only by rejecting both these approaches are we in a position to understand the complex historical, political, social, and cultural processes by which individuals construct and reconstruct the identities that give meaning to their lives.

For in the last analysis it is only with tolerance and a respect for the self-ascribed nature of ethnic and national identities that we can avoid the destructive tendency inherent in all nationalist ideologies to impose definitions of national identity from above, from the outside, definitions that all too often conflict with those arrived at through a process of self-ascription. Local Macedonians live in many different places—the Republic of Macedonia, Bulgaria, Greece, Canada, and Australia. They define themselves in many different ways—"our people," local Macedonians, Greek-Macedonians, Aegean Macedonians, Greeks, and Macedonians. *"Grkomani,"* and "Skopians," however, are not terms of self-ascription. People from Florina who identify themselves as Greeks are not *"Grkomani"*; they are Greeks. Similarly people from Florina who identify themselves as Macedonians are not "Skopians"; they are Macedonians.

The dispute between Greeks and Macedonians over which group has the right to identify itself as Macedonian is a dispute between the proponents of two nationalist ideologies over the possession of national identities, histories, and cultures, all of which from a nationalist perspective are regarded as the mutually exclusive property of one nation or the other. It is a dispute in which two nations have each attempted to place a trademark or copyright on what they consider to be their own name, their own famous ancestors, and their own national emblems. From an anthropological perspective, however, we can see that in this dispute two different national identities and cultures are being constructed from the same "primordial sentiments" (Geertz 1973d), from the same set of powerful symbols. And while territory must be the mutually exclusive possession of one state or another—a particular village can only be located in Greece or in the Republic of Macedonia—two different cultures can coexist in one place, just as two different peoples with two different nationalities can share the same name. From an anthropological perspective in which symbols can have more than one meaning, names more than one referent, there can be two kinds of Macedonians—Macedonians (in a regional sense) who are Greeks and Macedonians (in a national sense) who are not Greeks. Similarly, there can be two Macedonias—the Republic of Macedonia, an independent country in the central Balkans, and Greek Macedonia, a region in northern Greece.

While such a solution may create some confusion, it is clearly preferable to a solution that denies Macedonians who are *not* Greeks, or Macedonians who *are* Greeks, the right to identify themselves as Macedonians. It is also preferable to a solution that, in what could be called a kind of symbolic ethnic cleansing, simply denies the existence of a Macedonian nation and a Macedonian minority in Greece. For that solution is an expression of the same kind of ethnic nationalism that in times of economic chaos and political collapse can all too easily lead to a literal, not just a symbolic, form of ethnic cleansing, the kind of ethnic cleansing we have recently witnessed, to our horror, in the former Yugoslavia and other parts of the world as well.

Acton, John E. E. D. A.
  1967   *Essays in the Liberal Interpretation of History: Selected Papers, by Lord Acton*. Chicago: University of Chicago Press.
Adams, John Paul
  1980   The Royal Macedonian Tomb at Vergina: An Historical Interpretation. *Ancient World*. 3:67–72.
  1983   The *Larnakes* from Tomb II at Vergina. *Archaeological News*. 12:1–7.
Agelopoulos, G.
  1993   "Mothers of the Nation": Gender and Ethnicity in Greek Macedonia. Paper presented at a conference on "Ethnicity and Anthropology." Amsterdam.
Anderson, Benedict
  1983   *Imagined Communities*. London: Verso.
  1991   *Imagined Communities*. Rev. ed. London: Verso.
  1994   Exodus. *Critical Inquiry*. 20:314–27.
Andonov-Poljanski, Hristo, ed.
  1985   *Documents on the Struggle of the Macedonian People for Independence and a Nation-State*. 2 vols. Skopje: Kultura.
Andonovski, Hristo
  1976   The First Macedonian Primer between the Two World Wars—The Abecedar. *Macedonian Review*. 6:64–69.
  1978   The Ancient Macedonians and Alexander the Great. *Macedonian Review*. 8:10–15.
  1979   Rich Archaeological Discoveries in Vergina. *Macedonian Review*. 9:109–12.
  1985a   Makedonističkoto dviženje vo Kostursko. *Makedonija*. 387:26.
  1985b   Foreword. In *Abecedar: Jubilejno izdanie, 1925–1985*. Skopje: Makedonska revija.
Andriotes, Nicholas P.
  1957   *The Confederate State of Skopje and Its Language*. Athens.
Andronikos, Manolis
  1977   Vergina: The Royal Graves in the Great Tumulus. *Athens Annals of Archaeology*. 10:1–72. Also published as *The Royal Graves at Vergina*. Athens: K. Mihalas, A.E., 1978.
  1978   Regal Treasures from a Macedonian Tomb. *National Geographic*. 154:54–77.
  1980a   *The Search for Alexander: An Exhibition*. Boston: Little, Brown.
  1980b   The Royal Tombs at Aigai (Vergina). In Miltiades B. Hatzopoulos and Louisa D. Loukopoulos, eds. *Philip of Macedon*. Athens: Ekdotike Athenon. Pp. 188–231.

Andronikos, Manolis (*cont'd*)

1984 *Vergina: The Royal Tombs and the Ancient City*. Athens: Ekdotike Athenon.

Angelopoulos, A.

1979 Population Distribution of Greece Today according to Language, National Consciousness, and Religion. *Balkan Studies*. 20:123–32.

Anonymous

1980 Macedonians. In Stephen Thernstrom, ed. *Harvard Encyclopedia of American Ethnic Groups*. Cambridge, MA: Harvard University Press. Pp. 690–94.

Apostolski, Mihailo, and Haralampie Polenakovich

1974 *The Socialist Republic of Macedonia*. Skopje: Macedonian Review Editions.

Appadurai, Arjun

1990 Disjuncture and Difference in the Global Cultural Economy. *Public Culture*. 2:1–24.

Armstrong, John

1982 *Nations before Nationalism*. Chapel Hill: University of North Carolina Press.

Ata, A. W.

1986 *Cultural Pluralism, Ethnocentricity, and Inter-ethnic Relationships*. Melbourne: Catholic Intercultural Renewal Center.

Australian Bureau of Statistics

1991 *The Overseas-born in Victoria*. Canberra.

Australian Macedonian Weekly. Macedonian newspaper published in Melbourne, Australia.

Badian, E.

1982 Greeks and Macedonians. In *Macedonia and Greece in Late Classical and Early Hellenistic Times*. Studies in the History of Art. Vol. 10. Washington, DC: National Gallery of Art. Pp. 33–51.

Badone, Ellen

1992 The Construction of National Identity in Brittany and Quebec. *American Ethnologist*. 19:806–17.

Baerentzen, Lars

1987 The "Paidomazoma" and the Queen's Camp. In Lars Baerentzen, John O. Iatrides, and Ole L. Smith, eds. *Studies in the History of the Greek Civil War*. Copenhagen: Museum Tusculanum Press.

Balamaci, Nicholas S.

1989 What's in a Name? How to Lose an Ethnic Group. *Ethnic Forum*. 9: 65–74.

1991 Can the Vlachs Write Their Own History? *Journal of the Hellenic Diaspora*. 17:9–36.

Barker, Elizabeth

1950 *Macedonia: Its Place in Balkan Power Politics*. London: Oxford University Press.

Barth, Fredrik

1969 *Ethnic Groups and Boundaries*. Boston: Little, Brown.

Baudrillard, Jean
  1983   *Simulations.* New York: Semiotext.
Berger, Peter, and Hansfried Kellner
  1964   Marriage and the Construction of Reality. *Diogenes.* 46:1–24.
Berger, Peter, and Thomas Luckmann
  1967   *The Social Construction of Reality.* Garden City, NY: Anchor Books.
Blagoev, Spiridon
  1986   Colonization of the Border Territories of Aegean Macedonia, 1947–
          1965. *Review.* 30:183–97.
Borneman, John
  1992   *Belonging in the Two Berlins: Kin, State, Nation.* Cambridge: At the
          University Press.
Borza, Eugene N.
  1981   The Macedonian Royal Tombs at Vergina: Some Cautionary Notes.
          Archaeological News. 10 (4):73–87.
  1982a   The History and Archaeology of Macedonia: Retrospect and Pros-
          pect. In *Macedonia and Greece in Late Classical and Early Hellenistic
          Times.* Studies in the History of Art. Vol. 10. Washington, DC:
          National Gallery of Art. Pp. 17–30.
  1982b   Those Vergina Tombs Again. *Archaeological News.* 11:8–10.
  1987   The Royal Macedonian Tombs and the Paraphernalia of Alexander
          the Great. *Phoenix.* 41:105–21.
  1990   *In the Shadow of Olympus: The Emergence of Macedon.* Princeton, NJ:
          Princeton University Press.
Bottomley, Gillian
  1979   *After the Odyssey: A Study of Greek Australians.* Brisbane: University of
          Queensland Press.
  1992   *From Another Place: Migration and the Politics of Culture.* Cambridge:
          At the University Press.
Bottomley, Gillian, and John Lechte
  1990   Nation and Diversity in France. *Journal of Intercultural Studies.* 11:
          49–72.
Bourdieu, Pierre
  1977   *Outline of a Theory of Practice.* Cambridge: At the University Press.
  1991   *Language and Symbolic Power.* Cambridge, MA: Harvard University
          Press.
Brailsford, H. N.
  1971   *Macedonia: Its Races and Their Future.* New York: Arno Press. Origi-
          nally published 1906.
Brass, Paul R.
  1976   Ethnicity and Nationality Formation. *Ethnicity.* 3:225–41.
  1985   *Ethnic Groups and the State.* London: Croom Helm.
Braudel, Fernand
  1972   *The Mediterranean and the Mediterranean World in the Age of Philip II.*
          New York: Harper and Row.

Brown, Keith
  1992   Learning to Forget: The Many Pasts of Macedonia. Paper presented
          at the Eighth International Conference of Europeanists. Chicago.
Bulgarian Academy of Sciences
  1978   *Macedonia: Documents and Material*. Sofia.
Bureau of Immigration Research
  1990a   *Community Profiles: Greece-Born*. Canberra: Australian Government
          Publication Service.
  1990b   *Community Profiles: Yugoslavia-Born*. Canberra: Australian Govern-
          ment Publication Service.
  1991   *Birthplace, Language, Religion, 1971–86*. Canberra: Australian Govern-
          ment Publication Service.
Castles, Stephen, Mary Kalantzis, Bill Cope, and Michael Morrissey
  1990   *Mistaken Identity: Multiculturalism and the Demise of Nationalism in
          Australia*. Sydney: Pluto Press.
Chimbos, Peter D.
  1980   *The Canadian Odyssey: The Greek Experience in Canada*. Toronto:
          McClelland and Stewart.
Clifford, James
  1988   *The Predicament of Culture*. Cambridge, MA: Harvard University Press.
Clogg, Richard
  1979   *A Short History of Modern Greece*. Cambridge: At the University Press.
Clyne, Michael
  1991   *Community Languages in the Australian Experience*. Cambridge: At the
          University Press.
Connor, Walker
  1972   Nation-Building or Nation-Destroying. *World Politics*. 24:319–55.
  1973   The Politics of Ethnonationalism. *Journal of International Affairs*.
          27:1–21.
  1977   Ethnonationalism in the First World: The Present in Historical Per-
          spective. In Milton J. Esman, ed. *Ethnic Conflict in the Western World*.
          Ithaca, NY: Cornell University Press. Pp. 19–45.
  1978   A Nation Is a Nation, Is a State, Is an Ethnic Group Is a. . . . *Ethnic and
          Racial Studies*. 1:377–400.
Coronil, Ferdinand
  1992   Beyond Occidentalism: Towards Post-Imperial Geohistorical Cate-
          gories. In *Power: Thinking through the Disciplines*. (Conference Pa-
          pers). Comparative Study of Social Transformations Working Paper
          no. 72. Ann Arbor: University of Michigan. Pp. 1–29.
Coufoudakis, Van
  1992   The Future of Hellenic Macedonia. *Makedhonia*. 39(1):5–9, 24.
Cowan, Jane K.
  1990   *Dance and the Body Politic in Northern Greece*. Princeton, NJ: Princeton
          University Press.
Crampton, Richard J.
  1983   *Bulgaria, 1878–1918: A History*. Boulder, CO: East European Mono-
          graphs.

Crossland, R. A.
  1982 Linguistic Problems of the Balkan Area in the Late Prehistoric and Early Classical Periods. *Cambridge Ancient History*, 2nd ed., vol. 3, pt. 1, chap. 20c. Cambridge: At the University Press.
Dakin, Douglas
  1966 *The Greek Struggle in Macedonia, 1897–1913*. Thessaloniki: Institute for Balkan Studies.
Danforth, Loring M.
  1984 The Ideological Context of the Search for Continuities in Greek Culture. *Journal of Modern Greek Studies*. 2:53–85.
  1989 *Firewalking and Religious Healing: The Anastenaria of Northern Greece and the American Firewalking Movement*. Princeton, NJ: Princeton University Press.
  1990 The Denial of Macedonian Identity at the First International Congress on Macedonian Studies. Paper presented at the 89th Meeting of the American Anthropological Association. New Orleans, LA.
Daskalakis, Ap.
  1965 *The Hellenism of the Ancient Macedonians*. Thessaloniki: Institute for Balkan Studies.
De Bray, R. G. A.
  1980 *Guide to the Slavonic Languages*. Part 1. Columbus, OH: Slavica Publishers.
Denich, Bette
  1994 Dismembering Yugoslavia: Nationalist Ideologies and the Symbolic Revival of Genocide. *American Ethnologist*. 21:367–90.
De Vos, George, and Lola Romanucci-Ross, eds.
  1975 *Ethnic Identity: Cultural Communities and Change*. Palo Alto, CA: Mayfield.
Diaspora: A Journal of Transnational Studies. Oxford: Oxford University Press.
Dimevski, Slavko
  1973 The Archbishopric of Ohrid. *Macedonian Review*. 3:39–46.
Douglas, Mary
  1966 *Purity and Danger: An Analysis of Concepts of Pollution and Taboo*. London: Routledge and Kegan Paul.
Drummond, Lee
  1980 The Cultural Continuum: A Theory of Intersystems. *Man*. (N.S.) 15:352–74.
Eleftherotypia. Greek newspaper published in Athens.
Esman, Milton J.
  1977 Perspectives on Ethnic Conflict in Industrialized Societies. In Milton J. Esman, ed. *Ethnic Conflict in the Western World*. Ithaca, NY: Cornell University Press. Pp. 371–90.
  1986 Diasporas and International Relations. In Gabriel Sheffer, ed. *Modern Diasporas in International Politics*. New York: St. Martin's Press. Pp. 333–49.
Esman, Milton J., ed.
  1977 *Ethnic Conflict in the Western World*. Ithaca, NY: Cornell University Press.

Ethnikos Kiryx. Greek newspaper published in Melbourne, Australia.

Fabian, Johannes
  1983 *Time and the Other: How Anthropology Makes Its Object*. New York: Columbia University Press.

Featherstone, Mike, ed.
  1990a *Global Culture: Nationalism, Globalization, and Modernity*. London: Sage.
  1990b Global Culture: An Introduction. In *Global Culture: Nationalism, Globalization, and Modernity*. London: Sage. Pp. 1–14.

Fishman, Joshua
  1972 *Language and Nationalism*. Rowley, MA: Newbury House.

Fishman, Joshua, Michael H. Gertner, Esther G. Lowy, and William G. Milán
  1985 *The Rise and Fall of the Ethnic Revival: Perspectives on Language and Ethnicity*. Amsterdam: Mouton.

Foreign Broadcast Information Service Daily Report. Eastern Europe.

Foster, Lois, and David Stockley
  1984 *Multiculturalism: The Changing Australian Paradigm*. Clevedon, England: Multicultural Matters.
  1988 *Australian Multiculturalism: A Documentary History and Critique*. Clevedon, England: Multicultural Matters.

Fowler, Don D.
  1987 Uses of the Past: Archaeology in the Service of the State. *American Antiquity*. 52 (2):229–48.

Fox, Richard G., ed.
  1990 *Nationalist Ideologies and the Production of National Cultures*. American Ethnological Society Monograph Series, no. 2. Washington, DC: American Anthropological Association.

Fox, Robin Lane
  1980 *The Search for Alexander*. Boston: Little, Brown.

Fredricksmeyer, E. A.
  1981 Again the So-Called Tomb of Philip II. *American Journal of Archaeology*. 85:330–34.

Friedman, Victor
  1975 Macedonian Language and Nationalism during the Nineteenth and Early Twentieth Centuries. *Balkanistica*. 2:83–98.
  1985 The Sociolinguistics of Literary Macedonian. *International Journal of Language*. 52:31–57.
  1986 Linguistics, Nationalism, and Literary Languages: A Balkan Perspective. In Victor Raskin and Peter Bjorkman, eds. *The Real World Linguist: Linguistic Applications in the 1980s*. Norwood, NJ: Ablex. Pp. 287–305.
  1993 The First Philological Conference for the Establishment of the Macedonian Alphabet and the Macedonian Literary Language: Its Precedents and Consequences. In Joshua Fishman, ed. *The Earliest Stage of Language Planning: The "First Congress" Phenomenon*. Berlin: Mouton de Gruyter. Pp. 159–80.

Gans, Herbert J.
  1991   Symbolic Ethnicity: The Future of Ethnic Groups and Cultures in
          America. In Norman R. Yetman, ed. *Majority and Minority: The Dy-*
          namics of Race and Ethnicity in American Life. 5th ed. Boston: Allyn and
          Bacon. Pp. 430–43.
Geertz, Clifford
  1973a   Religion as a Cultural System. In *The Interpretation of Cultures*. New
          York: Basic Books. Pp. 87–125.
  1973b   Ideology as a Cultural System. In *The Interpretation of Cultures*. New
          York: Basic Books. Pp. 193–233.
  1973c   After the Revolution: The Fate of Nationalism in the New States. In
          The Interpretation of Cultures. New York: Basic Books. Pp. 234–54.
  1973d   The Integrative Revolution: Primordial Sentiments and Civil Politics
          in the New States. In *The Interpretation of Cultures*. New York: Basic
          Books. Pp. 255–310.
Gellner, Ernest
  1964   *Thought and Change*. London: Weidenfeld and Nicolson.
  1983   *Nations and Nationalism*. Oxford: Basil Blackwell.
  1987   *Culture, Identity, and Politics*. Cambridge: At the University Press.
Gessner, Volkmar, and Angelika Schade
  1990   Conflicts of Culture in Cross-Border Legal Relations: The Concep-
          tion of a Research Topic in the Sociology of Law. In Mike Feather-
          stone, ed. *Global Culture: Nationalism, Globalization, and Modernity*.
          London: Sage. Pp. 253–78.
Goodman, David, D. J. O'Hearn, and Chris Wallace-Crabbe
  1991   *Multicultural Australia: The Challenges of Change*. Newham, Victoria:
          Scribe.
Green, Peter
  1989   The Macedonian Connection. In *Classical Bearings: Interpreting*
          Ancient History and Culture. New York: Thames and Hudson. Pp.
          151–64.
Greenfield, Liah
  1992   *Nationalism: Five Roads to Modernity*. Cambridge, MA: Harvard Uni-
          versity Press.
Guidieri, Remo, Francesco Pellizzi, and Stanley J. Tambiah, eds.
  1988   *Ethnicities and Nations: Processes of Interethnic Relations in Latin Amer-*
          ica, Southeast Asia, and the Pacific. Austin: University of Texas Press.
Gupta, Akhil
  1992   The Song of the Nonaligned World: Transnational Identities and the
          Reinscription of Space in Late Capitalism. *Cultural Anthropology*.
          7:63–79.
Hall, Stuart
  1991   The Local and the Global: Globalization and Ethnicity. In Anthony
          King, ed. *Culture, Globalization and the World-System: Contemporary*
          Conditions for the Representation of Identity. Binghamton, NY: Depart-
          ment of Art History, SUNY at Binghamton. Pp. 19–39.

Hall, Stuart, et al.
 1978   *Policing the Crisis: Mugging, the State, and Law and Order*. London: Macmillan.
Hammond, N. G. L.
 1967   *A History of Greece to 332 B.C.* Oxford: Clarendon Press.
 1982   The Evidence for the Identity of the Royal Tombs at Vergina. In W. Lindsay Adams and Eugene N. Borza, eds. *Philip II, Alexander the Great and the Macedonian Heritage*. Lanham, MD: University Press of America. Pp. 111–27.
 1986   *A History of Greece to 332 B.C.* 3rd ed. Oxford: Clarendon Press.
Hammond, N. G. L. and G. T. Griffith
 1979   *A History of Macedonia*. Vol. 2, *550–336 B.C.* Oxford: Clarendon Press.
Handler, Richard
 1985   On Dialogue and Destructive Analysis: Problems in Narrating Nationalism and Ethnicity. *Journal of Anthropological Research*. 41: 171–82.
 1988   *Nationalism and the Politics of Culture in Quebec*. Madison: University of Wisconsin Press.
Handler, Richard, and Jocelyn Linnekin
 1984   Tradition, Genuine or Spurious. *Journal of American Folklore*. 97:273–90.
Hanson, Allan
 1989   The Making of the Maori: Culture Invention and Its Logic. *American Anthropologist*. 91:890–902.
 1991   Reply to Langdon, Levine, and Linnekin. *American Anthropologist*. 93:449–50.
Hatzopoulos, Miltiades, M., and Louisa D. Loukopoulos, eds.
 1980   *Philip of Macedon*. Athens: Ekdotike Athenon.
Hayden, Robert M.
 1992   Constitutional Nationalism in the Formerly Yugoslav Republics. *Slavic Review*. 5:654–73.
Hechter, Michael
 1978   Group Formation and the Cultural Division of Labor. *American Journal of Sociology*. 84:293–318.
Herzfeld, Michael
 1982   *Ours Once More: Folklore, Ideology, and the Making of Modern Greece*. Austin: University of Texas Press.
 1987   *Anthropology through the Looking Glass: Critical Ethnography on the Margins of Europe*. Cambridge: At the University Press.
 1991   *A Place in History: Social and Monumental Time in a Cretan Town*. Princeton, NJ: Princeton University Press.
 1992   *The Social Production of Indifference*. Chicago: University of Chicago Press.
Hill, Peter
 1988   Macedonians. In James Jupp, ed. *The Australian People*. North Ryde: Angus & Robertson. Pp. 685–91.
 1989   *The Macedonians in Australia*. Carlisle, Western Australia: Hesperian Press.

Hobsbawm, Eric
  1990   *Nations and Nationalism since 1780: Programme, Myth, Reality.* Cambridge: At the University Press.
Hobsbawm, Eric, and Terence Ranger
  1983   *The Invention of Tradition.* Cambridge: At the University Press.
Horowitz, Donald L.
  1985   *Ethnic Groups in Conflict.* Berkeley: University of California Press.
Human Rights Watch/Helsinki
  1990   *Destroying Ethnic Identity: The Turks of Greece.* New York.
  1991   *Destroying Ethnic Identity: Selective Persecution of Macedonians in Bulgaria.* New York.
  1993   *Greece. Free Speech on Trial: Government Stifles Dissent on Macedonia.* New York.
  1994a   *Human Rights in the Former Yugoslav Republic of Macedonia.* New York.
  1994b   *Denying Ethnic Identity: The Macedonians of Greece.* New York.
Iatrides, John O.
  1993   As Others See It: American Perceptions of Greece's "Macedonian Problem." Paper presented at the Modern Greek Studies Association Symposium. Berkeley, CA.
International Commission to Inquire into the Causes and Conduct of the Balkan Wars
  1914   *Report of the International Commission to Inquire into the Causes and Conduct of the Balkan Wars.* Washington, DC: Carnegie Endowment for International Peace, no. 4. Reprint 1993.
Jakubowicz, A.
  1981   State and Ethnicity: Multiculturalism as Ideology. *Australian and New Zealand Journal of Sociology.* 17:4–13.
Jelavich, Barbara
  1983   *History of the Balkans.* 2 vols. Cambridge: At the University Press.
Jupp, James, ed.
  1984   *Ethnic Politics in Australia.* Sydney: George Allen & Unwin.
  1988   *The Australian People.* North Ryde: Angus & Robertson.
Jusdanis, Gregory
  n.d.   Beyond National Culture. Unpublished manuscript.
  1991   Greek Americans and the Diaspora. *Diaspora.* 1:209–23.
Just, Roger
  1989   Triumph of the Ethnos. In Elizabeth Tonkin, Malcolm Chapman, and Maryon McDonald, eds. *History and Ethnicity.* Association of Social Anthropologists Monographs 27. London: Routledge and Kegan Paul. Pp. 71–78
Kalléris, J. N.
  1954–76 *Les anciens Macédoniens: Étude linguistique et historique.* 2 vols. Athens: Institut français d'Athènes.
Kapferer, Bruce
  1988   *Legends of People, Myths of State.* Washington, DC: Smithsonian Institution Press.

Karakasidou, Anastasia
   1992 *Fields of Wheat, Hills of Shrub: Agrarian Development and the Dialectics of Ethnicity and Nationality in Northern Greece, 1870–1990.* Ph.D. dissertation. Columbia University.
   1993 Politicizing Culture: Negating Ethnic Identity in Greek Macedonia. *Journal of Modern Greek Studies.* 11:1–28.
   1994 Sacred Scholars, Profane Advocates: Intellectuals Molding National Consciousness in Greece. *Identities.* 1:35–61.
Katačić, Radoslav
   1976 *Ancient Languages of the Balkans.* The Hague: Mouton.
Keefe, Eugene K., et al.
   1977 *Area Handbook for Greece.* Washington, DC: Foreign Area Studies of the American University.
Kemper, Steven
   1991 *The Presence of the Past: Chronicles, Politics, and Culture in Sinhala Life.* Ithaca, NY: Cornell University Press.
King, Anthony D., ed.
   1991 *Culture, Globalization and the World-System: Contemporary Conditions for the Representation of Identity.* Binghamton, NY: Department of Art History, SUNY at Binghamton.
King, Robert R.
   1973 *Minorities under Communism.* Cambridge, MA: Harvard University Press.
Kini Ghnomi. Local newspaper published in Florina.
Kitromilides, Paschalis
   1989 "Imagined Communities" and the Origins of the National Question in the Balkans. *European History Quarterly.* 19:149–94.
Kofos, Evangelos
   1964 *Nationalism and Communism in Macedonia.* Thessaloniki: Institute for Balkan Studies.
   1986 The Macedonian Question: The Politics of Mutation. *Balkan Studies.* 27:157–72.
   1989 National Heritage and National Identity in Nineteenth- and Twentieth-Century Macedonia. *European History Quarterly.* 19:229–67.
   1990 National Heritage and National Identity in Macedonia (19th to 20th Centuries). In Anastasios Tamis, ed. *Macedonian Hellenism.* Melbourne: River Seine Press. Pp. 54–85.
   1994 *The Vision of Greater Macedonia.* Thessaloniki: Friends of the Museum of the Macedonian Struggle.
Kostopoulos, Tasos, Leonidas Embeirikos, and Dimitris Lithoxoou
   1992 *Ellinikos ethnikismos: Makedhoniko zitima.* Athens: Kinisis Aristeron.
Kramer, Christina
   1993 Language in Exile: The Macedonians of Toronto. In Eran Fraenkel and Christina Kramer, eds. *Language Contact—Language Conflict.* New York: Peter Lang. Pp. 157–83.
Landau, Jacob
   1986 Diaspora and Language. In Gabriel Sheffer, ed. *Modern Diasporas in International Politics.* New York: St. Martin's Press. Pp. 75–102.

Larmeroux, J.
1918   *La Politique extérieure de l'Autriche-Hongrie, 1875–1908.* 2 vols. Paris: Plon Noarrite Cie.

Layne, Linda L.
1994   *Home and Homeland: The Dialogics of Tribal and National Identities in Jordan.* Princeton, NJ: Princeton University Press.

Lehman, Phyllis W.
1980   The So-Called Tombs of Philip II: A Different Interpretation. *American Journal of Archaeology.* 84:527–31.

Linnekin, Jocelyn
1991   Cultural Invention and the Dilemma of Authenticity. *American Anthropologist.* 93:446–49.

Lithoxoou, Dimitris
1992a   Dhio anekdhota dokoumenda yia tin istoria ke ti sinidhisi tis slavomakedhonikis mionotitas kata tin prometaksiki periodho. *Ektos Orion.* June 6. Pp. 36–42.
1992b   I mitriki ghlossa ton katikon tou Ellinikou tmimatos tis Makedhonias prin ke meta tin andalaghi plithismon. *Theseis* 38:38–66.
1993   I politiki tou eksellinismou tis makedhonikis mionotitas ston mesopolemo. *Politis.* 124:32–38.

Loukakis, A.
1981   *People of Australia: The Greeks.* Sydney: Hodder and Stoughton.

Lunt, Horace G.
1952   *A Grammar of the Macedonian Literary Language.* Skopje: Državno Knigoizdatelstvo.
1959   The Creation of Standard Macedonian: Some Facts and Attitudes. *Anthropological Linguistics.* 1 (5):19–26.
1984   Some Sociolinguistic Aspects of Macedonian and Bulgarian. In Benjamin Stolz, I. R. Titunik, and Lubomir Dolezel, eds. *Language and Literary Theory.* Ann Arbor: Michigan Slavic Publications. Pp. 83–132.

MacDermott, Mercia
1978   *Freedom or Death: The Life of Gotse Delchev.* London: Journeyman Press.

Macedonia: History and Politics (MHP)
n.d.   Athens: Center for Macedonians Abroad and the Society for Macedonian Studies. Ekdotike Athenon.

The Macedonian Affair: A Historical Review of the Attempts to Create a Counterfeit Nation.
n.d.   Athens: Institute of International Political and Strategic Studies.

Macedonian Information and Liaison Service.

Macedonian Newsmagazine. Skopje.

Macedonian Review. Skopje.

Mackridge, Peter
1985   *The Modern Greek Language.* Oxford: Clarendon Press.

Makedhonia. Official Publication of the Pan-Macedonian Association of the United States and Canada.

Makedhoniki Foni. Monthly Publication of the Pan-Macedonian Association of Melbourne and Victoria. Fitzroy, Victoria.

Makedhoniki Zoi. Thessaloniki.

Makedonija. Skopje: Matica na Iselenicite ot Makedonija.

Malkki, Liisa
    1992   National Geographic: The Rooting of Peoples and the Territorialization of National Identity among Scholars and Refugees. *Cultural Anthropology.* 7:24–44.
    1994   Citizens of Humanity: Internationalism and the Imagined Community of Nations. *Diaspora.* 3:41–68.

Martis, Nicolaos K.
    1983   *The Falsification of Macedonian History.* Athens: "Graphic Arts" of Athanassiades Bros.

Mavrogordatos, George
    1983   *Stillborn Republic: Social Conditions and Party Strategies in Greece, 1912–1936.* Berkeley: University of California Press.

McDonald, Maryon
    1989   *"We Are Not French!" Language, Culture, and Identity in Brittany.* London: Routledge and Kegan Paul.

McNeill, William H.
    1986   *Polyethnicity and National Unity in World History.* Toronto: University of Toronto Press.

Menounos, John
    1992   Greece of the Five Continents. *Makedhoniki Zoi.* Vol. 318. English Supplement. Pp. 2–4.

Mertzos, N. I.
    1987   *Emis i Makedhones.* Athens: I. Sideris.

Messing, Gordon M.
    1981   *Tsinganos* and *Yiftos*: Some Speculations on the Greek Gypsies. *Byzantine and Modern Greek Studies.* 7:155–67.

Minčev, Nikola
    1972   The Ideals of Goce Delčev Are Built into the Macedonian Reality of Today. *Macedonian Review.* 2:144–54.

Misirkov, Krste
    1974   *On Macedonian Matters.* Skopje: Macedonian Review Editions. Originally published 1903.

Moglena. Newspaper published by Macedonian human rights activists in northern Greece.

Molho, Anthony
    1991   The Jewish Community of Salonika: The End of a Long History. *Diaspora.* 1:83–99.

Morin, Francoise
    1982   Anthropological Praxis and Life History. *International Journal of Oral History.* 3:5–30.

Moskos, Charles C.
    1989   *Greek Americans: Struggle and Success.* New Brunswick, NJ: Transactions Publishers.

Mouzelis, Nikos
    1994   *O ethnikismos stin isteri anaptixi.* Athens: Themelio.

Myrivilis, Stratis
    1977   *Life in the Tomb*. Hanover, NH: University Press of New England.

Nagel, Joane
    1994   Constructing Ethnicity: Creating and Recreating Ethnic Identity and Culture. *Social Problems*. 41:152–176.

Nash, Manning
    1989   *The Cauldron of Ethnicity in the Modern World*. Chicago: University of Chicago Press.

Nea Elladha. Greek language newspaper published in Melbourne, Australia.

Neos Kosmos. Greek language newspaper published in Melbourne, Australia.

Ninou, Kate, and Loula Kypraiou, eds.
    1979   *Treasures of Ancient Macedonia*. Thessaloniki: Archaeological Museum of Thessaloniki.

Nugent, Neill
    1989   *The Government and Politics of the European Community*. Durham, NC: Duke University Press.

Nurigiani, Giorgio
    1972   *The Macedonian Genius through the Centuries*. London: David Harvey.

Okamura, Jonathan Y.
    1981   Situational Ethnicity. *Ethnic and Racial Studies*. 4:452–65.

Palmer, Stephen E., Jr., and Robert R. King
    1971   *Yugoslav Communism and the Macedonian Question*. Hamden, CT: Archon Books.

Panov, Branko
    1972   Cyril and Methodius and Their Pan-Slavic Work. *Macedonian Review*. 2:183–87.

Papadimitriou, Demetrios G.
    1978   European Labor Migration. *International Studies Quarterly*. 22:377–408.

Papaioannou, George
    1985   *The Odyssey of Hellenism in America*. Thessaloniki: Patriarchal Institute for Patristic Studies.

Pavlowich, Stevan K.
    1988   The Macedonian Orthodox Church. In Pedro Ramet, ed. *Eastern Christianity and Politics in the 20th Century*. Durham, NC: Duke University Press. Pp. 338–47.

Pellizzi, Francesco
    1988   To Seek Refuge: Nation and Ethnicity in Exile. In Remo Guideri, Francesco Pellizzi, and Stanley J. Tambiah, eds. *Ethnicities and Nations: Processes of Interethnic Relations in Latin America, Southeast Asia, and the Pacific*. Austin: University of Texas Press. Pp. 154–71.

Perry, Duncan M.
    1988   *The Politics of Terror: The Macedonian Revolutionary Movements, 1893–1903*. Durham, NC: Duke University Press.

Petroff, Lillian
    1995   *Sojourners and Settlers: The Macedonian Community in Toronto to 1940*. Toronto: University of Toronto Press.

Polenakovič, Haralampie
1972   The Miladinov Brothers, Heroes of the Macedonian Renaissance. *Macedonian Review*. 2:155–60.
Pollis, Adamantia
1987a   Notes on Nationalism and Human Rights in Greece. *Journal of Modern Hellenism*. 4:147–60.
1987b   The State, the Law, and Human Rights in Modern Greece. *Human Rights Quarterly*. 9:587–614.
1992   Greek National Identity: Religious Minorities, Rights, and European Norms. *Journal of Modern Greek Studies*. 10:171–95.
Popov, Chris, and Michael Radin,
1989   *Contemporary Greek Government Policy on the Macedonian Issue and Discriminatory Practices in Breach of International Law*. Melbourne: Central Organizational Committee for Macedonian Human Rights, Australian Sub-Committee.
Poulantzas, Nicos
1978   *State, Power, Socialism*. London: New Left Books.
Poulton, Hugh
1993   *Balkans: Minorities and States in Conflict*. London: Minority Rights Publications.
Pribichevich, Stoyan
1982   *Macedonia: Its People and History*. University Park: Pennsylvania State University Press.
Price, Charles
1975   *Greeks in Australia*. Canberra: Australian National University Press.
Pulevski, Ǵorǵi M.
1875   *Rečnik od tri jezika*. Belgrade.
Radin, Michael, and Chris Popov
n.d.a   *Macedonia: A Brief Overview of Its History and People*. Adelaide: Macedonian Cultural Society.
n.d.b   *The Way Ahead for Macedonian Human Rights*. Adelaide: Australian Macedonian Human Rights Committee.
Ramet, Pedro, ed.
1988   *Eastern Christianity and Politics in the 20th Century*. Durham, NC: Duke University Press.
Ristovski, Blaže
1983   *Makedonskiot narod i makedonskata nacionalna svest*. Skopje: Dvojna Kniška.
Robertson, Roland
1987   Globalization Theory and Civilization Analysis. *Comparative Civilizations Review*. 17:220–30.
Rossos, Andrew
1991   The Macedonians of Aegean Macedonia: A British Officer's Report, 1944. *Slavonic and East European Review*. 69:282–309.
1994   The British Foreign Office and Macedonian National Identity, 1918–1941. *Slavic Review*. 53:369–94.

Royce, Anya P.
1982 *Ethnic Identity*. Bloomington: Indiana University Press.
Sahlins, Peter
1989 *Boundaries: The Making of France and Spain in the Pyrenees*. Berkeley: University of California Press.
Sakellariou, M. B., ed.
1983 *Macedonia: 4000 Years of Greek History and Civilization*. Athens: Ekdotike Athenon.
Saloutos, Theodore
1964 *Greeks in the United States*. Cambridge, MA: Harvard University Press.
1980 Greeks. In Stephen Thernstrom, ed. *Harvard Encyclopedia of American Ethnic Groups*. Cambridge, MA: Harvard University Press. Pp. 430–40.
Sarantis, Theodoros
1984 *I sinomosia kata tis Makedhonias*. Athens: Ethniki Enosi ton Vorion Ellinon.
Sarides, Emmanuel
1985 An Ethnic-Religious Minority between Scylla and Charibdis: The Pomaks in Northern Greece. Paper presented at the Modern Greek Studies Association Symposium.
Schein, Muriel D.
1975 When Is an Ethnic Group? Ecology and Class Structure in Northern Greece. *Ethnology*. 16:83–98.
Schiller, Nina Glick, Linda Basch, and Cristina Blanc-Szanton, eds.
1992 *Towards a Transnational Perspective on Migration: Race, Class, Ethnicity, and Nationalism Reconsidered*. New York: New York Academy of Sciences.
Schneider, David
1968 *American Kinship: A Cultural Account*. Englewood Cliffs, NJ: Prentice-Hall.
1969 Kinship, Nationality and Religion in American Culture: Toward a Definition of Kinship. In Robert F. Spencer, ed. *Forms of Symbolic Action*. Seattle, WA: American Ethnological Society. Pp. 116–125.
1984 *A Critique of the Study of Kinship*. Ann Arbor: University of Michigan Press.
Scott, James C.
1990 *Domination and the Arts of Resistance: Hidden Transcripts*. New Haven, CT: Yale University Press.
Scourby, Alice
1984 *The Greek Americans*. New York: Macmillan.
Sesito, R.
1982 *The Politics of Multiculturalism*. Sydney: Centre for Independent Studies.
Seton-Watson, Hugh
1977 *Nations and States*. Boulder, CO: Westview Press.
Sheffer, Gabriel, ed.
1986 *Modern Diasporas in International Politics*. New York: St. Martin's Press.

Siguan, Miguel
  1990   *Linguistic Minorities in the European Ecomomic Community: Spain, Portugal, Greece.* Luxembourg: Commission of the European Communities.
Silberman, Neil Ascher
  1989   *Between Past and Present: Archaeology, Ideology, and Nationalism in the Modern Middle East.* New York: Henry Holt.
Simovski, Todor
  1978   *Naselenite mesta vo Egejska Makedonija.* Skopje: Institut za Nacionalna Istorija.
Smith, Anthony D.
  1981   *The Ethnic Revival.* Cambridge: At the University Press.
  1983   *Theories of Nationalism.* New York: Holmes and Meier.
  1986   *The Ethnic Origins of Nations.* Oxford: Basil Blackwell.
Spencer, Jonathan
  1990   Writing Within: Anthropology, Nationalism, and Culture in Sri Lanka. *Current Anthropology.* 31:283–300.
Stack, John F.
  1981   *Ethnic Identities in a Transnational World.* Westport, CT: Greenwood Press.
Stalev, G., and T. Kabrovski
  1991   *From the Macedonian Culture.* Sydney: Macedonian School Council of New South Wales.
Stohos. An ultranationalist weekly newspaper published in Athens.
Stoianovich, T.
  1960   The Conquering Balkan Orthodox Merchant. *Journal of Economic History.* 20:234–313.
Tambiah, Stanley J.
  1989   Ethnic Conflict in the World Today. *American Ethnologist.* 16:335–49.
Tamis, Anastasios M.
  1994   *The Immigration and Settlement of Macedonian Greeks in Australia.* Bundoora, Victoria: La Trobe University Press.
Tashkovski, Dragan
  1973   Samuel's Empire. *Macedonian Review.* 3:34–38.
  1976   *The Macedonian Nation.* Skopje: Nasha Kniga.
Thernstrom, Stephen A., ed.
  1980   *Harvard Encyclopedia of American Ethnic Groups.* Cambridge, MA: Harvard University Press.
Thongchai, Winichakul
  1988   *Siam Mapped: A History of the Geo-Body of Siam.* Ph.D. dissertation. University of Sydney.
Triantis, Stephen G.
  1992   Greeks and World Hellenism. Paper presented at a conference on "Greeks in English Speaking Countries." Melbourne, Australia. March.
Trigger, Bruce G.
  1984   Alternative Archaeologies: Nationalist, Colonialist, Imperialist. *Man.* (N.S.) 19:355–70.

Trudgill, Peter
    1974   *Sociolinguistics: An Introduction.* Harmondsworth, England: Penguin
            Books.
Tsaousis, D. G., ed.
    1983   *Ellinismos, Ellinikotita.* Athens: Estia.
United States Commission on Security and Cooperation in Europe.
    1990   *Document of the Copenhagen Meeting of the Conference on the Human
            Dimension of the CSCE.* Washington, DC.
United States Department of State
    1990   *Country Reports on Human Rights Practices for 1989.* Washington, DC.
    1991   *Country Reports on Human Rights Practices for 1990.* Washington, DC.
    1992   *Country Reports on Human Rights Practices for 1991.* Washington, DC.
    1993   *Country Reports on Human Rights Practices for 1992.* Washington, DC.
    1994   *Country Reports on Human Rights Practices for 1993.* Washington, DC.
Useem, John, Ruth Useem, and John Donaghue
    1963   Men in the Middle of the Third Culture. *Human Organization.* 22:
            169–79.
Urla, Jacqueline
    1993   Cultural Politics in an Age of Statistics: Numbers, Nations, and the
            Making of Basque Identity. *American Ethnologist.* 20:818–26.
Vakalopoulos, Kostantinos
    1986   *I Makedhonia sta plesia tis Valkanikis politikis. 1830–1986.* Thessaloniki:
            Barbounakis.
    1989   *To Makedhoniko zitima.* Vol. 1, *1856–1912.* Thessaloniki: Paratiritis.
Valinakis, G.
    1990   I Ellinoyugoslavikes sheseis ston politiko tomea. In *I Simerini Yugo-
            slavia.* Athens: Elliniko Idhrima Amindikis ke Eksoterikis Politikis.
            Pp. 67–76.
Van Boeschoten, Riki
    1990   Politics, Class, and Identity in Rural Macedonia: A Comparative Per-
            spective. Unpublished manuscript.
    1993a   Ethnicity and the Cultural Division of Labour: The Case of
            Macedonia. Paper presented at a conference on "Ethnicity and An-
            thropology." Amsterdam.
    1993b   Minority Languages in Northern Greece. Report to the European
            Commission. Unpublished manuscript.
Vasiliadis, Peter
    1989   *Whose Are You? Identity and Ethnicity among the Toronto Macedonians.*
            New York: AMS Press.
Verdery, Katherine
    1991   *National Ideology under Socialism.* Berkeley: University of California
            Press.
Vergina. Newsletter published by the Macedonian Academic Society. Mel-
            bourne, Australia.
Vermeulen, Hans
    1984   Greek Cultural Dominance among the Orthodox Population of
            Macedonia during the Last Period of Ottoman Rule. In A. Blok and

Vermeulen, Hans (*cont.*)
H. Driesser, eds. *Cultural Dominance in the Mediterranean Area.* Nijmegen: Katholieke Universiteit. Pp. 225–55.

Vidoeski, Božo
1971 The Macedonian Language and Its Affirmation in the World of Slavonic Studies. *Macedonian Review.* 1:211–16.

Vishinski, Boris
1973 Culture through the Centuries. *Macedonian Review.* 3:209–18.

Vissoulis, Pandelis
1988 *O Makedhonikos Ellinismos.* Athens: Eleftheri Skepsi.

Wace, Alan J. B., and Maurice S. Thompson
1913 *The Nomads of the Balkans.* New York: Dutton.

Wallerstein, Immanuel
1991 The National and the Universal: Can There Be Such a Thing as World Culture? In Anthony King, ed. *Culture, Globalization and the World-System: Contemporary Conditions for the Representation of Identity.* Binghamton, NY: Department of Art History, SUNY at Binghamton. Pp. 91–105.

Waters, Mary
1990 *Ethnic Options: Choosing Identities in America.* Berkeley: University of California Press.

Weber, Eugen
1976 *Peasants into Frenchmen: The Modernization of Rural France, 1870–1914.* Stanford, CA: Stanford University Press.

Wilkinson, Henry R.
1951 *Maps and Politics: A Review of the Ethnographic Cartography of Macedonia.* Liverpool: At the University Press.

Winnifrith, T. J.
1987 *The Vlachs: The History of a Balkan People.* New York: St. Martin's Press.

Wolf, Eric
1982 *Europe and the People without History.* Berkeley: University of California Press.

Xhudo, Gus
1993 Macedonia: The Trouble Within. *Terrorism and Political Violence.* 5: 311–35.

Zografski, Danchjo
1973 The Awakening and Creation of the Macedonian Nation. *Macedonian Review.* 3:234–47.

Zora. Newspaper published by Macedonian human rights activists in northern Greece.

Index

About the Author

LORING M. DANFORTH is Professor of Anthropology at Bates College. He is the author of *The Death Rituals of Rural Greece* and *Firewalking and Religious Healing: The Anastenaria of Greece and the American Firewalking Movement* (both available from Princeton University Press).